THE ANATOMY OF
HISTORICAL KNOWLEDGE

MAURICE
MANDELBAUM

THE ANATOMY OF
HISTORICAL KNOWLEDGE

THE JOHNS HOPKINS UNIVERSITY PRESS
BALTIMORE AND LONDON

This book has been brought to publication with the
generous assistance of the Andrew W. Mellon Foundation.

Manufactured in the United States of America

The Johns Hopkins University Press, Baltimore, Maryland 21218
The Johns Hopkins Press Ltd., London

Library of Congress Catalog Card Number 76–46945
ISBN 0–8018–1929–6

Library of Congress Cataloging in Publication data
will be found on the last printed page of this book.

CONTENTS

v

PREFACE

Prior to 1938, when my first book, *The Problem of Historical Knowledge*, appeared, there had been relatively little interest among British and American philosophers in the topics with which it dealt. That situation has changed. Beginning in 1942 with Carl G. Hempel's article on "The Function of General Laws in History," and reinforced by the slowly accumulating interest in Collingwood's posthumously published *Idea of History*, philosophers in the United States and Britain have been increasingly concerned with various aspects of the same or allied problems. In the last decades, the number of serious works in this area has grown so great that it would be difficult to discuss even the most important in a careful, critical, and fair-minded way. Therefore, I have made reference to subsequent discussions only when I have happened to find them especially apposite. I trust that this will not be taken as a mark of disrespect.

In the present work I have returned to the main issues with which my earlier work was concerned, but it is only natural that I should now treat these issues in a different way. In some cases this has been due to changes that have occurred in philosophy itself, particularly in this field. For example, the problem of "fact" and "value" looms less large at the moment than it once did. Taking its place in the forefront of attention is the question of what kinds of explanation are to be sought, or can be found, in history. My own conception of the problems has in some cases also changed. For example, I have become increasingly aware of the variety present in different kinds of historical inquiry. In what follows, I have attempted to focus attention on this fact, and to relate it to some of the problems with which philosophers dealing with history are concerned. It is in this area, and in my attempt to offer a more detailed and adequate exposition of my views concerning causation, that the novelty of the present work may chiefly lie.

I have had the honor to present various portions of this book, in varying forms, when I delivered the Rabbi Irving Levey Lecture at Princeton University, a Franklin J. Matchette Foundation Lecture at the University of California at Irvine, the Arthur O. Lovejoy Lecture at Johns Hopkins, and the Alfred Schutz Memorial Lecture at the University of California at San Diego. I thank my hosts at these institutions for their invitations, and these and other audiences for their friendly criticism.

I also wish to thank W. H. Dray and C. Behan McCullagh for their careful reading of my manuscript. Each saved me from many infelicities in exposition and from some important errors; I am most grateful to them.

PART ONE

HISTORY AND ITS MODES

Chapter One

Unity and Diversity in Historical Studies

In this book I shall attempt to clarify some problems that are of concern to philosophers and to historians who reflect on the nature of history as a discipline, on what constitutes explanation in history, and whether historical knowledge is as reliable as other forms of knowledge may be. Although these problems have long been discussed in one form or another, most of the issues that remain current began to be intensively discussed in the last decades of the nineteenth century. Since then, the philosophic literature concerned with historical knowledge has grown enormously, and the interest of historians appears not to have slackened. While I hope not to have overlooked any of the most significant contributions to various aspects of the arguments that have flourished, it is my aim to offer a consistent view of my own rather than to attempt an assessment of all the admittedly important

3

positions that have been advanced, criticized, and defended by others.

As a foundation for what is to follow, I shall first attempt to show in what sense one may claim that there is a fundamental unity in historical studies; I shall also attempt to indicate some of the important ways in which these studies differ from one another. When one considers the proliferation of forms of historical writing since the beginning of the eighteenth century and the differences in the interest and the practices of historians of different backgrounds, it may seem foolish to propose—as I shall do—that there is unity as well as diversity in historical studies. Practicing historians are thoroughly aware not only of the individual differences among historians, but of the long-term changes and the short-run fashions in the kinds of subject matter with which historians have been concerned. This diversity has been so apparent that one finds very few historians making a serious attempt to characterize in a careful or precise way what is distinctive about their discipline. On the other hand, when philosophers have been concerned with the problems of historical knowledge they have generally failed to recognize the diversity that exists in the field of historical studies: I know that my own work has suffered from that defect. In what follows I wish to lay equal stress on the unity and on the diversity that are present when one takes into account the whole range of historical studies. It is to a consideration of the question of unity that I shall first turn.

I

It is a commonplace in the literature of our subject that historians are concerned with particular events that occurred at specific times and places, and not with them only in so far as they represent events of a given type. To be sure, historians occasionally embark on analyses of similar events, comparing and contrasting their origins and natures, as R. R. Palmer in *The Age of Democratic Revolution* studied one facet of the political history of the eighteenth century. They also frequently choose some very limited topic for study because they take it to be typical of other phenomena in which they are interested, as a medieval French historian may study a particular village to find out about French village life at the time. Similarly, a historian may study the lives of persons belonging to a particular social class in Victorian England in order to gain a better understanding of the class structure and class attitudes prevalent there at the time. Such studies are sometimes said to involve "generalizations" because they move from what was true in specific cases to what generally held true at the time. It is important to note, however, that such generalizations are simply means of discovering and describing what was characteristically true of some particular place over some particular span of time. One should not suppose that because historians "generalize" in this way that they are attempting to formulate or confirm any generalization as to what always, or usually, occurs in situations of a given type. In this respect their aims are different from those characteristic of sociologists or social psychologists who might be dealing with the same materials. Thus, the familiar thesis that historians are concerned with the particular, rather than with establishing explanatory generalizations, appears to me sound. The classic formulation of this distinction is attributable to Windelband, who distinguished between the idiographic aims of the historian and the nomothetic objectives of the sciences.[1]

Unfortunately, those who initially introduced this contrast into discussions of historical knowledge formulated it in a way that involved many other issues. For example, the contrast between idiographic and nomothetic interests became entangled with the claim that each historical event is unique and unrepeatable, and that in this respect historical events are different from the events with which the natural sciences deal. From this claim it was thought to follow that while nature could be adequately described in terms of laws, laws were not in principle applicable in the domain of history. Unfortunately, this in turn was thought to imply that historians must use methods totally different from those used in the natural sciences. It is against this tangled background of issues that Carl Hempel's famous paper "The Function of General Laws in History" should be read. Unfortunately, these issues were not disentangled within that paper itself. For example, the question of the function of general laws in historical explanation is not equivalent to the question of what it is that historians are attempting to do, yet Hempel failed to draw this distinction. Most of his argument was in fact directed toward showing that historical explanations involve the use of general laws, but from this he drew the unwarranted conclusion that historical studies are not primarily concerned with the description of particular events.[2] Since this confounding of two distinct issues and other similar confusions continue to be present in much of the literature that stems from Hempel's extremely influential article, only a return to the original idiographic-nomothetic distinction, disentangled from other issues, will permit us to make a fresh start.

It is my claim that any work we take to be historical in nature purports to establish what actually occurred at a particular time and place, or is concerned with tracing and explaining some particular series of related occurrences. However, this does not entail that in fulfilling such a task the historian may not, at certain points, have to rely on generalizations in order to offer a coherent account of some of the occurrences with which he deals. For example, in attempting to give an account of a particular revolution, a historian often has to make use of certain general assumptions concerning how individuals generally behave in particular sorts of situations, such as those that arose in the course of that revolution. This does not involve any abdication of his primary enterprise as a historian, since before he can make use of any generalizations concerning their behavior he must establish the nature of the situations in which these individuals were placed, and he must also have established how they did in fact behave. The function of his assumptions concerning human behavior is that of linking the behavior of individuals and of groups to the situations in which they found themselves, rendering it intelligible why they acted as they did. Unlike a social psychologist who may be concerned with revolutionary movements, the historian is not attempting to show how certain factors that may be present in all human behavior can be used to account for the occurrence of revolutions. Also, unlike sociologists who attempt to establish theories of revolutions, historians are concerned with what actually occurred in specific cases, rather than with discovering the general sociological conditions that serve to explain those types of social and political change designated as revolutions.

The foregoing example should make it clear that the task of the historian is quite different from that of the psychologist or sociologist, whose approach to the same subject matter is nomothetic rather than idiographic. However, it would be misleading to assume that the historian's approach is in all cases as free from general theoretic components as the preceding example may have suggested. In some cases at least, he must have a broad acquaintance with social theory in order to recognize various alternative types of explanations that could be used to account for the facts with which he is to deal. As one illustration of where this is needed, consider the problem of a historian who wishes to trace the history of a particular set of beliefs and an associated pattern of actions, such as beliefs in witchcraft and the prosecution of persons as witches. A historian of witchcraft must seek to establish whether it is more plausible to hold that the spread of the beliefs and of the patterns of action with which he is concerned is best accounted for in terms of direct influence and imitation, or in some other way. For example, they might have arisen independently of each other because of the presence of similar psychological or sociological conditions in different places at the same time. In short, the historian will often be enmeshed in precisely the same sorts of problems that any anthropologist must face when he deals with the question of whether the distribution of a particular set of culture traits is to be accounted for by diffusion or whether it is an example of independent origins. This will almost always involve general knowledge based on a comparison of instances; it is not usually a question that can be satisfactorily solved merely by examining any one case.[3] However, the fact that a historian must make use of general knowledge of this sort, drawn from his familiarity with other cases, does not signify that his task in any particular case diverges from a concern with understanding and describing what actually occurred in that one case: His interest remains rooted in that case, and is idiographic.

I turn now to a second generic characteristic of historical studies, no matter in what field they are pursued: They depend upon inquiry, the purpose of which is to establish the truth concerning particular events that did actually occur. In this, historical studies are to be distinguished from stories, myths, and memories, with each of which they have on occasion been claimed to be intimately related. Let us first consider the fact that the element of inquiry distinguishes them from memory. While our own memories, or the records of the observations of others (which in an extended sense can be characterized as a form of "memory"), may give us information useful for conducting an inquiry into what has occurred, such information does not constitute more than a starting point for historical studies. The accuracy of our memory, or of the records, must be tested against other memories and records, and relationships must be established among a host of such remembered and recorded events. It is for this reason, and not for the reasons assigned by Benedetto Croce, that one must distinguish between history and the types of records Croce designated as mere chronicle: Chronicles purport to be a record of a set of facts that did occur, but a chronicle neither supports its statements by authenticating them, nor does it necessarily provide an account of the relationships in which they stand to one another. It is the task of the historian to take chronicles and all other related records of the past, and to establish, through inquiry, the various relationships that ob-

tained among these recorded facts. One of the merits of Collingwood's work on the nature of history was that he insisted upon the
essential role inquiry plays in anything we denominate as a historical
work. This thesis is, however, independent of other doctrines with
which Collingwood associated it, such as his contention that history is
the reenactment of past thought. To mark this difference, and also to
separate my use of the distinction between history and chronicle from
the view of history to which Croce subscribed, I might say that the
role of inquiry in history is not instrumental to reliving, reenacting, or
in any other way experiencing or bringing alive what is past. Its role
is to allow us to know what occurred, and to know it as fully and
accurately as we can. To put the matter in as strong an opposing light
as I can: History aims, and ought to aim, at being *wissenschaftlich*,
which is to say that in laying claim to truth it must be able to advance
external evidence that vouches for its truth; in default of this, it is not
to be considered a historical study.

Inquiry in history not only serves to distinguish it from memory
and from mere chronicles, but also distinguishes it from story and
myth. Neither the storyteller nor the mythmaker need seek to establish that the elements entering his account actually occurred; even if
he aims at conveying a truth through his story or myth, that truth will
not depend upon whether the elements through which it is elucidated
do in fact refer to actual events. Although there are works of art,
especially in painting and in fiction, that strive to depict specific
events, or to depict very concretely the kinds of events that did occur
at a particular time and place, such attempts are by no means characteristic of all works of art; and if one claims—following Aristotle—
that poetry is truer and of greater import than history, it is not to
such features of the work that one would be inclined to refer. Rather,
the truth one would usually wish to assign to a work of art or to a
myth, if one were to assign it such an attribute at all, would lie in its
revelatory character when taken as a whole. All of the events in a
story may be fictitious, and in some novels, such as Kafka's *The
Castle*, they may bear only ambiguous resemblances to events that
ordinarily occur in everyday life; yet the story can, like a myth, carry
a meaning that relates to human experience in such a way that we are
apt to regard it as true, and as profoundly true, or perhaps as false.
Fiction, however, is not history. One would be extremely silly to ask
of a novelist whether there was really some person exactly like a
character he had depicted in one of his novels, or to ask whether
anyone who had in some respects served as a model for one of his

characters had, in real life, stood in the same relations to other persons as had been depicted in the novel. It is not silly, however, but absolutely essential that we demand of a historian that he include within his account only such persons as really existed, and only such events and relationships among these persons as did really occur. Putting the matter more generally, we impose upon historical studies a truth condition that is not only different from any applied to art or myth, but one that may be more severe than the truth condition placed on the theoretical structures of the natural sciences by some philosophers of science. We ask that a historian's account of a series of events be true not only of that series when viewed as a whole, but that its account of all of the component elements included within the series also be true. If this demand were abandoned, history would not be a descriptive discipline, dependent for its truth on the accuracy with which it could infer what had actually occurred.

This claim, that historical studies characteristically aim at discovering and describing the nature of particular events and series of events, and that inquiry enables them to do so, is a claim that has often been challenged. Such challenges have occasionally arisen because historical accounts refer to the past, which (being past) cannot, of course, be directly observed. Both Charles A. Beard and Carl L. Becker sometimes appealed to arguments of this type. Taken by itself, however, this form of argument is not strong. One may note, for example, that the historical aspects of various natural sciences, such as geology, are not generally challenged simply because they concern the past. Nor is it usual—or plausible—to challenge all historical reconstructions which concern past actions; for example, we do not believe it intrinsically impossible to establish in a court of law what occurred in a specific case. Whatever difficulties may beset such inquiries, they are not usually subjected to wholesale challenge. It is therefore not surprising that skepticism with respect to our historical knowledge is only occasionally based on the fact that historians deal with the past; its most usual sources are to be found in other aspects of the subject matter with which historians are concerned. For example, it is often assumed that the particular interests, antipathies, and sympathies of historians cannot be disentangled from the materials with which they deal. Furthermore, different historical accounts are often taken to be so diverse and disparate that no general standards are applicable to those that were written at different times, arose out of different interests, and were guided by different assumptions. However, were it possible to show that differing historical accounts are not intrinsically unrelated, but that they tend to dovetail in spite of differences in the prejudgments of different historians, and that they explore different aspects or facets of a single body of connected data, then it might be claimed that these accounts supplement, corroborate, and serve to correct one another. Were this the case, it would not be necessary to abandon the assumption that there is a common standard for judging historical inquiries, however diverse they may be in content or in their approaches to that content. I shall later examine this problem in some detail. At this point I shall confine my attention to showing that the data used in differing sorts of historical accounts do in fact have important features in common, thus laying the groundwork for my claim that they constitute a connected set of data. The nature of these data constitutes the third and final generic characteristic of historical accounts with which I shall be concerned.

It has often been supposed that the data of history include all that is accessible, or becomes accessible, with respect to what any human being has done, said, felt, or thought over the whole of the past.[4] Such characterizations of what belongs to history are not unusual, and they appear to be attractive because they do not place antecedent restrictions on historians, except for the stipulation that history is concerned with the human rather than the nonhuman past. Yet, characterizations of this type are too inclusive, unless their scope is tacitly restricted to make them conform to the actual practice of historians. This becomes evident when one considers the fact that the thoughts, feelings, and actions of any individual may be seen in relation to various contexts, of which their historical context is only one. For example, a psychoanalyst is interested in the thoughts, feelings, and actions of his patient; a judge is interested in the thoughts, feelings, and actions of persons brought before him in a trial; and it is normal for any parent or child to attend to what other members of his family feel and think about many matters—otherwise neither parent nor child would know what to expect when behaving in one way rather than another. The historian, however, views the thoughts, feelings, and actions of individuals in a special context: He views them in their societal setting, that is, in terms of the various ways in which they affected, or were affected by, the society in which they took place. It is only insofar as individuals are viewed with reference to the nature and changes of a society existing at a particular time and place that they are of interest to historians; it is not the thought or action of any individual viewed merely as this specific individual with which the historian is concerned. For this reason I elsewhere characterized the domain of historians as "the study of human activities in their societal context and with their societal implications."[5]

That characterization suffered from one defect I now wish to correct: It tended to lay undue stress on the institutional structures of societies and left too little room for the consideration of those aspects of human culture, such as the arts, technology, or philosophy, that undoubtedly have some relation to the organization of the societies in which they are found, but which can also be the objects of independent historical inquiries. In what follows, much more will be said concerning the difference between institutionally oriented histories, which I have elsewhere referred to as "general history," and histories of specific aspects of culture, which I termed "special histories";[6] here it is necessary only to discriminate the way in which I shall be using the terms "society" (or "societal") and "culture" (or "cultural").

Social scientists, and social anthropologists in particular (e.g., A. L. Kroeber, M. J. Herskovits, S. F. Nadel, and Clyde Kluckhohn, among others), draw a distinction between "society" and "culture," but no standard definitions of these terms have become established. I shall be using them, and their cognates, in the following way. A *society*, I shall hold, consists of individuals living in an organized community that controls a particular territory; the organization of such a community is provided by institutions that serve to define the status occupied by different individuals and ascribe to them the roles they are expected to play in perpetuating the continuing existence of the community.

I wish to draw a distinction between a society, as thus defined, and my use of the term "culture." In doing so, I shall not conform to either of two usages currently found in the writings of most anthropologists. In one such usage the term is not primarily employed as a generic term, but is used to designate the particular way of life characteristic of a society, as when one might say "the culture of the Navaho differs from that of the Kwakiutl."[7] Another usage tends to restrict the term "culture" to a system of ideas and values that shapes the behavior of individuals in a society.[8] For my purposes at least, neither of these ways of defining culture seems adequate. Instead, I shall use the term in a generic sense, as E. B. Tylor originally did, and I shall include as elements of culture artifacts and the ways in which they are used, as did he.[9] The chief reason for defining it in this way is that various cultural elements need not be tied to a partic-

ular society, but can migrate from society to society. So too can
artifacts, as many familiar studies of the diffusion of culture traits and
culture complexes have shown. Also, no complex society is likely to
be as monolithic in its culture as speaking of "the way of life" or "the
values and ideas" of a society would seem to suggest. Although persons occupying different institutional roles in a society may share a
common culture in many respects, they may also belong to different
cultural subgroups within that society, being distinguished from one
another by speech, possessions, and dress, as well as by manners,
tastes, and morals.

I shall, then, use the term "culture" as a generic term designating
whatever objects are created and used by individuals and whatever
skills, beliefs, and forms of behavior they have acquired through their
social inheritance. Defined in this way, "culture" does *not* include
institutions, such as kinship systems or rules governing the distribution of property and the division of labor, which define the status and
roles of individuals within a society and regulate the organization of
its life. Rather, I am using "culture" as a generic term covering
language, technology, the arts, religious and philosophic attitudes and
beliefs, and whatever other objects, skills, habits, customs, explanatory systems, and the like are included in the social inheritance of
various individuals living in a particular society. Using these definitions of "a society" and of "culture," special histories trace various
aspects of culture as they arise and change in a society, or as they
cross the boundaries separating societies, whereas general history is
concerned with the nature of and the changes in particular societies.

Although the contrast I originally drew between general history
and special histories has not had any marked impact on discussions
of historiography, it has on occasion been referred to; what is of more
importance is that others have quite independently used the term
"general history" in essentially the same sense as that in which I used
it. Most notable among the parallels is the distinction drawn by Otto
Brunner, the medieval historian, between "history as a discipline"
and other historical studies, a distinction he developed in a lecture entitled "Das Fach 'Geschichte' und die historischen Wissenschaften."
He held that history as a discipline—"History, *tout court*," as it is
sometimes put—concerns the actions of human beings, both individually and in groups, in the context of a particular organized society;
the structures of such a society distribute relationships of power
among the individuals, and it is in terms of these power relationships
that the individuals act. In contrast to general history, taken in this

sense, which he called "*Geschichte im engeren Sinn*," Brunner characterized the special forms of historical study ("*die historischen Fachwissenschaften*") as dealing not with individuals and groups, but with their cultural products, such as philosophic and religious views, works of literature and art, which the historian investigates, interprets, and depicts.[10]

In a somewhat different manner, W. H. B. Court, the economic historian, raised the question of the relation between economic history and general history.[11] In this connection he distinguished between the history of single nations, which he referred to as "general or integral history," and what he referred to (not altogether happily, I think) as "universal history." While general history attempts to deal with all aspects of a particular society, and may thus be called "integral," an economic historian needs to transcend the confines of single nations, tracing the spread of economic institutions and dealing with whole trading areas, or even with all nations, from an economic point of view. Economic history, in this sense, is a special discipline, a *Fachwissenschaft* in Brunner's terminology, concerned with the nature of and changes in one aspect of human culture rather than attempting to depict the nature of a particular society and the changes in it.

To be sure, whether one deals with economics or art or religion, or with any other aspect of human culture, innovations and change take place in particular societies and form part of the life of that society; they are therefore of concern to the general historian who attempts to understand and depict the nature of a given society and its changes. Yet, these aspects of culture may also spread beyond the points of their origin and present the special historian with a distinct subject matter of his own. Thus, as both Brunner and Court suggest, and as I wish to emphasize, while the tasks of the general historian and of those dealing with special histories are different, they are none the less complementary, lending each other mutual support.

In the light of what has been said concerning general history (which deals with societies) and special histories (which deal with culture), it might be thought that I wish to minimize the historian's concern with individual human beings. This is not the case. That on which I wish to insist is merely the fact that in order for an individual to be of concern to a historian his character and actions must be viewed in relation to the place that he occupied and the role that he played in the life of a society or in relation to some facet of culture; and this holds, as well, for groups of individuals. Such relationships may of course be of different kinds. For example, a historian may be concerned with the actions of an individual because he had a certain institutional status within a particular society, or because of some important influence he had in changing that society, or simply because he may serve as representative of some aspect of the social or cultural life of that society. What is important to bear in mind is that the place individuals occupy in any historical account is relative to the social organization and the culture of the society the historian seeks to understand and depict.[12]

In order to avoid misunderstanding, it is also important to note that a historian's idiographic interest in some particular society does not signify that historians may not undertake comparative historical studies. These studies, which are becoming of increasing interest to the historical profession, often help to direct attention to aspects of societal organization or cultural activities that might be overlooked by any historians whose familiarity with different forms of organization and of culture tends to be restricted to what was most characteristic of the nature and changes to be found in the history of their own society. Furthermore, the striking presence of quite different features in other societies may call attention to the presence of analogous features in one's own. Thus, comparative historical studies help to prevent misinterpretations of other societies and their culture, and misinterpretations of our own. However, such studies need not involve an abandonment of the historian's idiographic approach, turning historians into psychologists or sociologists; they simply attest to the fact that adequate historical understanding, in any field, demands sophisticated inquiry: What is present and needs to be described does not always lie on the surface of those forms of social organization and of cultural life with which historians seek to come to grips.

In sum, it has been my contention that historical accounts are concerned to establish through inquiry, and to validate through evidence, occurrences that relate to the nature of and changes in a particular society, or—using the same methods—to trace continuity and change in those human activities that we may designate forms of culture.

II

It will be recalled that in introducing my contention that history as a discipline is concerned with societal facts and with the elements of culture produced by men in different societies, I indicated why I attach importance to showing that there is unity as well as diversity in historical accounts. If the events with which these accounts deal are intrinsically related, and if there are interlocking data that historians can use in establishing their relationships, then various historical accounts can serve to supplement, corroborate, and correct one another. Under these circumstances one would not need to abandon the assumption that there is some common standard for judging historical inquiries in spite of the diversity in their content and in their approaches. One important way of establishing that there are interlocking relationships among historical accounts is to take note of the phenomenon I have elsewhere termed the *scale* of such accounts.[13] Some historians survey longer time intervals than do others, because of the subject matter with which they choose to deal, and some are concerned with more inclusive entities than are others, who choose subjects of smaller scope and enter into them in greater detail; but these differences in scale do not make their accounts irrelevant to each other. One way of illustrating this fact is to say that in the field of general history (although not, as we shall see, in all special histories) the series of events with which the historian deals is an indefinitely dense series, just as is the geographical territory with which a cartographer deals. Let us examine what, precisely, this means.

A map maker always operates on some scale; let us initially suppose that he is drawing a map of the continental United States on a scale of two hundred miles to the inch. He may then draw a map of any one of the states on some other scale: for example, Connecticut at ten miles to the inch, Wisconsin forty miles to the inch, and Texas eighty miles to the inch. The Connecticut map can thus include more information concerning roads and towns than can the Texas map, but either map may be blown up further, to include more details. Such maps may also be supplemented by maps of the main arteries of the major cities that lie within the state, and these maps may be supplemented by street maps that show not only the main arteries but each city street. Further, the Department of Public Works in a city can usually supply maps identifying buildings and utilities on each block of each street, and, in the end, architectural blueprints might be found showing the floor plans of these buildings and even the details of wiring and carpentry in each of the rooms in the buildings. It is in this sense that I would characterize the possible maps of a territory as being indefinitely dense. Similarly, historical accounts of a series of events may, in many cases, form a dense series, with the various temporal and geographical segments of a nation's history being capable of being explored in further detail, insofar as the requisite data are available.

The applicability of this simile to historical studies should be obvious. Some histories are concerned with longer stretches of time than are others; also, the regional as well as the temporal scope of different histories varies, some historians being concerned with the political life of a nation as a whole, whereas others focus on what occurred in the politics of one region, or with political changes within a single city. To be sure, maps drawn on different scales do not present us with representations of the very same items: The details shown on a city map are not represented on a national map, nor—on the other hand—can a city map give indications as to what road one should choose in leaving that city in order to find the best route across the country. Nevertheless, maps drawn on different scales, if they are accurate, will fit together, allowing us to move toward an increasingly small target, or they will allow us to find our way from any particular starting point to other points that are extremely remote. In the realm of historical studies, one can also move in either direction: from broad horizons to more accurate and detailed vision, or from an acquaintance with what is most familiar to entirely unfamiliar territory. In each case, the historian will either follow connections that his own investigations uncover, or he will be helped by connections that other historians, working on a different scale, may have laid out for him. It is in this sense that historical studies using different scales reinforce one another, even though the details they depict will necessarily be different—and will be different precisely because different scales are used.

The interlocking of historical data is also to be found in the fact that different historians deal with what I shall term different *facets* of the same events. To illustrate this aspect of historiographical practice, one need merely bear in mind that any stretch in the life of a modern society can be viewed in terms of political changes, economic changes, the international relations of that society, or the like. To be sure, a historian dealing with any one of these facets will almost certainly be called upon to make reference to events that historians approaching the society from another point of view will also be forced to mention or investigate. Nonetheless, having approached a society from one point of view rather than another, a historian will not be obliged to trace all of the connections that are of importance to the historian who approaches the same society from another angle. Once again a comparison with map making may be helpful.

The same geographical territory—say, that of the United States—may be mapped in terms of its political subdivisions or, alternatively, in terms of its physiographic features; in the latter case the map need not reveal state boundaries, but it will show differences in altitudes in various areas of the country, which a political map will not do. Other maps of the United States will indicate our systems of transportation, but will not indicate the altitudes of various regions and need not indicate state boundaries. In short, maps drawn on the same scale and having reference to the same region may be concerned with very different aspects of the territory they map. Yet these maps fit together. On each of the maps, the Great Lakes and the Great Salt Lake must be shown in the same relationship to one another, and must bear the same relations to other points, such as Cape Cod and San Francisco Bay. If these geographical features of the same territory are not depicted in a consistent manner, we demand that one or another of the maps be revised. And so, too, in history.

To be sure, when historians depict different facets of a society controversies frequently arise as to which of the interlocking factors with which they deal is to be considered the more important: for example, whether in the case of concurrent changes in the economic and the political aspects of life in a society one of these can be held to be responsible for the other, or whether both result from strains due to some long-standing dysfunction in the organization of the society's life. Thus, it must not be assumed that in history the relationships between different facets of a society are inert and static, as is the case in geography. We shall later be forced to deal with these and similar problems of causation in history. We shall also have to raise the question of whether the adoption of some general theory, such as the Marxist theory of social structure and social change, makes it impossible to find a fit between historical accounts that deal with different facets of societal life. For our present purposes, however, where we are concerned with understanding the unity and diversity in historical studies, it is necessary only to take note of the fact that historians dealing with one and the same society often deal with different facets of that society, as well as deal with it on different scales, and for that reason there is great diversity—and there will always be great diversity—in the ways in which the same society will be described.

This has become especially noticeable since the hegemony of political history has been broken. To be sure, as Otto Brunner pointed out, history-as-a-discipline—that is, general history—always has the organization of society, and therefore relationships of power among the members of a society, in the forefront of attention. This, however, does not entail that it is primarily concerned with political life in any narrow sense: The relationships of power in many societies do not turn on such institutions as kingship, or on the relations between church and state, or on representative forms of government, as political historians were inclined to hold. It has become increasingly clear that in order to understand many of the major changes in a society— for example, those in the United States after the Civil War—it is wholly inadequate to focus attention on the course of political events alone. In addition, knowledge of the successive waves of immigration is needed, and so, too, is knowledge of the development of technology and its application to the manufacture and distribution of goods. These facets of our history have, of course, been closely linked. There also are many other aspects of American life that historians recognize as important and find it necessary to take into account. For the sake of increasing accuracy, checking what might otherwise be too facile overall generalizations, all of these studies must be pursued in considerable detail. Thus, within the scope of what I have termed "general history" we find historical accounts (written on very different scales) concerning our politics, economic organization, foreign affairs, changes in the forms of our family life and in the nature of our educational and religious institutions, and the roles played at various times by distinctions of wealth, ethnic origin, and race. Consequently there is boundless variety in what is investigated in an attempt to understand the nature of a single society and the changes that occurred in that society within a limited period of time. And historians are not, of course, interested only in some particular society, but deal with the nature and the interrelationships of many different societies.

Given this variety in the matters with which those whom I have termed general historians are concerned, what further areas of investigations are open for those who pursue special historical studies, that is, who are concerned with the special *Fachwissenschaften* as Otto Brunner designated them? It is with these studies, and with their differences from general history, that the following section is primarily concerned.

III

It is not usual to regard historians of literature, of science, of painting, or of philosophy as "historians," even though it cannot be denied that they are concerned with establishing and delineating historical connections in the fields within which they work. To be sure, what they establish often throws light on various aspects of what I have termed general history; it is also often the case that an awareness of the relationships within societies with which general historians are concerned is of crucial importance to these special histories. We shall shortly have more to say concerning these interlocking relationships, but it is first necessary to turn our attention to the differences between the kinds of inquiry involved in general history and the procedures followed by those who write special histories, such as histories of a national literature, a style of architecture, or a period in the history of science or philosophy. One such difference relates to the fact that in writing an account of some period in the life of a society—say, of France in the reign of Louis XIV—one is dealing with what continuously existed in a particular region over a stretch of time; insofar as their materials permit them to do so, there is in principle no limit to the detail into which historians can enter in exploring the nature of a society and its changes. Different historians may assign different degrees of importance to different aspects of a particular society, but even as its institutions change there are continuous ongoing connections among them. For example, though France not only changed during the reign of Louis XIV but has changed even more radically since, due to major fluctuation in its political structures and continuing changes in its economic organization, there has been, through time, a people occupying a given territory, with peoples of other languages, traditions, and forms of social organization around them; however much the social organization of French life has changed, France has remained throughout the last centuries a society different from those by which it has been surrounded, possessing a degree of continuity and a unity of its own.[14]

In contrast to the continuing existence of a society such as France, with which general history is concerned, let us consider the object of some special history, such as a history of French literature. The historian of a national literature, or of the literature of a period, is dealing with a collection of works that may be related to one another in a variety of ways, but in dealing with this collection of separate works, he is not dealing with anything that constitutes a single functioning whole. There are, so to speak, gaps between these works: Unlike the elements in the life of a society, they are not continuous, forming an indefinitely dense series which can be explored in ever increasing detail. One can, for example, imagine the main outlines of

French literature as having remained the same even had some individual plays or poems or novels not been written, or even if there existed others of which all traces have now been lost. To be sure, influences exist, and the special historian often searches for a connecting link between works that seem similar and yet puzzlingly different, but there is no guarantee that any such link ever existed: Genuine innovation, as well as influences, must be taken into account. While there are high-water marks and major turning points in a nation's literature, that literature does not constitute a single continuing event, as does the nation itself. This is true not only of literature and the arts, but of technology and of customs. It is the same difference to which I have already called attention, between habits and artifacts that individuals learn and create in the course of their lives, and which I designate the elements of a culture, and the institutional patterns in which these activities are carried on. As I pointed out, cultural habits may migrate from society to society; they are not rooted in any one form of life, and different individuals in the same society may not possess a common culture. In understanding the elements in a culture, how they arise, change, and spread, we must therefore not look to their institutional basis only, but must trace particular influences, allow for innovation, modification, and changes in use. It is in this way that historians of the special disciplines, and historians of customs and technology who are not dominated by an institutional bias, will proceed.

The difference between those who have what I would term an institutional bias, attempting to explain the elements in a culture solely in terms of the society in which these elements are found, and those who treat these elements in partial independence of that society can best be suggested by considering the relationship between an author and his works. One cannot understand a literary work simply in terms of its author's character and life; one must also take into account the traditions of his craft that he absorbed—or against which he rebelled—the reception accorded his own earlier work, and the relationships in which he stood to other authors and to the audiences he sought. Thus, there is a history of an author's work which—although an intimate part of his personal history—demands treatment in its own right if we are to understand the characteristics of what he produced. Similarly, to understand developments in the science of a period, or changes in architectural style, we need special histories and cannot view these forms of activity simply in terms of changes occurring in the societies in which they were produced. It is with the semiautonomous histories of the various aspects of cultural life that special historical disciplines, such as literary histories, histories of science, and histories of theology, as well as histories of language and of customs, are concerned.

To say that these histories are *semi*autonomous should call attention to the fact that even if they are not to be regarded merely as facets of the institutional life of a society, they frequently are deeply influenced by the nature of that life and the changes taking place in it. One cannot, for example, understand some changes that take place in the arts without finding in them reflections of how people reacted to events that occurred in their lives; nor can one always understand changes in the position of artists or of scientists in their societies without understanding changes in the institutional structure of those societies. Thus, the special historian often needs basic help from the general historian if he is to understand the materials with which it is his task to deal; and the general historian may derive help from the special historian in coming to understand how people viewed the events of their time, and how, for example, the development of science and technology paved the way for major forms of economic change. This interlocking of different forms of historical inquiry need be no more surprising than the manner in which inquiries into different facets of the institutional life of a society offer each other corroboration and mutual support.

While these connections between general history and special histories should not be underestimated, it remains true—as I have remarked—that historians of literature, of painting, of science, or of philosophy are not usually regarded as "historians," and their academic posts more often than not are outside departments of history. It is not difficult to understand why this should be the case. A historian of literature, for example, will almost always have to function as a critic as well as a historian, and he may therefore find a more natural place for himself among those who are concerned with the practice and theory of criticism, with hermeneutics, stylistics, and linguistics than among those whose interests are more purely historical, focusing primarily on the nature and changes within a society. Similarly, the historian of philosophy must have a concern with philosophic problems for their own sake, and to be a historian of art demands aesthetic sensitivity and some degree of connoisseurship. Furthermore, as I have pointed out, a great deal of the work of those dealing in special histories has to do with comparative studies, with studies of influence, and with the migration of cultural traditions over time; thus, the focus of their attention will not be like that of general historians, whose aim it is to understand the nature and the changes of particular societies.

To be sure, there has been a tendency among many cultural historians, and among some institutional historians, to obliterate any ultimate distinction between general histories and special histories; they do so because they assume that within any society, or in any age, there is an overriding unity that embraces all aspects of social life. Such a unity is sometimes held to be based on the dominance of some form of institutional structure, as has sometimes been held by Marxists; sometimes it has been identified with a pervasive *Zeitgeist*; at other times it is more modestly claimed that there are common intellectual presuppositions and common forms of sensibility that underlie traits common to the social institutions and to the cultural products of an age. Any one of these monistic tendencies will do much to obliterate the degree of independence that, I believe, must be preserved in various fields of historical inquiry. This can most clearly be shown by considering what is inevitably involved in the ways in which, for various purposes, we periodize history.[15]

Any periodization of history demands that we select some aspect of the life of a society, or some aspect of cultural life that we regard as important, as the basis for marking the beginning, middle, and end of the period with which we are concerned. One cannot assume, however, that what marks the beginning of a period when seen from a political point of view also marks the beginning of a new economic period, nor that a periodization in terms of some element of culture, such as painting or literature, will be synchronous with a periodization based on scientific discoveries or on philosophic innovation. This is not to say that it is misleading to offer periodizations of history, *if* the principle of periodization used is made explicit. What is to be rejected is the all-or-none approach of monistic views of history, in which periodizations are taken to be equally applicable to all aspects of a society and its culture. How great a distortion this can involve is most strikingly illustrated by the way in which the concept of *"the* Renaissance" has sometimes been used, even when that concept has been applied only within Italy. In literature, two major Italian authors of the Renaissance, Petrarch and Boccaccio, died in 1374 and 1375; but the Renaissance painter Raphael died 146 years later. Thus, the period designated as "the Renaissance" must be differently dated if one is concerned with painting rather than with literature. Similarly, were one to view the new science of the sixteenth and seventeenth centuries as a Renaissance phenomenon, as is sometimes done, the limits of the period would have to be greatly extended, since Galileo died 122 years after Raphael. In fact, the stretch of time from Petrarch's birth to the death of Galileo is approximately equal to that from Galileo's death to the present day. It is certainly implausible to assume that there was one and the same spirit successively developing in different areas of cultural life over that length of time. In fact, no investigations of the actual works produced in different fields during that period would support the notion that it is legitimate to regard "the Renaissance" monistically, as if it were a unitary phenomenon pervading all aspects of Italian cultural life from the fourteenth to the seventeenth century.

Nor is it only with respect to cultural periodizations that such a situation obtains. If one chooses different institutional facets of a society, one finds that even though they are intimately connected, one or more of them may have failed to change at the same accelerating rate as others. In such cases, of course, major dysfunctions may have arisen; but even if it is assumed that these will in time correct themselves (as sociological and anthropological functionalists tend to assume), the historian who wishes to look at what actually occurred within a particular period will have to take such dysfunctions into account. In taking "the long view," the monistically inclined historian conceals from himself and his readers what did actually occur. This holds as well for those who take "the broader view," looking only at a total result. In accounting for the outcome of a presidential election in the United States, it is assuredly necessary to take into account a variety of interests, dissatisfactions, antipathies, and enthusiasms which come together to give the final result. Yet, this result does not necessarily give an accurate picture of the basis for the votes in different regions of the country, nor among different classes of voters within these regions; the results of the election as a whole may therefore be relatively unintelligible until these fragmentary data are analyzed and it is shown in what ways they contributed to the final result. When a historian takes the broad view, or when he takes the long view, he is interested only in final results, not in tracing the nature of a society and the changes in it as these actually occurred over time. For a historian, I submit, this is a *contradictio in adjecto*, for regardless of the diversity to be found in the matters with which different historians deal, it is their commitment to idiographic concerns that leads us to regard them as historians.

Chapter Two

Varieties of Structure in
Historical Accounts

Traditionally, the general form of historical accounts has been that known as "narrative history." Even though other forms have increasingly replaced narrative histories, a number of philosophers have recently taken the narrative to be the best model for understanding the logic of historical explanation. Among examples of this view one may cite W. B. Gallie, *Philosophy and the Historical Understanding,* Arthur C. Danto, *Analytical Philosophy of History,* and Morton White, *Foundations of Historical Knowledge;* earlier forms of a similar tendency are to be found in W. H. Dray's continuous series model of explanation, in W. H. Walsh's account of history as "significant narrative," and in some aspects of the theories of Croce and Collingwood. I find this tendency unfortunate, as I have elsewhere attempted to make clear.[1] What is of concern to me here, however, is not criticism; instead, I wish to offer a positive analysis of alternative forms of structure to be found within historical works. I need merely make two preliminary remarks concerning the concept of a narrative as applied to historical studies.

In the first place, describing history as narrative suggests—and I assume is meant to suggest—that historiography is to be compared with telling a tale or story. This is misleading even when applied to the most traditional histories. A historian dealing with any subject matter must first attempt to discover what occurred in some segment of the past, and establish how these occurrences were related to one another. Once this research has been carried forward to a partial conclusion, he must, of course, think about how he will best present his findings, and this, and what follows upon it, may be regarded as "constructing a narrative." Such a narrative, however, is not independent of his antecedent research, nor is that research merely incidental to it; the historian's "story"—if one chooses to view it merely as a story—must emerge from his research and must be assumed to be at every point dependent on it. It is therefore misleading to describe what historians do as if this were comparable to what is most characteristic of the storyteller's art: The basic structure of a story or tale is of the storyteller's own choosing, and whatever may be preliminary to his telling that story does not serve to control the act of narration.[2] In the second place, as we shall see, the demands placed on a historian by his subject matter rarely permit him to follow any simple story line. To explicate the chain of occurrences with which he deals, he must, in most cases, provide a great deal of material concerning the antecedent background of these occurrences, and must also pay close attention to many contemporaneous events. The storyteller, on the other hand, is not under the same necessity: he starts *in media res* and he need merely introduce whatever earlier background or whatever references to ongoing events he regards as useful in highlighting his story. Therefore, narratives tend to have a simpler, more linear, and more self-contained structure than do historical accounts, even when the historian is sequentially tracing the changes that occurred over time with respect to the central subject with which his account is concerned. I shall therefore speak of the structure of the more traditional historical accounts as *sequential* in character, and avoid referring to such works as narratives.

As I have remarked, this traditional structure has been increasingly replaced by other ways of organizing historical works, but the sequential form remains one basic pattern of which we must take cognizance. There are two other such forms with which I shall deal in the present chapter: the *explanatory* and the *interpretive*. What must be emphasized at the outset is that these are not "pure" forms: No historical work uses one to the exclusion of the others. As we shall see, there will be points at which each of the three modes comes into play in any historical work; however, the overall structure of any historical study is likely to conform more closely to one of these forms than to either of the others. The fact that I shall not attempt to isolate and deal with any other forms does not indicate that I believe my classification to be exhaustive. I do, however, regard these three types of structure as more pervasive than any others one might distinguish.

I

For purposes of exposition, I shall first briefly consider the *explanatory* structure, which dominates some historical accounts and which can be of importance at almost any point in any form of historical inquiry. What I shall term an explanatory structure is present only when a person—in this case a historian—already knows (or believes that he knows) what has in fact happened, and seeks an explanation of why it happened. In such a case he starts from a fact taken as present and seeks to trace back its causes—that is, to establish what was responsible for its having happened. How we are to conceive of the cause, or the causes, of an occurrence is a problem that will occupy us in the second part of this book. What is here of importance is what may be called the direction of inquiry in an explanatory account. Speaking generally, inquiry starts from a given outcome and proceeds in a direction that is the reverse of the direction in which the events responsible for that outcome actually occurred; in other words, an explanatory account involves a tracing back of events from the present toward the past.[3] It is here that there emerges a first and fundamental point of difference between an explanatory structure and a sequential structure, for the latter—as we shall see—follows events in the order of their occurrence, and though the outcome of the series may in fact already be known by the historian, it need not have been known. On the other hand, in explanatory inquiries, the inquiry itself (although not the account that emerges from it) moves back from what is known to have occurred and seeks an explanation of it through tracing its antecedents.

Furthermore, in an explanatory account of a particular occurrence, the events with which the historian deals may be extremely diverse, not belonging together except insofar as each happened to contribute to the particular outcome the historian is investigating. For example, if he is to account for a sudden decline in a nation's foreign trade, he is not necessarily confined to events that occurred within that nation: The eruption of a war involving one of the nation's major trading partners and a blockade of that partner by its neighbors might well be important factors to be taken into account. In addition, a drought may have caused a decline in the nation's agricultural exports to other nations; so, too, may have a strike of dock workers. All such factors are relevant for the historian who wishes to explain what occurred, but it is obvious that they are often wholly independent of one another. Thus, an explanatory account of a particular effect draws upon factors each of which has its own separate history: The historian will not be following any one continuous series of events. In this respect, such accounts differ from the characteristic structure of sequential histories.

In a sequential history, the historian chooses a subject that has a degree of continuity in its history, and he seeks to trace the strand of events making up that history. Consequently, a sequential history seems to possess a single dominant story line—as narratives generally do—rather than being an analysis of independent factors that, together, bring about a particular result. However, the comparison between sequential historical accounts and nonhistorical narratives must not be overemphasized, not only because of the differences to which I have already alluded but because what we regard as a story usually leads to a specific conclusion, and it is with respect to that conclusion that the episodes were selected by the person telling that story. A historian, however, may write a history of some still incomplete series of events, as Thucydides did: He commenced his account of the war between the Athenians and the Peloponnesians when they first took up arms. In that case the historian follows occurrences as they occur, not knowing where they will eventuate, but keeping in mind that he is to include only those events that seem to have a direct bearing on the particular subject with which his history is concerned. His subject may be a person or a nation, a changing institution or a cultural movement; in any of these cases a sequential history has a unifying theme. When historians look back upon a completed life or the end of an era in a nation's history, or upon an earlier cultural movement or a set of institutional changes, it is of course easier to see what was relevant than when they are dealing with what is still an ongoing process; yet, even in these cases, the structure of a sequential account may be quite unlike the usual structure of a narrative—the reign of a king may have come to a close without coming to a climax, or an institution may have changed its forms and its functions without our viewing each of its earlier changes as preparatory to what it later became. In short, in much of history, if it be narrative, it is narrative sorely lacking in point. This fact, however, is apt to be concealed by cases in which the historian has chosen to depict some sequence of events in which we are fascinated by the manner in which—as in a story—the parts form themselves into a single unified whole.

We are now in a position to see the essential differences between an explanatory and a sequential approach to the materials with which historians are concerned. For the sequential historian there is a particular series of events he wishes to follow, seeing one grow out of another and observing how other events altered their progress, but how in the end they came to form a single history whose course he is able to render intelligible. In this, the direction of the flow of events and the direction of his explanation coincide. To be sure, at some points in this flow he may be puzzled, and he will then have to pause to give an explanatory account as to why, at this point, an event of a particular sort unexpectedly occurred; in general, however, a sequential account will follow the form of Dray's continuous series model of explanation—one event led to another, and it to the next, and so on to the end of the series. On the other hand, an explanatory account does not set out to give the reader a sequential view of what occurred, but seeks to answer a definite question: Granted that this event *did* occur, what factors were responsible for its occurrence? Sometimes tracing a continuous series of events provides an explanation with which we are satisfied, but historical analyses often take another form, tracing back a confluence of otherwise unrelated events and indicating how, at successive moments, they interacted. The difference between these approaches is sometimes as great as the difference between explaining the size of the population of the United States in 1976 by tracing a curve of growth and accounting for the rate of growth in any particular decade.

We must now turn to the third form of structure in historical works, the interpretive. Perhaps the simplest way of indicating how interpretive works differ from those whose structure is primarily sequential or primarily explanatory is to consider the task faced by almost any historian as he introduces his reader to the subject with which he is to be concerned. In that introduction he must portray the state of affairs existing at the time and place at which his account begins, insofar as its aspects are relevant to that with which he is to deal. Other aspects of what then existed, even if known, are not of concern: What is needed is to present a background against which future developments can be understood. The portrayal of these materials cannot consist in simply listing them, since the relations existing among them will be important to relationships among the events that later emerged from them. Thus, at the outset of any historical work an attempt is made to depict a particular state of affairs, not in all detail but in terms of what was most significant in its structure with respect to the later events with which the historian intends to deal.

Now, it is possible for a historian to enter upon a similar task not simply for the sake of presenting background for understanding further events, but for the sake of depicting that state of affairs itself. This, I take it, is precisely what historical accounts that are primarily interpretive in structure are intended to do. To be sure, they are unlikely to be restricted to depicting the structure of a state of affairs merely at some moment in time; they will be inclined instead to treat of such structures as enduring in a continuing form over some definite span. For example, G. M. Young in his essay *Victorian England: Portrait of an Age* dealt with England from 1831 to 1865; Burckhardt's *Culture of the Renaissance in Italy* is, of course, an interpretive history of even greater sweep. Since historical structures to some extent change over time, the interpretive historian will generally also be concerned with understanding and depicting these changes. Thus, in portions of his work he will adopt sequential modes of treating his subject matter. Further, he will at various points attempt to explain such changes, and thus from time to time his account will proceed much as explanatory accounts proceed. Nonetheless, a historian may envision his main task as that of revealing the characteristic feature of some form of life, rather than sequentially tracing or explaining the various occurrences that enter into his account. This motivation is evident in the works of Young and of Burckhardt to which I have alluded.[4]

It is easy to identify such works as examples of interpretive histories, but the genre is far more inclusive than these illustrations suggest. For example, if one takes Richard Pares's well-known Ford Lectures, *King George III and the Politicians*, one finds an attempt to portray "the ruling interests and motives of British politics in George III's reign; to explore the king's uncertain and undefined relations with the House of Commons; and to illustrate the conflicts which this uncertainty and want of definition produced from time to time."[5] While Pares's description involved elements of explanatory analysis and also some tracing of sequential connections, his emphasis throughout his lectures lay on the interpretation of relationships among individuals and groups who held and shared power. Nor is this an isolated example: Almost any cross-sectional study of political or social life is bound to have a strong bias toward an interpretive structure, even if, later, explanations are offered as to how the relationships among the various segments of the community came to be as they were. Thus, interpretive studies cannot be confined to a study of the interplay of elements in the culture of a people; they often deal with institutional relationships as well. Of this we shall have more to say later.

II

It is now time to turn from this first general characterization of the three types of historical structure to a closer consideration of their interplay. I shall first address myself to the relations that are likely to exist between sequential and explanatory accounts, and in this connection we shall see in further detail why the current tendency to identify history with narrative is basically misleading, especially insofar as general history is concerned.

In general histories, the nature and changes of a social order are what serve as the focus of a historian's interest, and any such order involves a complex network of relationships even where a historian may wish to confine himself to only one facet of the society—say, to its political aspects. In order to depict the political life of a society one cannot follow any simple narrative sequence. This is evident if one considers even a sharply delimited segment of political life, such as a single presidential election campaign. It would be a gross distortion of the subject matter if the historian were to view the events constituting the campaign as a single linear series in which each step is causally related to a particular antecedent and itself leads to a specific consequent, as (for example) Morton White's analysis of the basic skeletal structure of historical narration would have us assume.[6] Usually there is an overall strategy in a political campaign, and that strategy originally depends upon an analysis of the established voting habits of different segments of the population, and upon a recognition of the current interests, disaffections, and needs of various geographic, economic, and ethnic groups. Thus, to understand the stratagems each political party employs, one must grasp their relationships to longer-enduring factors that are not themselves links in the sequential chain of events constituting the "story" of the campaign. Moreover, much that happens in a national election happens at different times and in different parts of the nation, and the ultimate outcome of a campaign, even in an age of rapid, widespread communication, may depend not upon what happens day by day, but upon where it happened, and by whom it is known to have happened, and how it relates to what the opposition had already claimed. In other words, an election, unlike a chess match, is not won or lost by a series of neatly arranged sequential moves and countermoves; any merely sequential narrative, or "campaign story," is therefore not likely to give its readers much insight into why the elements in that story occurred or why they had the effects they did.

Rather than viewing an election as a linear sequence of events, it is more accurate to view it as a whole made up of parts, with an understanding of that whole depending upon an understanding of its various parts and of their relations to one another. Such a whole is, of course, temporal; it is not a whole that is present all at once. Some of its parts will precede others, but many may be present at the same time; some will depend upon others, but many may be independent of most of the others, nonetheless contributing something to the whole of which each is a part. What is true of a single process, such as an election campaign, or the enactment of a single measure by the Congress, is obviously true of any major ongoing changes in the political life of a nation. The interplay of centers of political power, and the decisions reached, the setbacks, the recouping of losses, and the final results achieved cannot be charted in a linear pattern in which each relevant event is to be viewed as a discrete link in a single continuous chain. The relations between the events with which political historians deal are always set against an institutional background, without which the relations between the various events cannot be understood. Furthermore, it is rarely the case that the political life of a nation exists in isolation from its economic and social changes or is unaffected by its relations to other nations. Under these circumstances, the model of historical accounts that narrativists propose is so oversimplified as to be radically misleading.

Nevertheless, there is one important aspect of the view of those who adopt this model that can be retained even after one drops all other analogies between writing history and telling a story: This aspect is the claim that, in describing what actually occurred and in tracing the relationships between these occurrences, one is in fact offering what a historian will take to be an *explanation*. In other words, contrary to what has been held by Hempel and others, there is what Fred D. Newman has termed "explanation by description": In order to explain actual events, one need not in all cases show that they followed from a set of antecedent conditions according to some general law.[7] This is a consequence of what has already been said in the preceding paragraph: An understanding of a whole may come through understanding its parts and their relations; and while these relations among the parts may sometimes have to be explained with reference to general laws, as we shall see in chapter 5, this is not in all instances necessary.

Consider what has been said of an election campaign: To explain its outcome we do not in fact relate that outcome to some antecedent set of conditions by means of a general law; we analyze the campaign as an ongoing process in which the tactics employed by each contending party proved to be successful or unsuccessful with particular groups of people in particular localities, and we take into account how events over which neither party may have had control also affected the outcome. Understanding what constitutes the electoral process in a particular nation (or its subdivisions) permits one to analyze that process into its components and to offer a description of these components and of how they affected one another; this is to offer what historians generally would take to be an explanation of the campaign's outcome. Some historians or political scientists or sociologists may wish to generalize from such analyses, formulating a general law concerning relationships between particular economic conditions or wars or psychological factors and what have been the results of presidential elections in the United States; however, as we shall see, it is doubtful whether there can be any satisfactory laws of sequence of that type, even in the physical sciences.[8] While there are indeed generalizations that historians must often use, the point to be noted is that one is giving what a historian would count as an explanation when, within a sequential history, one is able to follow the train of events that make up the series as a whole. Unless the relations between the particular episodes remain opaque—which they often are not—tracing the components within a process does yield an explanation of why, when the situation was as it was at a given time, it later became radically altered. In short, as our contemporary narrativists insist, to complete "the story" is to give the explanation; but my point is that in a historical account "the story" is by no means a simple narrative story.

Furthermore, I wish to insist that the relations between the particular episodes within a historical account may remain opaque: It may not be in the least clear how one well-authenticated part of a process was related to another, even when one suspects that there must be some relation between them. In such cases the sequential structure of a historical account must be supplemented by explanatory or interpretive analyses. Consider, for example, the case in which it is obvious that a historian must make mention of a deep economic recession in order to explain the outcome of a particular election. Campaign speeches, newspaper editorials, and voting patterns may yield abundant evidence that there was such a connection. Yet, it may not be at all clear from the documents available to the historian how such a recession was itself connected to any foregoing events. To establish such a connection, he may have to call upon economists who, by the use of well-established generalizations concerning economic processes, can explain the connection between the recession and earlier politically motivated policies. In order to apply such generalizations to the events with which he is concerned, the historian may also have to employ what I have termed the interpretive method, which forces him to look for institutional relationships of which he may not previously have been aware. Thus, an opaque relationship in what otherwise seems to be a straightforward sequential account may lead historians to seek new factors in the situation, and the background of earlier sequential accounts will thereby have become more complex. This, of course, is one way in which a discipline such as economics has led to fundamental changes in the traditional forms of historiography.[9]

Analogous relationships between sequential accounts and explanatory or interpretive inquiries are to be found when we turn from general histories to the field of special histories, such as histories of science or literature or architecture or philosophy. In these fields, however, the sequential structure raises problems not present in the case of general history. These problems arise because the subject matter of a special history—as we have noted in chapter 1—is some phase of culture, not a particular society or its institutions. Therefore, the special historian deals with a collection of activities and works, rather than with any entity that has a continuous existence. Nevertheless, when one reads a history of French literature, of Gothic architecture, or of chemistry, the literary works, the buildings, or the discoveries that make up the history form a related series; they are not merely random collections, sequentially arranged. Obviously, this is because the historian has arranged them as he has; but why, one may ask, should that arrangement have been chosen?

The answer that may first come to mind is that one can see how each of these works may have influenced some of the succeeding ones; thus, the series is formed through the skeins of influence the historian follows. This, however, leaves out of consideration a more basic factor: the definition of his subject matter that led the historian to his selection of those materials to which primary attention was to be devoted. As we shall see, only after his subject matter has thus been delimited does the tracing of influences become important in establishing the continuity to be found in any special history. One can appreciate the importance of a definition of the nature of a cultural element when one notes, for example, that different literary historians define "literature" in different ways. For some, it includes only fiction, drama, poetry, essays, and journals, whereas others would also include sermons and correspondence, and perhaps historical, scientific, or philosophical writings viewed from the point of view of their relations to other literary forms.[10] Furthermore, whether one uses a broad or a narrow definition of "literature," some would wish to include only works considered to be of high literary merit during their author's own time or subsequently, whereas others would include popular fiction, popular verse, widely distributed political tracts, and so forth, taking into account breadth of distribution and general interest, as well as literary merit. Similar considerations apply, *mutatis mutandis*, to histories of architecture, of science and technology, philosophy, or any other special history. Given this situation, it is not strands of influence, but the historian's conception of his subject matter that, in the first instance, dictates the principles of inclusion of certain materials in his work and governs the exclusion of others.

We find, of course, that literary historians (for example) do not deal with the whole of past literature, but set themselves more specific tasks: They may deal with the works of a single author or of a school, with a style or a genre, with the literature of a period or of a nation. Yet, what is included within their more specific topic depends upon what they are willing to regard as literature, and also upon how, for example, they delimit the period or the genre they wish to investigate. This primary delimitation of the materials with which a literary historian deals is analogous to the fact that the materials that fall within the scope of a general historian's interest are, in the first instance, determined by the subject he has chosen, by the aspect or aspects of it with which he is concerned, and by the scale on which he wishes to pursue his inquiry. There is, however, a point at which this analogy breaks down. As we have noted, the general historian deals with some continuing societal structure, analyzing its parts and following its changes, whereas a literary historian, or the historian of any other branch of culture, deals with a series of works that, although they are seen as belonging together, are not parts of any actual single whole. It then becomes necessary to raise the question of how a literary historian can justify the fact that he includes certain works and excludes others when he comes to write his sequential account of, say, a nation's literature, or of a genre such as the novel. While his definition of literature or of the novel provides an initial delimitation of his material, there will undoubtedly be many examples that fit his definition with which he will not deal. Unlike a general historian, he cannot then say, "These do not belong to the subject with which I am dealing," for that with which he is dealing is a *class* of objects, not a continuing whole and its parts.

At this point the literary historian, or any other special historian, is likely to invoke the concept of "importance": He will attempt to include all *important* examples of the class of works with which he is dealing, but will be willing to exclude those he believes lacking in importance.[11] The term "importance," however, conceals within itself a number of meanings. In the present context, for example, an important work may be one of outstanding literary value; or it may be one that had a significant influence on other literary works by virtue of its theme or its technique; or it may be regarded as important because it influenced social and political thought, or moral and religious belief, and would therefore be included by those literary historians who adopt one of the broader definitions of literature. Of these alternatives—for each of which many examples can readily be cited—it is only the first meaning of "importance" that does not include an obvious and explicit reference to the factor of influence. Even in that case, the way in which the concept of "outstanding literary value" is frequently used may suggest a tacit reference to the factor of influence, for works so designated are usually those that are considered classics—that is, works whose readership and influence have persisted. Should this be challenged, and were there to be no reference to a work's influence contained in value judgments regarding literary merit, the role of influence would nevertheless be deeply ingrained in any literary history, since the *history* of a literature, or of a genre, does not confine itself to criticism and to the comparison of individual masterworks. Therefore, in a literary history, or in any other form of special history, the question of influence and the spread of influence stands at the heart of the problem of continuity.

In tracing influences in literature—to remain with it as an example —the historian sometimes has explicit evidence to guide him: Letters, diaries, the author's conversations with others, and the like provide the historian with suggestions as to the works and events that may have most influenced an author. Such materials are, of course, of great biographical value, but one cannot take an author's explicit comments on other authors or events (nor can one take any absence of such comment) as an accurate reflection of the degree to which he was in fact influenced by them. In literary history, as in anthropological investigations of the spread of culture traits and of culture complexes, one must be guided by resemblances that are found, as well as by the probability that there has been an opportunity for the dissemination of influence.[12] Letters, diaries, and the like can directly attest to the existence of contact, and thus to the opportunity for influence; however, the literary historian has other, less direct evidence he can use concerning opportunities for influence: the availability of the relevant works in their original form or in translation, discussion of these works in periodicals known to have been read by the author in question, and the like. Yet, it is through resemblances that most clues as to influence are originally discovered; and after the possibility of contact has been established, it is on the strength of these resemblances, and the unlikelihood of their having been accidental, that the historian's argument for influence must finally rest.

In noting resemblances and tracing influences among literary works, the historian of literature is led to weave a complicated pattern of relationships: Even in the simplest cases, there will not be any single line of influence to follow, in which *a* influenced *b*, and *b* influenced *c*, but in which *c* was influenced by nothing but *b*. Any work, *c*, will have been written by some person, and the influence of *b* on his work—no matter how strong—will not explain *c*, since the author's own experience and style, as well as the need not merely to repeat what has already been done, will have affected his work. Nor is it likely that the work of an author will be affected by one model only: Whatever the influences from the past or from his contemporaries that affect him, they are not likely to remain discrete, but will blend and affect his various works in different ways. Therefore, even if one were to write the history of some limited literary form, in moving from one author to another the literary historian must take much into account beyond the specific form he is to trace. He must be prepared to treat the most important works written in this form in their own contexts, and not merely as illustrations of that form; furthermore, in some cases he may also be expected to account for the fact that the form with which he is concerned arose and flourished when it did. For example, it would be a poor history of the epistolary novel in the eighteenth century if one were led by similarities in their form to treat *Pamela, La Nouvelle Héloïse,* and *The Sorrows of Werther* without consideration of Richardson, Rousseau, and Goethe, as if these novels were related only to each other and not to the lives and other works of those who wrote them. It would also be an impoverished history of the epistolary novel if no attempt were made to show what these works had in common beyond their epistolary form, and how such common elements were related to other aspects of the literature and thought of the time. It is for this reason that I have characterized the task of a literary historian as one of weaving a complicated pattern of resemblances (and, of course, also contrasts) among the works with which his definition of literature and his chosen aspect of that literature has led him to deal. And since he is a *historian,* and is not merely classifying works according to resemblances in abstraction from questions as to when they were written, or by whom, he will seek to account for these resemblances in terms of influences: In other words, he will seek not merely to analyze the resemblances and differences he finds, but to *explain* them.[13]

Not all such explanations will be of the same type, since many sorts of influences can affect any literary work. For our present purposes it will be sufficient to classify them under four general heads, which may be roughly described as follows: (1) influences coming from other literary works; (2) influences coming from the other arts, or from religion, the sciences, or philosophy; (3) factors in an author's own personality and in his experiences that can be related to individual works or to his creative work as a whole; and (4) political and social factors in the life of his time by which his work can be shown to have been directly influenced. This classification of the sorts of influences one may expect to find in literature is not intended to apply to all kinds of special histories, but it does have applicability in fields other than in literature—for example, to the history of the pictorial arts or of philosophy.

I shall not attempt to deal with these different forms of influence individually, but shall merely use them to illustrate how, in the sequential structure of a literary history, or in other forms of special history, explanatory elements are introduced. For example, when there is a sudden break in the literary traditions of a nation, the literary historian will attempt to explain that change. In some cases he can appeal to influences coming from sources other than literature, whether these arose in other arts or were to be found in intellectual or social changes; in other cases he may find testimony that the old forms have worn thin and no longer attract, and a major innovator has appeared. In such cases the innovations may have been directly related to the life experiences of one or a few major innovators; in other cases they may have resulted from a rebellion against current fashions and a search for renewal in earlier indigenous traditions or in exotic forms. The power of novelty is not to be underestimated, and when it is found in a major creative figure, his work may set a pattern for his generation and, for a time, for others who come after him.

In other cases, where one is not dealing with swift, revolutionary changes, but with new emphases and a new tone, the influence of individuals may also be strong, but the literary historian will be more apt to look for the explanation of such changes in the intellectual and social life of the period with which he is concerned. This point need not be labored: The literary historian does not merely depict the changes he finds, but seeks to account for them in terms of the different influences that have effectively shaped the works and have channeled the influences of the authors with whom he has chosen to deal.

It is at this point that one can most clearly see the importance of interpretive accounts for the literary historian, or for any other type of special historian. Unless a background has already been presented in which the relationships between social, political, religious, philosophical, scientific, and other important factors in the life of the period have been depicted, there will be virtually no materials upon which to draw when the literary historian wishes to explain the changes he finds and the effects these changes have carried in their train. Therefore, he must, at various points, present a cross-sectional depiction of the condition of the society with which he deals and of the various elements entering into its culture, or he must presuppose that his readers will have knowledge at hand regarding these factors when he introduces them in explaining the persistence or the changes of the forms and themes with which he deals. In presenting such interpretive portraits, a historian need not confine himself to discussing works of major importance. In fact, he is unlikely to do so. Many works that are not of outstanding merit nor of significant influence may find their way into a literary history, or into any other form of special history. These are works taken to be more or less "typical," that is, works that to a marked degree are paradigmatic of a style or a form of sensibility, or of reactions to the political, social, or intellectual aspects of the times. For example, while it is unlikely that any examples of the eighteenth-century Gothic novel would be included in histories of English literature if the literary historian were to be concerned only with outstanding literary value or with subsequent influence, such novels do represent a facet of English sensibility, and are usually included in histories of English literature in that guise, being taken as harbingers of some of the attitudes associated with "Romanticism."

Since the literary historian will, as we have seen, introduce explanatory elements into his sequential account of almost any aspect of literary history, and since such explanatory interpretations presuppose interpretive analyses of the society and its culture, it is obvious that in the field of special histories, no less than in general histories, a sequential account will not take the form of a simple narrative exposition; it will involve crisscrossing relationships, in which the historian picks up first one thread and then another and weaves them into an intricate pattern that follows the complex of relationships with which he is concerned.

III

A similar intricate pattern of relationships is to be found in historical accounts that are interpretive in their basic aim and structure. In them, however, the sequential patterning that arises through tracing influences is less in evidence. While an interpretive account is not usually confined to a single cross section of time but spans a period, as I have noted in the case of Young's *Victorian England* and Burckhardt's *Culture of the Renaissance in Italy*, the emphasis in such works is on the manner in which aspects of society or of the culture of the period, or both, fit together in a pattern, defining a form of life different from that which one finds at other times or in other places. It is of interest to consider what lends structure to interpretive accounts as thus conceived.

In the first place it is to be noted that since the historian is seeking to depict the nature and relationships of various aspects of life at one particular place and time, his account will have to fit into a chronological, sequential framework of greater duration than that of the continuing state of affairs with which he is directly concerned. As we see in Young and in Burckhardt, he will initially need to provide a background for the specific period he is to interpret. In providing such a background, his position is the converse of that of sequential historians: They must inform their readers of the state of affairs obtaining at the outset of their sequential accounts, whereas the background the interpretive historian must supply is a sequential background that sets the stage for the patterns of life with which he is to be concerned. Thus, the ongoing processes in which a particular state of affairs is embedded contribute one element of structure to interpretive historical accounts, and the chronology of events within the period cannot be neglected. To be sure, the interpretive historian need not be concerned with all of the known facts leading up to an initial state of affairs, nor with all the events that later occurred because of them; not every change that may have occurred in the preceding period will be relevant to the later state of affairs with which the interpretive historian is concerned. Nor will every event that has a legitimate place within a sequential account of a period also be relevant to an interpretive history, although many events will have a place in both.

While the presence within any interpretive history of elements derived from various sequential histories—such as those concerned with political, economic, literary, or religious life—provides a structural framework or principle of organization that cannot be wholly neglected, a second and even more significant factor in structuring any interpretive historical account is the historian's view of what aspects in the times were most characteristic, pervasive, and fundamental for the pattern of life he is attempting to portray. Sometimes such convictions are derived from general sociological theories, or from some particular philosophic or historical bias, but they need not be: Many historians in fact deny that the same aspects of life are always, and in all societies, equally fundamental. Whatever the source of his interpretation may be, the interpretive historian will attempt to show how the period with which he is concerned may be viewed—or may *best* be viewed—in terms of some basic theme or themes. This type of selective organization differs at least in degree (and, as I shall later argue, also in kind) from the structure to be found in other forms of historical account. While it is true that the work of *any* historian presupposes that certain events or aspects of life are taken to be more important than others, in historical works that aim to be primarily interpretive it is the interpretive theme itself, and not a particular series of intrinsically related occurrences, that serves to explain why the elements the historian discusses have been brought together.

Under these conditions, it may seem that I acknowledge that an interpretive historian has free rein, and can in effect offer almost any interpretation of a period that fits the theme he has chosen. This, however, is not the case. Different historians may, of course, adopt different positions as to which basic themes provide the greatest insight into a period, and thus in what light the period may best be viewed, but there is a standard against which such claims are measured. That standard is how well a given interpretive theme is supported by a wide range of evidence. Thus, regardless of what may have led a historian to offer one rather than another interpretation of a period, it is on the basis of evidence that interpretive histories—no less than other histories—are to be judged.

To understand the limits that evidence places on the historian's interpretation of a period, one must first note that interpretive history is not an independent enterprise that can proceed without using the results of other historical inquiries not primarily interpretive in their aims and their structure. This is merely to say that in order for an interpretive historian to get to know the form of life in a given period he must draw upon other studies, embracing the political, economic, literary, religious, artistic, and other developments that occurred within that period; otherwise he will not have materials to interpret. To be sure, the interpretive historian should be more than a synthesizer of already familiar materials; there may be a great deal of research he himself must do after he has found the framework that for him best characterizes the form of life in the period with which he is concerned. Yet, even this further research must cohere with what has already been known concerning the period, and it is usually his own prior knowledge of many aspects of the period—rather than prior sociological or philosophical commitments—that suggest to the interpretive historian in what light those phases of the period in which he is interested can best be viewed. At this point his interpretation must be able to withstand criticism: Others who are knowledgeable in the same fields will judge whether the interpretation is supported by the evidence adduced, and will also want to consider whether important contradictory evidence exists. Furthermore, interpretive accounts are praised or condemned on the basis of whether the fit between the interpretation and its evidence leads one to see other points at which the interpretation is applicable to the period in question, or whether the interpretation is plausible only because its author arbitrarily restricted his attention to those aspects of the period that illustrated the theme he had chosen to push. Historians—no less than scientists— apply general principles such as these in estimating the fit between an interpretation and the evidence needed to support it, and they apply such principles concretely and in detail with respect both to what has been said and to what has been left unsaid and should have been said in any particular work.

Interpretive historical accounts are not only judged as wholes, in which case the primary basis of judgment would seem to be a question of what evidence was adduced, or what should have been taken into account; they are also judged in a more piecemeal fashion. As is the case with respect to other types of historical works, one expects them not only to be enlightening when taken as a whole, but also to be sound in their parts. Therefore, an interpretive account of a period that is not also sound in its interpretation of the specific elements with which it deals within that period will be liable to criticism. At this point it is well to recall that interpretive accounts always presuppose, and at various points include within themselves, materials drawn from a vast number of relevant sequential histories. Similarly, as we have noted, within any interpretive account there will be suggestions as to how one is to explain particular changes that took place within the period under consideration. Where one part of an interpretive account comes into conflict with specific facts or relationships that may have been generally agreed upon by competent historians, it will presumably be the interpretive account, not the sequential or explanatory ones, that will be damaged. Such damage may not be irreparable to the interpretation as a whole. The conflict may simply lead one to substitute some element other than the one in question as evidence for the interpretation offered. In other words, when ample evidence exists, emendation and not reinterpretation may be all that is called for. However, in cases of basic conflict it will be the interpretive account, not the sequential or explanatory accounts, that will call for alteration.

This fact does not signify that interpretive accounts are inferior to other forms of historiography; it follows from the fact that we are here speaking of the elements within interpretive accounts, and not of the interpretation as a whole. Such elements serve as evidence for the interpretation, and whatever account is given of these elements must hold up against the same sort of critical scrutiny one uses in testing the continuities depicted in sequential accounts or the linkages among events that are taken as explanations of any particular outcome. In other words, the overall interpretation of a period that is offered by a historian will not serve as a justifying ground for his view of the various elements that are of concern to him in that period. It is these elements that serve as evidence for his interpretation, since the interpretation as a whole cannot serve as evidence for the accuracy of the elements upon which it is supposedly based. Thus, with respect to whatever is included within any interpretive historical account, the standards of criticism to be used are the same as those employed in examining the reliability of the elements present in any other type of historical account.

IV

In concluding this discussion of the types of historical accounts that I have differentiated, I wish to emphasize once again that although the structure of any particular historical work will be predominantly of one of these types, in every such work there will be passages—and frequently long passages—in which the other forms are present. Thus, as we have noted, explanatory accounts will be introduced into works that are primarily sequential or interpretive in nature, and a sequential framework makes its appearance in both explanatory and interpretive accounts. As we have also noted, at least a rudimentary form of interpretive historiography is also to be found in sequential and explanatory histories because of the necessity for depicting the initial state of affairs that any sequential or explanatory account takes as its point of departure.

There are, however, even tighter sets of bonds that tie these forms of historiography together. The chief of these is that the same events are susceptible of treatment in all three types of accounts: Whenever these accounts deal with the same society or societies over roughly the same span of time (if they use roughly similar scales), each will include discussions of many of the same events. The elements that thus make their appearance in different types of historical accounts must be described and interpreted in noncontradictory ways if the accounts containing them are to be considered reliable with respect to them. Thus, so long as two or more historians are concerned with the same events, their works will not be irrelevant to each other, no matter how different their basic approaches may be. It therefore follows that historians who work in the same fields, or in fields that commit them to being concerned with the same events, are not to be regarded as working at crosspurposes, even if differences in their assumptions and their methods might otherwise lead one to regard them as opponents rather than as co-workers.

I do not wish to suggest that all disputes between historians will be resolved and that all historians will ultimately reach consensus in their views regarding the events with which they are mutually concerned. I merely wish to insist that insofar as the antagonisms one finds are based on radical differences in methods—as distinct from antagonisms based on personal hostilities, pride of place, or the like —one should not assume that it is in principle impossible to reach a substantial measure of agreement as to what occurred in given societies and how it happened that these events did occur. Should this contention appear to be hopelessly out of touch with the realities of the disagreements that exist among historians, there are several points to be noted, only two of which I shall mention here. First, it is to be noted that I have not claimed, and would not claim, that different interpretive histories, *when taken as wholes*, are mutually compatible; I have argued only that the adequacy of their treatments of the elements they introduce can be assessed, and that their adequacy with respect to the evidence they adduce, or fail to adduce, can also be assessed. It remains possible that after this has been done the weighting of the elements in the interpretation as a whole may differ from historian to historian, and there may not be any way in which such differences can be decided independently of more general sociological or philosophical commitments, or independently of purely personal preferences.[14] Second, I wish to stress once again that different historians work on different scales and are concerned with different aspects of the life of a specific society at a given time. Therefore, the proliferation of works on what superficially appears to be "the same subject" need not be taken as indicative of a need for continual attempts to start afresh and to rewrite all that has been written concerning our human past. If, as we shall see in subsequent chapters, it is normal to find that works written on different scales and concerned with different aspects of a society prove to be interlocking, the pro-liferation of historical accounts, each of which makes a point of its own, does not entail that we should commit ourselves to any form of historical relativism.

In the final chapters I shall once again take up this question, which was the issue with which philosophers who wrote about the problems of historiography were at one time most concerned. In general, how-ever, this interest subsequently shifted, and problems concerning the nature of historical explanation came to dominate the field. Such problems are, of course, relevant to questions concerning the objec-tivity of historical knowledge, but they deserve discussion in their own right. In the following chapters I shall be concerned with some of them; only in chapter 5, however, will I deal specifically with history. This is because I believe that questions concerning historical explanation cannot be adequately discussed without raising issues that involve a general theory of what constitutes causal explanations. That topic, in turn, involves a careful consideration of the relation between causes and laws. Since the views I hold on these matters are undoubtedly heterodox, I shall develop them in the next two chapters at considerable length. Then, in chapter 5, I shall suggest some of the ways in which these analyses are applicable to the various types of historical study I have already delineated. I can then address the question of objectivity once again.

PART TWO
CAUSATION

Chapter Three

Causal Beliefs in
Everyday Life

Among the many changes in philosophic opinion that have taken place during the past thirty years one is of special concern to the following discussions. This has been a change in the dominant view of what constitutes a proper analysis of the concept of causation. The view that prevailed until recently may be designated in different ways, depending upon which of its aspects one wishes to emphasize. It is often characterized as the Humean view, which calls attention to what was undoubtedly its most influential source. It has also been referred to as the regularity view because it takes the cause-effect relation to be equivalent to an empirically established regularity between two types of events, one invariably following the other. It might also have been designated in more technical terminology as the nomothetic view, since it holds that the concept of causation is otiose and should be abolished from our philosophic and scientific vocabularies except when referring to some particular instance of an empirically established law.

These variant formulations are not to be regarded as strictly equivalent. For example, Hume's psychological account of the role of the imagination in causal attributions differentiates his position from most subsequent formulations of the regularity view; furthermore, his emphasis on the importance of causal beliefs in all aspects of our lives is incompatible with the position of those who, holding the nomothetic view, have wished to rid us of any reliance upon common-sense notions of causation. Nevertheless, these three variant formulations (to which others could be added) constitute a type of philosophic position regarding causation that, in spite of some critics, tended to dominate all others for at least one or two generations.[1]

The fact that this domination has come to an end may best be signalized by mention of one highly influential book, *Causation in the Law*, by H. L. A. Hart and A. M. Honoré.[2] It is no exaggeration to say that since its appearance in 1959 the whole tenor of discussions of causation in Anglo-American philosophy has changed. In their preliminary analysis of causal concepts, Hart and Honoré drew a sharp contrast between the plain man's notion of causation, which they found to be dominant in history and the law, and the regularity view, which they accepted as being, on the whole, applicable in the sciences. In short, they did not challenge the prevailing view within one domain, but argued that it was inapplicable in another. A willingness to follow this general strategy—especially a willingness to hold that scientific concepts and procedures are not necessarily applicable to the affairs of everyday life—has been one characteristic feature of philosophy in the last decades. There is some reason to believe that this strategy is losing its appeal. Instead of segmenting philosophic issues in order to deal with them piecemeal, there is now a tendency to try and connect the distinguishable parts of these larger problems that had initially been separated through linguistic analysis. With respect to causation, J. L. Mackie has recently attempted to bring various aspects of the problem into a single focus in his distinguished book *The Cement of the Universe: A Study of Causation*.[3] In what follows I shall not attempt to deal with all of the problems with which he and others have dealt, for there are many logical issues that are not, I think, especially relevant to historical causation. On the other hand, I shall devote more attention to the phenomenological features of those situations in which we make causal judgments than one finds in Mackie, or in any other discussion of causation with which I am acquainted. I do so in order to focus attention on problems that specifically concern *causal* attributions, rather than on questions concerning those generalizations that, in the natural sciences or elsewhere, we take to be *laws*.

So long as the regularity view was dominant, such a distinction could not be tolerated. Now, however, philosophers of different schools are often willing to distinguish between causally explaining why a particular event occurred and formulating a generalization that states that whenever an event of a specific type occurs it will be followed by an event of some other designated type. As we have noted, Hart and Honoré assumed that this distinction coincided with a difference between our causal attributions in the contexts of everyday life and the characteristic structure of scientific explanation. I believe that their assumption was mistaken. I shall therefore attempt to show in the present and following chapters that although the causal explanation of a particular event does not rest on knowledge of what occurs in all cases of a particular type—and thus that the regularity view is mistaken—one should not conclude that this provides a basis for distinguishing between common sense, history, and the law on the one hand, and the sciences on the other.[4]

My concern in the present chapter will be with our causal beliefs in everyday life. What I shall attempt to provide is a broad range of examples of different types, uninterrupted by discussions of any alternative interpretations of these examples. However, since my interpretation differs so markedly from the views held by Hume, and also from those held by Hart and Honoré, I feel obliged to explain on what grounds I find their positions unacceptable. This I shall do in two brief appendices.

I. THE PERCEPTION OF CAUSATION

It is not uncommon to find that some terms frequently used by philosophers are rarely used in everyday life. "Cause," with its cognates, is one such term. This should not suggest that the concept of causation is remote from everyday concerns; on the contrary, it may signify that the causal relation is so pervasive in experience that our ordinary language has a variety of expressions that serve, in a rough manner, to distinguish among the many forms it takes. For example, if we use the expression "x *produces* y," a more immediate, less remote relationship is suggested than if we say "y was *a consequence* of x*," yet it is wholly legitimate to treat each expression as involving the relation of cause and effect. Again, when we use verbs such as "kill," we have in mind a causal relation between some action, or some state of affairs, and the death it brought about, yet neither the word "cause" nor any of its derivatives is used when we say that "x killed y." Similarly, we distinguish between pushing an object and pulling it, but both pushing and pulling may legitimately be taken as instances in which a causal agency brings about an effect. In all of these cases one may rephrase the original statement using the term "cause" without introducing a significant change in cognitive meaning; it is therefore false to assume that simply because philosophers have used the more general term they have invented a coinage that has no corresponding use in everyday life. Their use of "cause" would be dangerous only if it led them to identify that term with some one or some few types of causal relationship, neglecting all others. This is a danger I wish to avoid.

It is especially important not to confine our discussion of everyday causal attributions to too narrow a range of examples, since all causal notions, whether in science or elsewhere, and no matter how sophisticated and altered they grow to be, have their original roots in everyday experience. Only if we direct our attention to a wide variety of apparently disparate examples will we guard against oversimplification and avoid a distortion of our everyday causal notions. In my opinion, the primary source of many oversimplifications and distortions has been the conventional view that when we speak of the cause-effect relationship we *always* have in mind a temporal sequential relationship in which some specific prior event is the cause of a subsequent event. The pervasiveness of this view is probably due to the influence of Hume's analysis, for it is not a view to be found in Aristotle, nor in Western mediaeval or Renaissance philosophy, nor among the Rationalists. Yet, even Hart and Honoré take this conventional view for granted and treat it as if it were clearly adequate in all causal situations, whether in science or in everyday life. To be sure, there are many cases in which what is taken to be the cause of an event *is* some specific event that was precedent to its effect. On the other hand, there also are many cases in which the conventional view does not conform to our ordinary causal descriptions; we do not always regard the cause and its effect as two distinct and discontinuous events.[5] In such cases, a cause and its effect appear as related aspects of a single event whose continuity we directly perceive, rather than as different, separable events. I shall first deal with these cases. It will then be possible to show that even when the conventional view is apparently correct it does not provide a satisfactory mode of analysis for the causal relationship.

To speak—as I shall—of directly experiencing a connection between a cause and its effect is, of course, to challenge Hume, and for that reason Appendix A is designed to show that his argument against the possibility of perceiving the connection between cause and effect is by no means compelling. Now, however, I wish to present cases in which it is legitimate to speak of perceiving causal connections.[6]

If we consult our direct experience, uninhibited by Humean objections, and if we consider only those cases in which we believe that we directly see a causal connection, we will not, I believe, describe what is seen just as Hume and others have described it. Although it has become usual to speak of the causal connection as existing between two events, in many cases in which we think we are seeing causal power, it is *within* different phases of a continuous happening, and not *between* two distinct events that we experience connection. In such cases what we see as "the effect" is the end point of a series of changes; what we see as "the cause" of this effect is what led up to it in that continuous series. To be sure, this is not always the way in which we describe a cause-and-effect relationship: It is certainly not the way in which I would describe the causal connection when I switch on a light. I shall deal with cases of the latter type in the next section of this chapter, and we shall then find that such causal attributions depend upon regularity of sequence. Thus, my belief in the connection between my flicking the switch and having a light come on is a belief that must be acquired in the way that Hume said *all* causal beliefs are acquired. Now, however, I am dealing not with all causal beliefs, but only with those in which we would describe ourselves as directly seeing what Hume denied we can ever see: direct connection or transference of power. As examples of such cases I shall first cite two readily familiar instances in which a spectator watching a game may be said to see the connection between cause and effect.

When we see a football player running with the ball and then brought down by a hard tackle, we have witnessed an event that is seen as having a certain unity. That it has this unity for us may in part be due to the fact that we know the rules of football, but it is very doubtful whether this is the total explanation of its experienced unity.[7] That question is not, however, my immediate concern. My concern is to locate where in the event we see a causal connection, and what it is that we take to be the cause and what the effect. In this case, as in others, one must start from the effect, for in the cause-effect relationship nothing is denominated as a cause independently of our actually recognizing it as the cause of a particular effect. Now, the effect in this particular case can be described in several different but entirely compatible ways: for example, as the fact that the player who carried the ball was halted by being brought down by the tackler, or that the play was stopped on the five-yard line by number 99, the tackler. (The fact that there are alternative compatible descriptions, differing in *scale*, is a point that will later be of fundamental importance to us.) In each of these descriptions the cause of the effect was the effective tackle, but the tackle was not another event preceding the effect, as one would expect if one were to think of cause and effect in terms of the regularity model. The tackle *was* the bringing down of the ball carrier, not a precedent event; or, on the alternative description, number 99 stopped the play on the five-yard line, short of a touchdown, *in* effectively tackling the ball carrier.

Those who wish to hold to the notion that the cause must always be some event precedent to and distinct from the effect may seek to escape from the foregoing descriptions by regarding the tackling as a series of sequential events of exceedingly short duration, each of which caused its immediate successor, with the last item in the succession being the ball carrier's being brought to the ground in the grasp of the tackler. However, such an analysis would not only fail as a description of what it is that we really see in such a case (for we cannot discriminate what is actually occurring at each of these assumed successive states), but it would also fail to establish that, properly analyzed, what caused the effect was a linear sequence of successive events. It would fail in this respect because we recognize, either directly or from our own past experience, that there is present a simultaneous conflict of forces when a tackler tackles a runner: It is not a question of a series of successive independent movements taking place, each of which is followed by a distinct response; forces are at every instant exerted by tackler and runner, by gravity and by inertia, with the interaction of these forces ending in this effect.

It might be objected that in my description I have given a peculiar and truncated causal analysis since I have omitted relevant precedent actions, such as the fact that the tackler had to catch the ball carrier in order to tackle him; thus, it might be argued, we must carry the cause further back in time, to what preceded the effect. There is, of course, no reason not to include the speed with which the tackler pursued the ball carrier as part of the cause of the effect; however, if we do so we are not considering as "the effect" that the ball carrier was brought down by the force of the tackle, but that the play ended at the five-yard line, and not in a touchdown. In *this* description of the event, the speed of the tackler in overtaking the ball carrier is part of the cause of the effect, but it obviously is not a cause that preceded the event (the play that ended on the five-yard line); rather, it is included within it.

Let me now use my second illustration, that of a three-cushion billiard shot, in order to make the same point once again.[8] In this case, too, we must distinguish between alternative descriptions of what we take to be the event that ends in a particular effect. When our attention is focused on the actual collision of the cue ball with the red ball, we see the red ball move *when* it is hit; we do not actually see it being hit and *then* moving. Thus, the cause of its moving is its being hit. If, after the collision, we are asked why it moved with such force, we are likely to answer that it was because the cue ball had struck it with great force, but even here, when we are forced to use the past tense, we are referring to what was seen as a single continuous process, rather than as being two successive, independent events: In the collision, we have seen the force of the first ball apparently transferred to the second. Now, to say that the red ball moved because it was hit, or moved with great force because it was hit with great force, may not be considered very enlightening, but they are answers that we give and we get in everyday life. What is revealing about them is that even though we use the past tense when we look back upon what we saw, what was taken to be the cause was not an occurrence precedent to its effect: It was the *being struck* that was the cause of the ball's moving, and it was the force with which it was at that instant struck that caused it to have the force with which it started to move. (If, as the ball then slows down, we should be asked what is slowing it down, we would have to admit that we don't *see* what is doing so, but we may say "it is losing force"; if we are asked what that means, we can explain that friction with the table's surface is slowing the ball down. In either case, once again we would be using the present tense to describe the relation of cause and effect.)

To be sure, we can take a longer view of the event in question in the search for a precedent cause, just as it was possible to do in the example drawn from football; though here, too, the stratagem will be unavailing. We may, for example, say that the red ball moved with great force, in that particular direction, because the player was making a three-cushion shot and therefore struck the cue ball in a manner that would make it strike the red ball just as it did, sending the red ball in that particular direction; and we can say that this was necessary if the cue ball was to travel with sufficient force toward the first of the three cushions it was to strike before touching the opponent's cue ball. Once again, however, such a description includes the cause —what the player did—within the event itself, the event being a three-cushion shot that was successfully completed.

This view of what we in many instances take to be the cause-effect relationship may be illustrated by briefly citing other examples drawn from everyday life.[9] For example, a teacher is at the blackboard writing a sentence, and the students watch as he writes. The view of some may be obstructed, but others will see that as his hand moves, holding the chalk, the individual letters and words are formed until the sentence is complete. The completed sentence as written on the board is the effect: It is the state of affairs in which the event ended. But was the cause some separate and distinct precedent event? Not if the cause is taken to be the writing of the sentence, for this was constituted by forming the letters that formed the words that made up the sentence, and this was part and parcel of the event itself. Nor will this conclusion be escaped by saying that it was the chalk moving on the board, or that it was the movement of the hand that was the cause, for these occurred, *seriatim*, at precisely the time that the letters were being formed. Nor is there escape in adopting the longer-range point of view, seeking the cause in the teacher's intention to write just this sentence and no other, for the effect—the written sentence—would not have occurred unless the teacher not only had intended to write the sentence but had actually written it. Thus, the event has simply been assigned a longer time span, including the teacher's intention; however, that intention (which is now seen as causally related to the effect) is not to be taken as preceding the event, but is viewed as a part of it.

Cases of a cause-effect relation that are similar in structure to that of writing a sentence can be multiplied almost indefinitely if one considers those cases in which ordinary acts of pulling or of pushing objects occur. For example, if I am dragging a heavy object at the end of a rope, or pushing a piece of furniture from one part of a room to another, however short a distance or however far I move it—and whether I ever get it to the spot to which I intend to move it—the cause is not some separate *prior* event but consists in all that is involved in the act of hauling or pushing: It is included within the boundaries of the event itself. Furthermore, just as in the case of writing, such an event may be viewed either as a purely physical process where an individual's motions bring about a specific effect, or as an intentional act; in either case, however, what brings about the effect is a part of the process that eventuates in that effect.[10]

The significance of these cases in the present context is that they illustrate the fact that in many of our everyday uses of causal notions these apply to what occurs within what is seen as a continuous, ongoing process. Stating this conclusion with somewhat greater precision than it was convenient to employ in discussing the preceding examples, in each case the effect to be explained is some particular state of affairs that has been singled out for attention. In these causal attributions, such a state of affairs is viewed not as an isolated event, but as the end point of a process; what we take to be the cause of that state of affairs is the process leading to it, out of which it eventuated. We may, of course, distinguish various phases or various components within that process, but in our examples these were not seen as a series of separate and discontinuous events. To be sure, should we wish to do so, we can imagine the process, *once it has occurred*, as if it had been made up of a series of separate, successive states, but this form of cinematographical analysis (as Bergson called it), in which continuous processes are treated as if they were composed of a series of discontinuous, independent happenings, does not reproduce what we perceive when we perceive causal connections. What is seen as the process leading up to the particular state of affairs to be explained is what is taken to be the cause of that specific state of affairs.[11] In short, in those cases in which we may be said to perceive causation— and it is only with such cases that I am now dealing—the connection between cause and effect lies in the fact that both are seen as aspects of a single ongoing process, of which the effect is viewed as its end point or result; the cause of this result is the process itself. Michael Scriven may perhaps have had this in mind when, in the article I have already cited, he held that cause and effect are not (in such cases) separate, but are only conceptually distinct.

Wherever the foregoing analysis applies, the supposed mystery of how we perceive the connection between cause and effect simply does not arise in anything like its traditional form. To be sure, the question of why, for example, a complex set of motions is seen as a continuous process, and not as a random set of motions, will still demand psychological explanation, but this is not a problem peculiar to the cause-effect relationship, as those who follow Hume have generally supposed. On the contrary, it will form part of the more general problem of the ways in which stimuli that comes to us either successively or simultaneously are organized into wholes. Hume's puzzle as to how we could possibly be said to *see* any connection between cause and effect arose only because he started from the assumption that in the cause-effect relationship we are always dealing with what were originally seen as two separate wholes. Because of this assumption he sought some special relationship that could account for the fact that we see them as tied together. When, however, one does not assume that two separate events are originally given, the problem of explaining our perception of a causal relation takes a quite different form: We must seek to explain what leads us to see an event as a single process, possessing a unity of its own. With respect to many aspects of this larger problem a great deal of experimental evidence is available, but none of it tends to support Hume's atomistic sensationalism.

Among the factors we may with some assurance say give unity to an object or to an event are those that were singled out for attention by Gestalt psychologists in investigating such principles of organization as "good continuation" and "closure." One may seek to explain such factors and their modes of operation in a variety of different ways, depending upon one's theoretical framework, but their prominence in the perception of the unity and stability of objects, and of the connections within what are perceived as continuous events, can surely no longer be questioned. It is not part of my purpose to attempt to sort out the various factors that may be responsible, nor to say how they operate under variant conditions: As the experiments of Michotte indicate, even slight changes in the patterning of the stimuli lead to a shift in whether visually apprehended movements are seen as the uninterrupted motion of a single object (as in "the tunnel effect") or whether they are seen as two motions, one of which causes the other. Nevertheless, there is one type of factor to which I shall call attention, since it is relevant to another set of examples of causal perception with which I should like to deal. This factor, which is present in many cases in which we have the conviction that we are seeing a cause bring about an effect, has been designated by others as a *correspondence* between the cause and effect.[12]

To indicate what is meant by a correspondence between cause and effect, one can point to instances of the following sort: When a hot object is applied to another object, we are not surprised that the hot object should heat and not cool the other. It also seems entirely natural that marks left by something black, such as charcoal, should be black, or that impressions in the sand should have contours structurally similar to the objects that made them. Similarly, when one object strikes another it does not appear puzzling that the motion of the second should continue in the same line, and that the harder it is struck the greater the speed expected. Of course, in any given instance these expectations may not be fulfilled; in fact, we may be extremely surprised by the unexpected ways in which one object will be affected by another. All that the factor of qualitative similarity (which has been called "correspondence") helps to explain is why in some cases it is easier than in others to see a sequence of events as having continuity and unity. That fact it *does* help to explain.[13]

I come now to the new set of examples for the sake of which I introduced this brief discussion of correspondence. In these examples I am interested in the fact that in everyday life we often think of a complex set of events as a causally related series when they possess similarities in structure even though we do not necessarily relate each to the others in a simple linear pattern. In such cases their similarities serve to unify and connect them without our being aware of direct connections among the specific parts of the whole.[14] In these cases it is *as if* the qualitative similarities among the events were expressive of some underlying causal factor that manifests itself in each of them. For a simple illustration of this phenomenon we may consider Duncker's example of temporal correspondences with respect to form: "The rhythm of sounds of knocking corresponds to the rhythm of the motions of knocking."[15] In this connection, consider a simple rhythmic pattern of three knocks on a door, the first two being closely spaced, with a slight interval before the third. Regardless of whether it is we who are knocking or whether we are watching someone else knock, we do not relate each knocking motion to its own sound, but the three knocks are grouped in a pattern that also characterizes the sound. It is this similarity in pattern that connects what is felt or is seen with what is heard. That a pattern can play this type of role will be important in those more complex cases of causal connection I now wish to discuss. What it is important to note in these cases—which I take to be frequent in our everyday life—is that a complex patterning of phenomena is often experienced as expressive of some causal power that we do not directly experience but can only name.

Take, for example, the experience of watching a summer thunderstorm gather and break on a hot, still day. There is often a brief moment when one feels a breeze spring up, and the air cools and the leaves rustle, and soon branches bend, then toss in the wind; there is thunder, and the rain comes. There is here a clear sequential order of which we are aware. However, we do not experience this order as being a single linear progression from *a* to *b* to *c* to *d*. The rising storm is felt through all these effects together: The sudden breeze that cools the air also rustles the leaves, but their connection is felt and seen in the change all about us, not through the knowledge that the breeze that I feel also rustles the leaves. What gives unity to what is experienced in watching a storm grow is a crescendo of change: change in the air and in the light and the sky, but above all in the increase of movement and sound as the storm gathers and breaks. This patterning of events seems expressive of causal forces without our being clearly aware of what the forces are: It is "the storm itself" that brings the wind and the rain and the thunder, and we do not trace the individual relationships that exist among these aspects of it. This is quite different from what we found in our earlier examples, which may be said to have been serially ordered. In those earlier cases it was possible to trace how each successive phase of an on-going process was a part in that process. For example, in watching a successful three-cushion shot, we follow the line that the cue ball follows: Set in motion by the stroke, it hits the red ball and then a cushion, caroms off to hit a second and then a third cushion, and touches the opponent's cue ball before coming to rest. Whatever phase of this process one might wish to analyze further, one would still remain within this single, causally connected series. In the case of the storm, however, what is experienced as common to the individual elements that enter into its stages is that each is included within a developing pattern, that each is passing through a transformation similar to that which is also characteristic of the others. In such cases what is experienced may better be described as "orchestrated" relations rather than causal relations. Nevertheless, in such cases we are aware of what appears to be some causal power. Not experiencing it in the specific elements, but only in the pattern that is created by them, we are led to attribute that power to a mere "something" underlying the whole series; but what that "something" may be we cannot truly say. Insofar as direct experience is concerned, we can only say that it was the storm itself that caused the wind, the thunder, and the rain.[16]

I now turn to another sort of case of the same general type, in which we find ourselves in the presence of continuities that we experience as expressive of causal forces, though we are not directly aware of the factors on which that continuity depends. Among such cases are those in which a pattern of motions appears as determined, yet as determined by a source that remains hidden from us. For example, in watching a dog eagerly following a scent we see a pattern in his action—his nose to the ground, his body taut, rushing along a trail we ourselves cannot see, losing it, sniffing about, finding it, following it. We are aware of pursuit, but what gives unity to the dog's action is not any part of what we directly perceive. In this case, however, we *know* that dogs do follow scents, and this knowledge helps us to interpret what we see. However, even without that knowledge we would see the dog's behavior as goal-directed. This is evident in other instances where what is seen as goal-directed behavior leads us to look toward the goal in order to discover the cause of the behavior, as when we see pedestrians on a crowded street suddenly turning to stare in a particular direction. Similarly, in cases in which the goal-directedness appears as being not *toward* but *away from* something, that behavior is used as a way of ascertaining its unknown cause, as when we attempt to locate the source of an animal's pain or discover what a child is afraid of.

The universality and importance of this factor in interpreting human behavior can scarcely be overestimated, but that is not my present concern. I use these illustrations merely to show that we can be aware of the presence of unseen forces without directly experiencing them. Our awareness of them rests on the fact that the complex motions we do see have a common factor: They are seen as belonging within a pattern that runs through them all. In the immediately preceding illustrations the patterning depended upon the goal-directedness of the motions, but this need not always be the case. For example, two figures or shadows approaching and receding in rhythmic fashion, as if dancing, give us a strong impression of being connected, even though we see no connections between them.[17] Similarly, in human situations such as exhibitions of ballroom dancing in the Astaire films, when the partners give no sign of "leading" or "following," it sometimes appears as if the dancing were done *through* them, rather than *by* them: The pattern seems to have a force of its own. This is often even more strikingly displayed by large choruses of dancers following intricately patterned routines, or by expert drill teams.

Still another example of how patterned motion can give us a strong impression of some underlying force we do not directly perceive is to be found in some of the ways in which the ocean appears to us. In the rising and swelling and sinking of waves, the rhythmic pattern seems to express an underlying causal force. Similarly, if from the beach we watch a single wave rising and swelling, cresting and breaking, its rhythm gives us a sense of its underlying power, even before it crashes on the beach. Were it to be supposed that this sense of its power is to be attributed to what we *know* and not to what we see, I might point out that we know a great deal about the power of a pile driver but the repeated fall of its hammer, the sound this makes, the vibrations we feel, are merely repetitive and are not experienced as rhythmically unified; thus, they give us no sense of an underlying power such as we feel when we watch the crash of a wave.

The immediately foregoing sets of phenomenological observations were designed to show that we do sometimes experience what may be designated as causal power within a complex event even when we do not directly experience anything we would denominate as the cause of that event. I have suggested that in such cases it is the rhythmic patterning expressed through the various aspects of the event that gives us the impression of a force underlying what is presented to us. If these remarks are accepted, we have seen another reason to doubt a Humean type of analysis of our causal beliefs. In these cases, no less than in cases such as those in which we see one football player bring down another with a hard tackle, the causal relation is not one that exists between two separate events, one succeeding the other; rather, in the particular cases with which I have just been dealing, it is the patterning in a series of events that leads us to suppose that *behind* those events a causal power is being exerted. This does not signify that a Humean type of analysis may not be applicable in many other cases; it is to an examination of such cases that I now turn.

II. ON REGULAR SEQUENCES

I have already mentioned one case—that of switching on a light—in which Hume's account would seem to be adequate. In that case, the cause and its effect appear as distinct, with one occurring just after the other, and we can readily picture either the cause or the effect as occurring without the other. Furthermore, in such a case Hume is entirely correct in holding that we cannot indicate, on the basis of direct inspection, what it is that connects the flicking of the switch and the light's coming on. The awareness of a connection between these events would therefore seem to be wholly dependent upon past experience. Hume is also correct in holding that after repeated experiences of a similar sort some intimate connection seems to develop between the prior event and what follows. It must be admitted that there are indeed a great many cases in which past experience thus engenders convictions of "necessary connection."

On the other hand, there are many instances in which the same feeling of necessary connection never arises. For example, experience establishes that bread nourishes and that plants need light and moisture to grow. Such generalizations are derived from past experience, but in these cases we do not develop any inclination to hold that the connection between the cause and its effect has been directly experienced. Thus, these cases differ from those in which the effects of habituation are so strong that the causal relation seems to be directly experienced. In fact, there is a whole spectrum of cases ranging from those in which past experience engenders the feeling that the connection is experienced, to ones in which we would not make such a claim, even though we believe in, and rely on, a causal connection between what happened at one time and what happened much later. The existence of these variations does not, I believe, overthrow what the previous argument attempted to establish: that cause and effect are not to be construed as distinct events, but are to be regarded as components within some single ongoing process. To show that this is the case, I shall consider a number of different examples, and I shall start with the sort of instance that might be thought to be most advantageous to the Humean form of analysis: that of switching on a light.

In such a case, as I have noted, it is clearly past experience that leads us to connect the two successive events, since we cannot discern any direct bond of connection between them; nevertheless, our recognition of a causal relation between these events, though it was acquired on the basis of past experience, seems no less immediate than that which is present when there is a direct perception of causality. I shall attempt to explain on what basis such instances take on this immediacy of recognition, whereas it is lacking in other regular sequences that serve as a basis for causal attributions.[18]

In order to pave the way for an answer to that question, I shall first ask why in such cases—unlike those cases in which I have claimed that there is a direct perception of causality—the cause and its effect are seen as two distinct events. There are, I believe, three perceptual characteristics that, either alone or in combination, lead us in these cases to view the cause as discontinuous with the effect. The first of these characteristics is that they are not spatially contiguous. For example, I flick a wall switch and a ceiling light comes on. Unlike what is presented when two billiard balls collide, or when a child traces a line in the sand with a stick, spatial contiguity is lacking. This is one factor that separates the events, leading us to see them as distinct. Nevertheless, this factor is not in itself decisive, since there are other instances in which changes occur in two spatially separated objects and yet they appear as belonging together to form a single event: For example, two persons walking or running may be seen as connected in their actions, with one leading and the other following, or with one pursuing the other.

A second factor that separates flicking the switch and having the lights come on, and which makes them appear as events that are distinct and separable, is an absence of what, following Duncker, I have termed a "correspondence" between the cause and the effect. A manual, mechanical movement, such as pushing a button or flicking a switch, bears no direct resemblance to the sudden appearance of a bright light. This, too, enhances their distinctness. Nevertheless, it cannot be doubted that given the requisite prior experience (for I am here dealing with causal judgments that depend upon regular sequence), we do look upon the flick of the switch as immediately connected with the light's coming on.[19] Thus, there must in this case be some factor that compensates for the lack of spatial contiguity and lack of correspondence.

What seems of crucial significance in establishing this felt connection is not the sheer number of occasions on which we ourselves have switched on lights or have seen them switched on; rather, it is what I shall call their "instantaneous succession." So long as the context in which these events occur permits us to notice the immediacy of their succession (as opposed to whatever other changes are simultaneously occurring around them), the two events will come to be seen as linked. That this is the case should not be surprising: As conditioning experiments show, rapid temporal sequence is an extremely effective bond in linking two events. However, in order that we should see the two events as instantaneously successive, each must itself be of short duration, seeming to be almost (if not quite) instantaneous.[20] This may be illustrated in the following way: If we were always to turn on a light by means of some contrivance such as a crank or a pulley that took an appreciable time to operate, and if while operating it the light came on, we would learn through experience to expect the light when we worked the crank or the pulley. However, if there were no distinctive, quasi-instantaneous event immediately preceding the appearance of the light, such as a click of the crank or a hesitancy in the pulley, the experience of a direct link between what we are doing and the light's coming on would be lacking. On the other hand, were there to be such a click or hesitancy, we would regard *it*—and not the whole operation of cranking or pulling—as the cause of the effect. Thus, for there to be "instantaneous succession," both the cause and the effect must themselves appear as quasi-instantaneous.

In cases such as that of turning on a light by flicking a switch, each of the foregoing characteristics is present and contributes to our seeing the two events as distinct, even though they are experienced as causally related: The events are separated in space, they are qualitatively very different, and each appears as quasi-instantaneous. Thus, what provides linkage between them is their exceedingly rapid succession. Consequently, in such cases we can in fact do what Hume thought it possible to do in all cases: We can, without distorting our original experience, consider each event separately, as isolated from the other. To be sure, instantaneous succession without past experience would not lead us to link two noncontiguous, dissimilar events. Nevertheless, *after* repeated experience, events of this type appear to be linked in a way not found among events in which instantaneous succession is lacking. We have to learn from experience, through a comparison of instances, which foods do not agree with us, how much water is needed by different types of plants, and the like. All such relationships are causal, but there is no definite moment at which a connection between them appears. Thus, their connection is not *experienced*, but is a connection we recognize as having obtained in the past. It is in such cases, where no linkage is felt in any one particular instance, that attention most readily switches from what is true in one case to what is true in cases of a particular type.[21]

Contrary to the assumptions of Hart and Honoré, such cases are by no means confined to scientific explanation, nor to the explanation of nonhuman events: They arise with great frequency in all aspects of everyday life. To be sure, not all causal attributions are of this sort, yet in our daily experience we often explain a particular event through citing what generally happens in other cases of the same type.[22] Consider, for example, how we may explain to a child that the toy car he dropped in the water sank and was lost, but his sister's rubber ball was not. We will assuredly appeal to some general rubric concerning things that float and ones that do not: Things that are made of rubber float, or things that are light and not heavy float, etc.

In short, we appeal to generalizations as to how things of a given type behave in situations of a certain type, and this is our explanation of the particular case. Nor is this true only of explanations we use to fend off the questions of children: I may explain to you why the crops are good this year by citing the weather, which is of a sort that always results in good crops, or I may explain why one bed of rose bushes is healthier than another by citing the fact that it was fertilized with A and sprayed with X, A and X being particularly effective with roses of this type. Similarly, with respect to human conduct, a mother may explain to her child why her husband became angry by saying, "You know that when you act that way your father loses his temper." Explanations that rest on subsuming a particular case under previously familiar types of cases are to be found in all aspects of life.

It will readily be seen that such explanations serve useful purposes and are often satisfactory as answers to particular questions. However, even though they may have adequate pragmatic justification, they ought not to be treated as if they were sufficient as explanations of the occurrences that, in a shorthand manner, they are used to explain. This becomes evident as soon as one notes how much additional knowledge is presupposed in their use. For example, one must know something about the conditions necessary for the growth of plants and about the factors that inhibit growth before an explanation involving hot and humid weather, or fertilizers and sprays, can provide an answer to why one year's crop, or one garden plot, was more successful than another. These truncated explanations serve to supply missing pieces of information that belong within a more comprehensive explanation and help to complete it. This is their use, but also their limitation: Unless the other pieces of the puzzle were already in place, the truncated explanation would fail as an explanation.

Because this limitation is often not noted by contemporary philosophers, or because it is not taken seriously, the claim is frequently made that explanations are always context-determined. This claim would be correct if one were to equate supplying a missing piece of information, or citing a rubric that generally applies in a certain type of case, with providing an explanation of some particular occurrence. However, as we have just noted, these shorthand responses serve as explanations only when one already possesses a framework of relevant factual and theoretical knowledge into which they fit, and which they help to complete. Therefore, what is context-dependent is not the actual explanation of the occurrence, but only what particular sort of information may, under the circumstances, be needed to complete it. The information we seek, or that we supply when we respond to requests for explanations, will depend upon what sort of puzzlement apparently lies behind the question posed. Bearing this in mind, one can see that truncated explanations will always be context-dependent, with different answers being properly given to different persons, or upon different occasions. However, there is no reason to suppose that these differing explanations are either incompatible or mutually independent. On the contrary, what provides the basic structure into which the varying shorthand explanations must fit will not itself differ from case to case, but will be the same. Therefore, it will be less misleading if instead of saying "*explanations* are context-determined," we say that "answers to questions that are asked or implied are context-determined." We need not then speak as if the same occurrence (or, more strictly speaking, the same occurrence viewed on the same scale and with respect to the same facets) may have two correct but quite different explanations; we can say, more accurately, that the two inquirers were puzzled by the same occurrence for different reasons. In other words, neither had grasped the correct explanation, but the failure of each was due to a different reason: Each lacked a different piece of the correct explanation.

What the characteristics of a genuinely adequate explanation may be is a problem that lies in the background of all that is to follow. At this point, however, I shall limit my argument, seeking to show only why we cannot be satisfied by shorthand, context-determined explanations, even in the affairs of everyday life. One major source of difficulty in such explanations is that they rest on the assumption that the cause of an event is some simple prior event. Once this assumption is made, it becomes necessary to draw a distinction between *the cause* of an event and what are merely *conditions* that make for, or permit, its occurrence. As the next chapter will show, that distinction bristles with difficulties and should be abandoned. Here, I merely wish to expose the fact that even when we are explaining ordinary occurrences in everyday life, the distinction between causes and conditions is artificial and fails to establish the adequacy of our shorthand explanations.

III. ON CAUSAL EXPLANATION

In examining the problem of whether one can in fact distinguish between a cause and the accompanying conditions, let us first take as an example the fact that one sometimes explains an exceptionally good harvest in terms of that year's prevailing weather. Although "the cause" is taken to be the weather, it is nonetheless true that a whole set of other conditions must have been fulfilled for the harvest to have been good. Since we assume that farmers will have the skill and opportunity needed to plant and to tend their crops, and we also assume that the crops will grow when properly planted and tended, we regard the weather as the most variable of the factors relevant to the success of a crop in a particular year. Therefore, it is the weather we single out as being responsible for the harvest. (Whether peasants during the Thirty Years' War would have done so is another question.) However, it should go without saying that the quality of the seed that is sown and the judgment of farmers in knowing when it is best sown, their knowledge of how to tend their crops and their ability to do so unhampered by social upheaval or natural catastrophes, are all equally essential to having a successful harvest at the end of the season. It is therefore my claim, which I shall later defend at greater length, that it is not in the end possible to distinguish "causes" from "conditions," though in some particular contexts of inquiry, where a great deal can be taken for granted, it is often convenient to do so.

What leads to the easy acceptance of these pragmatic oversimplifications is that there are, as we have seen, a great many cases of regular sequences in which we view a cause and its effect as two distinct and separable events, rather than as elements within a single ongoing process. So long as the anticipated sequence occurs, any hiatus between a cause and its effect is not disturbing. However, in those instances in which what has usually occurred fails to occur, we are forced to go beyond these simplistic explanations and find some conditions that are usually present but are in this case absent, or some conditions that are usually absent but are in this case present. Thus, shorthand explanations that take into account "the cause" but not accompanying "conditions" explain what occurs only in "normal" cases; in so-called abnormal cases we must refer not only to "the cause" but to "conditions." This should make the distinction suspect. Furthermore, while shorthand explanations often serve our purposes, even in everyday life any prudent man who wishes to test the adequacy of a generalization will look not to positive instances only, but also to what constitute apparent exceptions. As the old adage holds, it is the exception that proves—that is, *tests*—the rule.

Consider the following cases. We flick a switch and a light comes on, and we regard the first as the cause of the second. Similarly, in all societies people have learned that if some things are eaten they will cause sickness or death, that other things help allay pain or induce visions, and in all societies—or in almost all—it is recognized that sexual intercourse causes pregnancy. In such cases it would seem as if nothing were involved beyond regular succession, that there need be no inherent connection between what is regarded as cause and what is regarded as its effect. Yet, such cases admit of exceptions. The light will not come on if the power has been cut off, or if the elements within the switch do not make contact, or if the filament in the bulb is broken. One can pack into the gap a whole series of "conditions" that must accompany "the cause" in order to bring about the effect, but what one is then doing is substituting these conditions for the continuous process that occurs whenever a light is actually switched on. Similarly, what is eaten and usually causes illness or death does not always do so, nor does sexual intercourse always result in pregnancy, even apart from contraception. To explain the differences between cases in which the expected effect follows and those in which it does not, we must trace the processes intervening between the event that is called the cause and that which we regard as its effect. In tracing these processes we quickly discover that what appeared as two distinct events from our ordinary common-sense point of view were in fact simply parts of one continuous process: For example, the light coming on is merely the terminal state of what occurred within that electrical system when we switched on the current. Similarly, the ingestion of a poison sets up processes in the digestive tract that, through their connection with other organs, in some cases leads directly and without interruption to death, whereas in others it may lead to vomiting and then to recovery. The difference between the results in the latter type of cases need not be a difference in the poison ingested, but in the reactions of the person's system to that particular poison when, at a particular time, it was administered in a particular amount. In this example, as in the preceding one, it is to be noted that the actual outcome, or "effect"—whether it was death or recovery—is not to be viewed as an event distinct and separable from that which brought it about: It is simply the terminal state of a process whose initial phase was the ingestion of the poison and which continued as the body absorbed the poison, with a consequent series of disruptions of organic function, ending either in vomiting and recovery, or in death. When we refine our shorthand explanations in order to account for those cases in which apparently similar causes produce variant effects, the cause can no longer be seen as a prior event distinct from the continuous process that terminates in the effect, nor does it make sense to separate *"the* cause" from "the conditions" without which the effect would not have occurred.

A second and quite different sort of difficulty arises if we attempt to treat the cause as a specific event distinct from its effect, rather than viewing both as elements within a single ongoing process. This difficulty consists in the fact that we would, as a consequence, some-times not be able to distinguish between cases in which it is warranted to say that the first event is itself causally related to the effect, and those cases in which a prior event is merely a sign accompanying another event that is responsible for what occurs. A hackneyed example of this problem is provided by the relationship between changes registered by a barometer and changes in the weather. For example, a rapid decline in barometric readings is taken as presaging a storm, but not as causing it. One might perhaps claim that this is because there is no invariant experienced sequence between events of these types: Storms are experienced by those who know nothing of barometers. Furthermore, other signs of an oncoming storm are fa-miliar to us, whether or not we happen to observe changes registered on barometers. Thus, events of these types are not experienced as constantly conjoined. However, on the regularity view this would not be an adequate reason for denying that changes in barometric read-ings cause storms: Those who analyze causation in terms of regular sequences do not in other cases hold that a failure to note particular regularities in some cases should count against a belief that there is a causal relation between two types of events *if* whenever we look for this sequence we are able to find it. It is beyond question that even though we do not always check a barometer when we notice weather changes, we can find regularity in the changes of barometric readings and changes in the weather whenever we *do* make a careful check. It is therefore necessary to seek some other reason why this regularity is not accepted as indicating a direct causal relationship between changes in barometric readings and the onset of storms.

The reason lies, I submit, in the fact that nothing in our previous experience of sequential relationships has provided us with a basis for seeing changes in these readings as an initial state in a continuous process that terminates in a storm. Spatial contiguity, correspon-dence, and instantaneous succession are all lacking. Yet, there are other cases in which we learn through experience that two states of affairs are causally linked, even when these signs of linkage are not present. The difference in this case is that there is nothing in our experience to suggest that an object such as an indicator on a barometer directly affects what occurs in the environment. Apart from the human purposes it is designed to serve, any slight change in the position of the indicator will appear as being merely an effect of something else, and not as the cause of any further effects. In fact, it is only on the basis of complex scientific theories that we understand the connection between readings on this simple household instrument and the onset of a storm. The connecting links are not directly observed, but involve a complex set of processes of which we learn only when we go beyond our everyday experience. In order to give a causal explanation of their linkage we would have to say something like the following: Changes in pressure result in changes in temperature, and under these conditions a movement of air sets in, the cooling of moist air leads to condensation, and therefore to a downpour. In all of this, through scientific theories, we are tracing a continuous process and are not simply specifying a number of different conditions that are present in one place at a given time. It is the existence of the process that permits us to say how the changes in barometric readings are connected with the storm: They are connected insofar as they themselves are effects of the same changes in atmospheric pressure that result in the storm.[23]

In the foregoing instance it is easy to see why no one is likely to be misled into thinking that changes in barometric readings cause storms. In the first place, as I have pointed out, spatial contiguity, correspondence, and instantaneous succession—each of which can contribute to a perception of causality—are all lacking. In the second place, we would not even know how to interpret "barometric readings" without the sort of knowledge that makes it evident that barometers are constructed to serve as indicators of certain specific processes, and not to cause other physical processes to occur. Nevertheless, there are some instances in which a regular sequence between two types of events may lead one to regard the first as having a causal relation to the second, even though the first is in fact only an indicator that one may expect the second to occur. Such cases are subsumed under the familiar fallacy of *post hoc ergo propter hoc*.

That there is a recognized fallacy of this type argues strongly against the regularity view, since the fallacy is present when one takes a sign for a cause, even though the sign regularly accompanies the effect and serves as an indicator that the effect will ensue. It would, for example, be an instance of this fallacy if a physician were to fail to distinguish between the symptoms of a disease and the factors responsible for the course the disease follows, trying instead to establish causal connections among the various symptoms. Even the layman draws this distinction. If I suddenly feel feverish, and the next day my joints ache, my breathing is constricted, and I develop a cough, I do not attribute these to my fever, nor to each other. Unlike a physician, I may not understand the conditions on which these effects depend; nevertheless, the fact that I have so often experienced them together, in this particular constellation, does not make me regard them as causally related to each other; instead, they are taken by me to be symptoms of processes going on within me, the nature of which I do not directly experience or understand.[24] In this case, as in others, we must distinguish symptoms from causes; in other words, some particular effect, or some series of effects, may serve as a reliable sign of an ongoing process without its being true that this particular effect causes that process or that the series of effects cause one another.

It is important to note that in drawing this distinction between the cause of an event and what merely serves as a sign indicating that some event has occurred, is occurring, or will occur, we do not remain on the level of those everyday shorthand explanations in which causation purportedly depends upon regularity of sequence between two types of events: Even within our everyday personal experience, when we are not relying on any advanced theoretical analyses, we presuppose connections that we do not actually observe in the instance immediately at hand. Thus, it is not in the sciences only, but in everyday life, that explanations of events reach deeper into the nature of ongoing processes than the regularity-of-sequence view would lead one to suspect. We have now seen this to be true in two sorts of cases. In the first type it was true of cases in which a particular expected effect did not occur, as when we flicked a light switch and the light failed to go on; we have now found that it is also true when we distinguish between causes and indicators, or signs. In cases of both types, the new level of causal explanation that must be reached is not one in which we are involved in connecting a series of distinct and separable events, but one in which we are tracing a continuous, ongoing process.

In addition to the preceding sorts of difficulties, which would arise if one attempted to remain on the level of explanation in which the cause of some occurrence is viewed as a distinct and antecedent event, we may note that in any advanced science an explanation consists not in correlating the occurrence of two types of events, but in finding systematic connections among various factors—such as pressure and volume, or mass and distance—that are applicable to events of the most diverse types. (See Appendix A for my criticism of Hume with respect to this point.) In other words, advanced scientific explanations consist in stating functional relations that, when taken in conjunction with the initial and boundary conditions, serve to explicate what has happened in the particular case at hand. Explanations that merely correlate one type of occurrence with some occurrence of another type lack the explanatory and predictive power that any advanced science possesses: They fail to make clear how the same functional laws apply with equal force to very diverse types of occurrences, thus offering uniform explanations for events that, on the surface, appear to be utterly disparate. In short, the sciences are not confined to explaining events according to rubrics that connect particular types of events on the basis of a series of observed correlations: The theoretical component of any reasonably advanced science demands that this model of explanation be abandoned, and with its abandonment the Humean view of causation necessarily disappears.

It must not be assumed, however, that the mode of explanation characteristic of an advanced stage of science does not have analogues in some of the explanations given in everyday life.[25] Among the instances one might cite are those in which we explain the way an object behaves when placed in a particular set of circumstances by appealing to one of its qualities, rather than by citing some antecedent event. I have already mentioned one such case in passing: We explain to a child why a toy car sinks but a rubber ball floats by appealing to the fact that "the car is heavier." To be sure, exceptions and counterexamples to such an explanation quickly push us to more adequate generalizations, and ultimately to the Archimedean law of displacement; however, on a common-sense level we often use shorthand explanations of this type. What is of interest about them in the present context is the fact that the cause is not some antecedent event distinct from the effect: It is in terms of the properties of the object itself that we seek to explain how it behaves. This is quite obviously true in innumerable explanations in everyday life. We explain some aspects of the behavior of a particular animal through reference to the kind of animal it is; or, to choose merely one other example, we explain what occurs when we put sugar in our coffee by referring to the solubility and the sweetness of the sugar. To be sure, some antecedent event may have been necessary to evoke the particular instance of animal behavior in which we are interested, just as it is necessary for me to drop the lump of sugar in my coffee to sweeten it; nevertheless, this does not mean that citing the antecedent serves to explain the particular aspect of the event in which we are interested. Rather, we are interested in why, under these circumstances, this animal behaves in a way in which animals of other species do not, just as we are interested in why lumps of sugar sweeten coffee but pebbles do not. Crude as such explanations may be, that to which we appeal is how objects of this type—that is, those having certain properties—behave under certain types of circumstances.

In going beyond these crude shorthand explanations, which resemble those satirized by Molière, we must offer further analyses of both the relevant properties of the objects and the relevant conditions in the circumstances. Such analyses do not, however, lead us backward in time to some prior events: They are analyses of how the present properties of the object are functionally related to other aspects of the conditions that are also present when the event occurs. This point can be illustrated by citing Hume's own example of the collision of two billiard balls. If our concern is not confined to the general characteristics of occurrences of this type, but if we wish to explain what actually occurred in one particular instance, Hume's analysis of the causal relation quickly proves to be inadequate. The way in which two billiard balls behave upon impact is not always the same: It varies, for example, with the amount and the direction of the spin imparted to the cue ball, as is evident in the difference between shots that "draw" and those that "follow." Let us also notice that different billiard balls, even though they behave in roughly similar ways, do not behave in an identical manner, for some are made of ivory and others of less elastic material. Experience is undoubtedly essential if we are to learn how objects of different types behave, and also how the effects of the impact of one billiard ball on another can be modified by the spin that has been placed upon it: I am not here arguing against Hume's appeal to past experience as the source of our knowledge of these connections. What I wish to point out is that his assumption that the causal relation is a linear, sequential relation between two distinct events is mistaken: An analysis of the cause of a particular occurrence involves tracing the various factors that are jointly responsible for the occurrence being what it was, and not being different. Such an analysis is in fact an analysis of the occurrence itself, and does not lead us to search for antecedent, independent causes. In fact, as our previous arguments were designed to show, so long as we remain on the level on which we say that a cause and its effect appear as two distinct and separate events, we cannot formulate generalizations that will adequately explain (a) why in some cases a regular sequence, which is expected, fails to obtain; nor (b) how we are to distinguish between what causes an effect and what is merely an accompanying sign of a causal relation; nor (c) why it is that different objects that are in many respects very similar do not always react in the same way when placed in similar circumstances. These reasons should, I believe, be sufficient to lead one to abandon Hume's view of the causal relation, once one has broken with his psychological and epistemological assumptions. In the next chapter I shall further develop the alternative view I have here been suggesting, by showing how that view applies in the case of scientific explanations. First, however, it will be well to draw together what has been said up to this point concerning our causal beliefs in everyday life.

IV. CONCLUSIONS

In summary, it should be obvious that our common-sense causal explanations are of very different types. In the first place, as we have seen, there are cases in which there is direct perception of what appears as a causal relation; on the other hand, the conviction that there is such a relation between one event and another often depends not upon direct perception but upon our having discovered that there are regularities in sequences of this type. In the second place, there are differences between those cases in which a causal relation appears to obtain between two events that are seen as distinct and in principle separable, and those in which cause and effect appear as comprising different aspects of one single event. Furthermore, we have seen that there are cases of other types. For example, some complex occurrences appear as dependent upon a cause we do not directly experience, but whose presence is adumbrated through a patterning in what we experience. In addition, we have noted that there are cases in which an effect is regarded as being dependent upon some particular property of an object, rather than as being a result attributable to some antecedent occurrence.

These differences in the various types of causal attributions in everyday life will first occupy us. We shall then turn our attention to the conclusions that follow from our argument that in all cases— when these cases are pressed—causal explanations lead us to view a cause and its effect as linked together in such a way that they may be said to constitute aspects of a single ongoing process, rather than being distinct events.

A. Concerning the Types of Causal Explanations in Everyday Life

Because of the influence of Hume's analysis of the causal relation, and because of the persistence of psychological assumptions similar to those he made concerning what we can take as "given" in sense perception (as distinct from what must be assumed to be contributed by activities of the mind), it is still difficult to convince most philosophers that there are cases in which a causal relationship is directly perceived. Perhaps the following clarification will help to dispel that reluctance.

In many primitive societies throughout the world, one finds beliefs identical with, or similar to, the belief in mana, a secret or spiritual power present in some objects or person, but not in others.[26] Mana can flow between objects and persons; it can be acquired by touching or eating that which possesses it; its presence brings strength, and its loss means loss of power. Though we view this as an instance of superstitious belief, vestiges of that belief are found in a wide variety of phrases, actions, and bits of folklore still evident in our society. If, for example, someone has achieved some notable success, we may jokingly say, "Let me touch you." Furthermore, in some cases this belief is connected with the notion of "correspondence," where cause and effect are linked by a qualitative similarity. For example, children are told that carrots will give them rosy cheeks and curly hair, just as in primitive societies the meat of a bear has been supposed to give strength, and meat of deer has been supposed to make hunters fleet. Belief in such direct transferences of qualities is, of course, superstitious; and if one were to explain our causal beliefs in a Humean way such superstitious beliefs should never have arisen, precisely because they *are* superstitious: Being false, they could not possibly have arisen through any observation of regularly repeated sequences. Their source must therefore lie elsewhere, and it lies at exactly the point that we have seen to be most essential in the perception of causality: a qualitative correspondence between what is taken as cause and as effect.

The fact that such qualitative correspondences sometimes lead us to believe in connections that do not exist shows that we should not in all cases rely on what we directly perceive. This, however, does not signify that we do not perceive it, nor that it may not be a reliable form of perception in other cases. For example, under certain circumstances we think that objects in our environment are moving when it is we who are moving, and under other circumstances the reverse is the case; however, such cases of induced movement, though deceptive, do not prove that our perception of movement is under all circumstances unreliable. So, too, in the cases of our perception of causality. As Michotte has shown, our perception of causal relationships between movable objects sometimes accurately depicts relationships that hold in nature, and sometimes these perceived causal relationships look equally convincing but go against all physical laws concerning what occurs upon impact. In both cases we perceive a relationship that we regard as a causal relationship, but in one case the perception is consonant with the laws of motion and in the other not.

It is here, of course, that regularity of sequence becomes important: It is a test that is used in everyday affairs when we check on the reliability of the causal attributions we make, and which others also make. Given a constant conjunction of one type of event and another, we expect the second whenever the first has appeared, and many of our shorthand explanations of causal connections in everyday life depend upon our having experienced such constant conjunctions. Nevertheless, as we have had occasion to note, the satisfactoriness of these shorthand explanations is often dependent upon the fact that they fit into a background of theory that allows us to connect the cause with the effect: The *connection* is not, as Hume claimed,[27] simply a matter of having observed a constant *conjunction* between the two types of events. Furthermore, as we have seen, such shorthand explanations, though they are often serviceable in everyday affairs, tend to break down and demand supplementation whenever we have to explain cases in which the conjunction does not hold, or cases in which we do not regard constant conjunction as indicating a direct causal relation but only a relationship in which, because of some genuinely causal factor, one event serves as a sign of the other. Finally, in those cases in which we attribute the behavior of an object under certain circumstances to the properties it possesses, rather than to whatever antecedent occurrence led to its being placed in these circumstances, a Humean analysis of what is to be taken as the cause of a given effect is not relevant.[28] Yet, in daily life we do attempt to explain many effects in terms of the properties inherent in objects that act in a particular manner, and the scientific search for invariant functional relationships is an extension of such common-sense attempts.

Bearing these points in mind, two general conclusions emerge concerning the types of causal explanations that are characteristic of everyday life: First, it should be obvious that these explanations are diverse, and should not in all cases be regarded as representing a direct perception of causality; nor, on the other hand, should they in all cases be thought to be dependent on observations of sequential regularities. Second, these illustrations show that, except in cases involving the direct perception of causality in a particular instance, a strong admixture of theory is apt to enter into our everyday causal explanations, and this element may well be continuous with the kinds of theoretical framework found in the sciences. Therefore, it should not be assumed that there are fundamental and irreconcilable differences between scientific generalizations and causal explanations in everyday life.

B. The Underlying Common Form of Causal Explanations

The illustrations through which I have attempted to lead the reader to the foregoing conclusions were also intended to show that the conventional form of description of the cause-effect relationship is inadequate: Only in shorthand explanations of a specific effect is the cause of that effect taken to be an *antecedent* event that is not itself a phase in the single, ongoing process that terminates in the effect. And, as we have seen, once the truncated nature of these shorthand explanations is understood, and the explanatory schemas on which they rely are brought to light, they too can be seen to share a common form.

To draw together what has been said about that form, it will be helpful to recall one pragmatic feature of any causal explanation: that each such explanation has as its point of departure the observation of something considered as *an effect*, the explanation required being one that answers a question as to why that particular effect occurred. The pragmatic aspect of this situation resides in the fact that when we ask why a particular effect occurred, we are treating a given occurrence under some aspect, and not with respect to all of the ways in which it might be described. Thus, when we inquire into the cause of an effect, we are always asking for its cause under some particular description. Since it is undoubtedly true that persons with different backgrounds, knowledge, and interests will view the same concrete occurrence in different ways, they will choose different aspects of that occurrence as standing in need of explanation. Thus, what questions are asked, and what effects need to be explained, will depend upon who it is who asks for causal explanations.

It might at first glance seem that the introduction of this pragmatic dimension would lead to a chaos of conflicting explanations. In fact, just the reverse is the case. In the first place, it is precisely this pragmatic dimension that keeps us from an endless quest in our search for causes: While each answer to any specific causal question may raise further causal questions, this does not mean that the initial question was not adequately answered. Furthermore, there would be no reason to expect conflict between the answers to the various causal questions that could be raised with respect to some concrete occurrence: So long as each question referred to some actual aspect of the occurrence, and so long as these questions were not confused with one another, the causal explanations should be no less compatible than are the differing aspects themselves. This point has been illustrated in several of our earlier examples, but it can equally well be applied in all. It is in fact a principle that can be expected to obtain in every case. It may be stated as follows: While no single explanation will answer all causal questions that can be asked concerning any concrete occurrence, any well-formed question that is correctly answered will fit into a consistent pattern of explanation. We shall have further occasion to note this feature of causal explanations in our later chapters. As we shall see, it will be of special importance in understanding how historical explanations cohere. Before turning to that question, however, I shall examine some traditional problems concerning causation, necessity, and laws. In doing so it will become clear that my analysis of the causal relation has wider applicability than has yet been suggested, and is by no means confined to the concerns of everyday life.

Chapter Four

Causes, Necessity,
and Laws

Of the many philosophic problems that have traditionally been discussed with respect to causes, necessity, and laws, I shall confine my attention to three: first, problems that arise if one attempts to separate "causes" from "conditions," as well as some that arise if one rejects that distinction; second, how the concept of causation is related to the concept of explanatory laws; and, third, in what sense or senses of "necessity" we must assume that necessity is present in causal relationships. The views I hold with respect to each of these questions have already been suggested in the preceding chapter and the appendices, but further discussion is needed so that we may later see in what ways, and to what degree, historical studies involve causal explanations and explanatory laws, and what role, if any, the concept of necessity plays in interpreting the past.

I. ON CAUSES AND CONDITIONS

One usual feature of modern philosophic analyses of causation is that a distinction is drawn between the cause of an event and whatever conditions were responsible—in addition to that cause—for its occurrence. So far as I know, no analytical history of this distinction has been written. What is of interest to me, in the present context, is the fact that at least two important modern philosophers, Hobbes and Mill, dealt with the problem in a way that largely undercuts the validity of the distinction. Mill's discussion is complex and vacillating, as Hart and Honoré have shown; I shall therefore take what Hobbes says as my point of departure. His view is most clearly summarized in one statement in which he contrasts what he terms the *"causa sine qua non"* with "the entire cause" of an occurrence. He says: "That accident either of the agent or patient, without which the effect cannot be produced, is called *causa sine qua non, or cause necessary by supposition,* as also the *cause requisite for the production of the effect.* But a CAUSE simply, or *an entire cause, is the aggregate of all the accidents both of the agents how many soever they be, and of the patient, put together; which when they are all supposed to be present, it cannot be understood but that the effect is produced at the same instant; and if any one of them be wanting, it cannot be understood but the effect is not produced."*[1]

It is not entirely easy to say what Hobbes, in this passage, wished to designate by the term *causa sine qua non,* except that it must refer to some single factor that is necessary to the occurrence of a given effect, but which, alone, is not sufficient. Yet, Hobbes clearly asserts that both the *causa sine qua non* and the *entire cause* are necessary—in some sense or senses of "necessary"—if the effect is to occur. To clarify his meaning, I suggest that the *causa sine qua non* be taken as referring to whatever condition is necessary for an event *of a given type* to occur. On the other hand, to explain the occurrence *of some particular event* one must discover its entire cause. Thus, the *causa sine qua non* of an event would be some factor that must be present in the entire cause of a specific event in order that any event of that type should occur. On this interpretation, the *causa sine qua non* should not be regarded as "the most important" of the total set of operative factors that brought about a specific effect; instead, it would be distinguished from other operative factors not in terms of its efficacy, but only because it is always present when cases of the same type occur. Unless Hobbes's distinction is interpreted in this way, I do not see that it would have been worth making, since *every* factor in the entire cause is necessary for the production of some particular event, and any of these factors could, therefore, equally well be designated as a *causa sine qua non*. To be sure, had Hobbes been one of our contemporaries, one might assume that by a *causa sine qua non* he merely wished to designate whichever factor might most usefully be singled out in order to explain to someone who was puzzled by the occurrence of some event why that event had occurred. Perhaps Hobbes's phrase "cause necessary by supposition" might be taken as suggesting this interpretation. On the other hand, it would not be easy to square such an interpretation with the fact that Hobbes's whole discussion of causation is couched in ontological terms, focusing on the ways in which the properties of bodies explain events. It therefore seems essential to interpret Hobbes as holding that a *causa sine qua non* may be a necessary condition for explaining an event insofar as it is an event of a given type, but that only the whole set of conditions, making up the entire cause, is both necessary and sufficient to explain the occurrence of that event itself, when it occurred and as it occurred.

While it is assuredly useful to try and discover what constitutes a necessary condition for the occurrence of any event of a particular type, we are often justifiably interested in discovering precisely why some very specific, unique event occurred as it did. To do so, we must discover what constituted "the entire cause": It is not sufficient to single out some one factor and denominate it as "*the* cause," distinguishing it from what are merely accompanying "conditions." This fact may be illustrated in the following way.[2]

If one is to explain how it came about that some specific conflagration destroyed almost an entire house within less than an hour, but that one wing of that house suffered only negligible damage, one must take into account a complex set of conditions, such as the fact that a lighted match was carelessly dropped into a wastebasket full of papers, that the basket was near inflammable curtains, that the walls were easily combustible, that some windows had been left open and provided a draft, that the construction of the whole house, with the exception of one wing, was not built to resist fire, but that a fireproof wall separated that wing from the rest of the house. These conditions are all necessary to explain the series of events in this particular case, but they are not, of course, relevant in all cases in which there are devastating fires. In another case a fire may have been deliberately set

by an arsonist who laid a trail of easily ignited chemicals and then set
fire to it. The end result might in each case have been the same, but
a causal account of what happened would involve tracing out, in as
much detail as possible, how the fire had started and spread, for not
every act of carelessness nor of arson ends in the almost total destruc-
tion of a house. The whole process, and not merely its origin, would
be needed to explain the damage that actually occurred.

This is not to say that one cannot generalize and state conditions
necessary for there to be any fire whatsoever, whether it be a house
that burns, or a fire that burns in a coal furnace, or a match or a
forest that burns. Knowledge of that sort is often extremely important
in helping us understand what has occurred in a specific case. Nevertheless, it is no substitute for a causal analysis. Because any such
condition will apply equally to all occurrences of the same type, it
will not—by itself—be adequate to explain the time and nature of
any particular occurrence. In fact, one should not even assume that
we must in all cases refer to some universally necessary condition
(that is, to some *causa sine qua non*) when we are seeking to explain
what occurred in a particular case. For example, although we know
that the presence of oxygen is a necessary condition for the occurrence of a fire, when we attribute one fire to arson and another to a
match being dropped in a wastebasket, we are dealing with events on
a common-sense level, and are not analyzing them on a microlevel.
On that level of explanation we do not—and need not—include the
fact that oxygen was present. In this case, as in many others, the only
necessary condition, or *causa sine qua non*, is not discernible in our
everyday experience; it will be some feature of the microstructure
that is present in all cases of the same type. Similarly, when we
explain how a fire spread, citing the presence of combustible materials, we need not explain (and on a common-sense level we cannot
explain) why these materials were in fact combustible. As we noted
in another context, different levels of explanation must be recognized: One may supply an adequate answer to a particular causal
question without answering all further causal questions that answer
may raise.

This point, with which we are already familiar, follows from the
fact that in our causal explanations we always start from some effect
that is taken as given, and we seek to account for *that* effect, that is,
to find its cause. In any such analysis, new causal questions will arise,
since each of the events that is part of the cause of an effect is
presumably itself an effect of other causes. However, to answer our

first question we need not also answer those further questions it may engender: The quest for explanatory closure, as Hempel has termed it, is a wholly fruitless quest. Thus, it should not be assumed that in offering a causal explanation of a particular occurrence we are committed to an endless and therefore senseless task. There will always be satisfactory stopping points since the specific questions that were actually asked will have found their answers.

There are two additional points to which I here wish to call attention in order to avoid the possibility that they might entangle us in needless difficulties. The first is the fact that although we use a singular term, "*the* cause," in causal explanations, our use of the singular does not entail that the cause is a single, simple event. In speaking of "the effect" we also use the singular, but in describing any specific event or state of affairs we must always refer to a multiplicity of factors that, together, constitute it. Therefore, even though we use a singular term in speaking of the cause of an event, it does not follow that a tenable distinction can be drawn between any one causal factor and whatever further "conditions" were responsible for the occurrence of the event we are attempting to explain.

In the second place, I wish to point out that my argument concerning causes and conditions is not intended as an analysis of ordinary language. As we have already seen, there are many occasions in ordinary life in which we give and accept truncated causal explanations; in such cases we are indeed apt to speak as if there were a fundamental difference between the cause of an effect and whatever attendant circumstances were also necessary for its occurrence.[3] However, when we go beyond such shorthand, truncated explanations, the distinction between causes and conditions breaks down, and the cause of an effect must be taken as including all of the so-called conditions that were essential to the occurrence of the effect to be explained.

In order to prepare the way for this argument, let us return to Hobbes's conception of the *causa sine qua non*, since it might be thought that his contrast between it and "the entire cause" permits us to draw a distinction between causes and conditions. This, however, is not the case. As we have seen, Hobbes's *causa sine qua non* is to be taken as referring to whatever factors must always be present in order for a certain type of effect to occur, as oxygen is necessary in all instances of burning. This being so, the *causa sine qua non* will not serve to distinguish "the cause" from the accompanying conditions, since (in most cases) the presence of oxygen would not be identified as the cause of a particular fire. It would simply count as one among a number of "conditions" without which the fire would not have occurred. This follows from the fact that those philosophers who distinguish between causes and conditions use the term "cause" to apply to some "firing cause," as the matter is often put: Whatever may have been continuously present prior to the effect—as oxygen is present before a match is struck—is not regarded by them as the cause of the effect, but only as an accompanying condition of its occurrence.[4] This point of view was developed in an original way by C. J. Ducasse in characterizing what he took to be the difference between the cause of an event and a condition of that event's occurrence:

"The *cause* of an event B was an event A which, in the then existing circumstances, was *sufficient to* the occurrence of B. . . .

"A *condition* of an event B was an event A which, in the then existing circumstances, was *necessary to* the occurrence of B. . . ."[5]

In introducing the notion of "the then existing circumstances," Ducasse was guarding against holding that any given type of event A is always sufficient to cause the occurrence of B, or that some condition A will, under all circumstances, be a necessary condition of B.

I shall not argue the merits or demerits of this specific formulation, but shall take it as more or less typical of those cases in which there is an attempt to hold that the cause of an effect is to be distinguished from the accompanying conditions necessary for that effect. On this view, the cause is some one specific occurrence that, given the requisite conditions, is sufficient to bring about the effect. If such a conception of a cause is to be regarded as adequate, it must hold in all cases, and not in some only. In criticizing it, I shall first show that there are cases in which one cannot draw a line of this sort between causes and conditions. I shall then extend my argument by relating it to what has been shown in the last chapter: That any account of causal relations in which cause and effect appear to be distinct and separate events presents a truncated and inadequate view of their relations.

Among the most obvious cases in which one cannot draw a clear and decisive line between causes and conditions are some found in physiology and medicine. Others at least equally clear arise in connection with the analysis of human motivation; and, as we shall later see, the cases that may be clearest of all occur in history and the social sciences. To choose one obvious instance from the physiological sphere, consider the disease of tuberculosis. In the *Encyclopaedia*

Britannica we find that it is said to be caused by the tubercle bacillus, but the disease is then more correctly described as follows:

Fundamentally, tuberculosis consists in an inflammatory reaction of any particular tissue to the invading bacilli, and since tubercle bacilli are relatively little virulent, this tissue reaction is subacute in character. It consists in the formation round the bacilli of a microscopic agglomeration of cells constituting the so-called "tubercle." . . . Though in the earliest stage the tubercle is microscopic, when several are formed close together they become visible to the naked eye.

The passage continues by describing what occurs if resistance to the infection is low, and what occurs if resistance is high; it concludes:

Tuberculosis, when it has reached the stage at which it is clinically recognizable, may be regarded as the end-result of a slow progressive unrecognized bacterial invasion.[6]

What is to be noted is that *the effect*, a case of tuberculosis, is regarded as the end result of a process beginning with the bacterial invasion. However, what is important is not merely the invasion but also the tissue reaction to it; the actual end result will be dependent upon those factors that, together, constitute the body's reaction to the invasion and the presence or absence of secondary infection. In speaking of any particular case of tuberculosis, we must therefore take into account not only the initial invasion, but the whole complex process that terminates in the spread of the infection or its containment. So long as we are attempting to explain what occurred in a particular case, it would be false to regard the bacilli as responsible for the effect. The actual outcome will have depended on an interplay of the various factors present in this specific case; no one among them is entitled to be isolated from the others and designated as "the cause" that brought about the effect. It is only if one considers tuberculosis as a *type* of disease that one speaks of the tubercle bacilli as "the cause" of that disease; but one is not then using the term "cause" to refer to some event that was sufficient, under the circumstances, to produce a given effect, but to some factor that is a necessary feature present in all instances of the disease. In short, instead of giving a causal explanation of a specific event, one is formulating a law concerning all events of a given type.

By drawing upon the literature of the physiological sciences one can multiply almost indefinitely cases in which it is obvious that what is responsible for a particular effect cannot be identified with any single causal factor; that one must take into account, as equally efficacious, the ongoing processes within the organism that are also determinative of that effect. Thus, so long as we are speaking of specific events and not of types of events, there is no justification for singling out some one immediately antecedent event, and identifying it as "the cause" of what occurred, when the presence of other factors was no less essential to the occurrence of that effect. Thus, it is my claim that the line between what is taken to be "the cause" of an effect and what are merely "conditions" of that effect disappears. This is true not only with respect to physiological explanations based on scientific inquiry but, as we saw in the preceding chapter, it also obtains in our common-sense explanations of what follows when a person swallows a poison. We shall later see that such cases are not confined to physiological processes, but arise in the physical sciences as well.

It might be thought that even though the distinction between causes and conditions breaks down when one attempts to explain processes in the world of nature, the distinction can be maintained when we seek to understand human actions. This, however, proves not to be the case.

As a first example, take a sudden outburst of anger when a person resents a remark and lashes back with a threat of violent reprisal. Can we say, quite simply, that the cause of the anger was only the remark that was made? If we do, it is likely to be inexplicable why in this case such a remark evoked sudden anger whereas if it had been made at another time to the same person, or to another person, it might have been shrugged off; or the person against whom it had been directed might even have been mildly amused. To explain the reaction—whatever it may be—one must take into account more than the remark itself: One must view the remark in the context of who made it, and of the circumstances under which it was made. One must also understand whether at that time the person to whom the remark was made was irritable and frustrated, or whether he was relaxed. One must also understand his longer-run dispositional tendencies to react in one way rather than another whenever his ego is involved in situations of a given type. In short, both the "conditions" characterizing the circumstances and "conditions" obtaining with respect to the person himself form part of *the cause* of his reacting in one way rather than another to any remark directed against him. It is only in shorthand explanations that we identify the cause of his anger with nothing but the remark. Yet, even then, we must assume the presence of the other factors if we are not to be puzzled as to why that person reacted as he did, since we know that such remarks do not universally lead to violent displays of anger.

Another example drawn from our everyday understanding of human behavior is to be found in the ways in which we often explain fear reactions. If a child or an adult appears terrified of some situation we are not in most cases content to explain that terror simply in terms of some aspect of the situation he confronts. To be sure, there are cases in which some single, simple event, such as a sudden loud noise, seems sufficient to account for the reaction of fear. When this is the case, it seems legitimate to draw a distinction between the cause of an event—the sudden loud noise—and what are construed to be merely conditions requisite for the effect—for example, that the person did not anticipate such a noise and did not recognize its source when it occurred. In other cases, however, when we are dealing with fears, rather than with what might be called startle reactions, the cause is clearly not regarded as a single, simple, antecedent event. It is not, for example, the presence of a cat alone that terrifies a child; we seek to explain the terror through some fact such as the child's having been badly scratched by another cat. To seek to distinguish between cause and condition in such a situation is hopeless, and can be recognized to be hopeless when we note that much of the child's terror often depends upon the circumstances under which he first notices the cat in the room—whether it is stalking softly or is being carried by a person the child knows. Similarly, to explain a person's sudden terror if he finds himself lost in unfamiliar surroundings, we cannot isolate any one factor as the cause of his fear. To be sure, we may say that it is the threateningness of the surroundings, or his recognition of a peril, that causes his terror, but these characteristics of the situation in which he finds himself are not isolable from the unfamiliarity of the surroundings, nor from the apprehension linked to this unfamiliarity. To seek to isolate any one of these factors, making it distinct from the others in the interest of finding some single cause, is to distort such experiences. One can, for example, be aware of possible dangers and yet not feel terror if one is in familiar surroundings and knows what paths of escape may be open; or one may be in unfamiliar surroundings and enjoy them as exciting, precisely because they are unfamiliar, not finding them in the least terrifying. Much will of course depend upon the character of the person, for in the case of the timid we expect a different reaction from that expected of those who throughout their lives are assertive and self-confident. Are such character traits to be counted as "causes" or as "conditions" of our reactions? To attempt to draw any such line is, I submit, to be misled into thinking that whatever may occur in some cases—as in those cases in which fear is a type of startle reaction—must occur in all.

It should now be clear from each of the preceding examples that there are many cases in which we cannot isolate any factor as *the* cause of a specific effect, relegating other factors to the status of being merely the conditions under which that cause operates. Nevertheless, there are cases—such as that in which a startle reaction occurs—in which it seems plausible to speak in this way. Usually these are cases in which there is an instantaneous succession of what are seen as two distinct events. However, as we noted in the preceding chapter, such cases constitute shorthand explanations, and are quickly seen to be inadequate when any exception occurs. To explain, for example, why a person who generally displays a startled reaction on hearing a loud noise does not appear startled on one particular occasion, we may have to take into account the fact that in this case he was expecting the noise. Thus, it is not merely a loud noise that explains his normal startle reaction, but the presence of an unexpected loud noise. In introducing the factor of unexpectedness into our explanation we are taking into account not merely an *event*, but a state of the person; and one cannot explain a person's reaction in any one instance without taking it into account. Thus, the line between the event that appears as "the cause" and "the conditions" that are relevant to the effect is a line that disappears. The case is, then, precisely like that in which a flick of a switch is usually considered to be the adequate, sufficient cause of a light's coming on, but when an exception occurs—as when the bulb is burned out, or the power has been cut off—we must go beyond our usual shorthand explanation, in which some single event is taken as the cause of the effect.

Two different types of objections will quite possibly be raised against the preceding argument. The first would seek to show that if one abandons the distinction between causes and conditions, treating them as being of equal importance, it will become impossible to offer an adequate explanation of any occurrence, since the list of conditions that can be shown to be necessary for that occurrence will be inexhaustible. A second objection might be that, in breaking down the distinction between causes and conditions, abandoning the notion that the cause of an effect is some specific antecedent occurrence, one would be surrendering an essential aspect of the causal relationship:

its temporal nature. I shall first briefly show that the first objection is unwarranted, and then show how the second is to be met.

In order to answer the first objection, it is necessary to show that there is not an inexhaustible list of relevant conditions that must be taken into account in order to offer an adequate explanation of any occurrence. One step in showing that such an objection is unwarranted has already been taken. As I have repeatedly argued, in explaining an event we come to a natural stopping point when we specify the elements in the process that terminated in that particular event; we are not committed to offering further explanations as to why each of these elements itself occurred. This is no less true on the view I have been defending than it is on the conventional view. Those who believe that an occurrence is to be explained by citing some single antecedent event need feel no obligation to offer a further explanation of the occurrence of that antecedent, nor of *its* antecedent and all prior antecedents. *Mutatis mutandis*, this will also be true of the view I am maintaining.

There is, however, a second reason why it may be thought that abolishing any ultimate distinction between causes and conditions leaves one open to the charge that it will then become impossible to offer an adequate explanation of any event. This reason consists in the fact that what is taken to be the cause of an event is always some actual occurrence, whereas the sum of the conditions relevant to any occurrence could include an indefinitely large number of "negative conditions." By a negative condition would be meant any event that, had it occurred, would have prevented the occurrence of the event we wish to explain. Thus, to choose an example made familiar by Mill, the success of a surprise attack on a military encampment may have been dependent upon the fact that the sentinel was asleep and therefore failed to give the alarm. In what I have said, no room seems to have been left for such negative conditions, since it has been my claim that an effect is to be explained by tracing the actual course of events that terminated in it. Furthermore, it would seem that such negative conditions could be multiplied at will, for we would also have to take into account the fact that no other soldier happened to be awake and to have seen the enemy approaching the perimeter; that no enemy sapper had happened to stumble on a mine; that no special sensors had been installed, though they were to have been supplied, et cetera, et cetera.

To escape this criticism we need only note that not all so-called negative conditions have the same status. The sentinel *was* asleep, no one awakened, and the sappers were successful in avoiding the mines. These are all actual occurrences. They are no more to be described as "negative conditions" than standing still rather than walking is a negative state of affairs. In the case before us, the only truly negative conditions would relate to what did not actually happen, but might have happened *if* the sentinel had in fact awakened, or *if* a sapper had triggered a mine. In raising these hypothetical questions one is not offering a causal explanation of what actually did occur: One is not identifying anything that can rightly be termed a causal condition of the actual event one is attempting to explain.[7]

In support of this claim, let me cite another example that has sometimes been used in an effort to show that negative conditions are as causally effective as are positive occurrences. A person dies because he has ingested a poison *and no antidote was given*. It is pointed out that had the antidote been promptly administered the person would presumably not have died; therefore, the failure to administer the antidote was one causal factor responsible for his death. Now, in such a case there could be many reasons why an antidote was not administered. Perhaps no one else was present, or none who were present realized that a poison had been ingested, or no antidote to that poison was known. Any one of these states of affairs would serve to explain why something did *not* occur that might, under other circumstances, have occurred. Yet, to say what might have happened if any number of things had happened other than what actually happened is surely not to give a causal explanation of the particular case at hand. In pointing out what might have happened had the circumstances been different, we are only calling attention to the fact that death is not a *necessary* consequence of having taken this poison; we are not giving an account of what in this case actually caused the person's death. It is, of course, important to know whether there is or is not a necessary connection between an occurrence of a particular type and some particular type of effect; as we shall see, this background of knowledge is often helpful when we seek to establish the actual cause of some particular effect. Nevertheless, as I have already indicated, and as we shall have further occasion to see, the determination of what is a necessary condition of a type of event is not to be identified with the discovering the cause of a particular event of that type.

It is not merely a confusion between these two different, although related, questions that has led to an interest in the role played by so-called negative conditions in causal analyses; in addition, there is our interest in fixing responsibility when the events analyzed concern the actions of men. For purposes of assigning praise and—especially— blame, what a person fails to do is often no less important than what he actually does. Thus, to omit doing something that one is expected to do is particularly relevant to what Hart and Honoré called "attributive causal judgments." However, as I argue in Appendix B, when historians make attributive judgments concerning matters such as "the causes of the Civil War," their judgments presuppose explanations of what did in fact occur. I should not expect Hart and Honoré to take issue with that claim; nonetheless, they introduced negative conditions into their causal explanations—generally in the form of omissions, that is, in terms of what some person failed to do. For example, in one discussion of negative conditions as causally explanatory, they cited an example analogous to Mill's example of the sleeping sentinel: A gardener fails to water a garden and the plants die. To substantiate my discussion of the sentinel case, I should like to examine this case as well, since (unlike Hart and Honoré) I do not believe that it establishes that negative conditions have the same status as positive occurrences in our nonattributive causal explanations of what did in fact occur.[8]

Let us initially put aside all questions of blame, and accept it as a simple matter of fact that the plants did die because the gardener did not water the garden. The question that then arises, and with which we must deal, concerns the sense in which his not watering the garden is a negative condition similar to all other negative conditions one might cite in a case such as this. For example, as Hart and Honoré point out, had anyone else watered the garden, even had the gardener not, the plants would not have died. Nevertheless, Hart and Honoré rightly hold that in such a case we do not say that the failure of any neighbor to water the garden was a cause of the plants' dying; yet we do in fact say that the gardener's failure was the cause. They hold that this is so because of the role played in our causal explanations of what we regard as normal and what we regard as abnormal. They would have us believe that we distinguish between the gardener's not-watering and a neighbor's not-watering because one expects that a gardener will water; his failure to do so is therefore abnormal, and we will, as a consequence, pick out that failure as the cause of what occurred. There is, however, another and quite different reason why we would say that the gardener's failure to water is what caused the plants to die. A gardener, having been hired to tend a garden, is counted on to do so. Seen in this light, his absence is not properly viewed as "a negative condition," as we view the fact that it did not happen to rain, or that no neighbor saw that the plants needed watering. Rather, the gardener's not coming breached an agreement he had undertaken. He did something other than that which he had agreed to do. In this respect his action is similar to that of a sentinel's sleeping at his post; each is a dereliction of a duty, whatever extenuating circumstances there may have been. Gardeners and sentries bear responsibilities that off-duty soldiers and neighbors do not bear; if they fail to perform the duties they are counted on to perform, we do not treat this as mere happenstance, but as something actually done, and we view what was done in terms of its consequences. It is for this reason, I submit, that we attribute what happened to the garden to the gardener's failure to come, and not to any other circumstances that might have saved the garden, had they indeed happened to occur.

Let me now turn from a defense of my view against those who would attack it because it fails to take account of the role of "negative conditions" in causal explanations, to meet another challenge: that the view I hold either omits or distorts the temporal aspect of causal relations. Actually, I believe that the account I have given has some distinct advantages in this connection. For example, one problem that has sometimes appeared worrisome with respect to the temporal aspect of the causal relation arises out of the assumption that a cause and its effect are two distinct and separate events, for on this assumption one is forced to ask at what instant the cause brings about its effect.[9] If, as I have claimed, the effect is not to be regarded as an event separable from its cause, but is simply the terminal state of a single ongoing process, this problem does not arise. It might be argued, however, that my position escapes one worrisome problem only to fall into others that may be more serious. The first and most basic of these problems is how one is to construe "the cause" of a specific effect, if cause and effect are not distinct and, in principle, separable.

As should already be clear, what I wish to designate as the cause of an effect is simply the process that terminates in the effect: The cause is the whole set of actual ongoing occurrences or events that resulted in this, and no other, particular effect. As I have noted, the fact that we most often use the singular, and speak of "*the* cause" of an effect, should not be taken to mean that the term cannot refer to a conjunction of factors, but must refer to some single, simple event. Furthermore, as I have also pointed out, when we ask for a causal explanation of some particular effect, we are not asking a limitless question. In the first place, we are not asking for an explanation of all aspects of some one concrete occurrence, but only of one of its aspects, under some one description. In the second place, we are asking what was responsible for *it*, not what were the causes of its cause. Finally, as I have also pointed out, we must not allow the shorthand causal explanations we often use in daily life to serve as paradigmatic cases of causal analyses, since these always presuppose that we can flesh them out through an appeal to more general schemas of explanation; in fact, we often find ourselves forced to do so when apparent exceptions arise. It is therefore to fuller causal explanations that I have looked for paradigmatic examples, not to their truncated versions. In such cases, as I have tried to show, we must include within the cause of an effect all of the elements that entered into the actual process that terminated in the effect. It is at this point that what is to be considered as relatively novel in my account of the causal relation most clearly appears.

As we have noted, Mill and Hobbes recognized that the real or entire cause of an effect consisted in a complex set of conditions and not in some one event only. In their discussions, however, each of the elements entering into the real or entire cause was considered as a separate or independent condition present in the agent, or in the patient, or in the circumstances obtaining at a particular time and place. In contrast to that conception of the cause as a compound of separate elements that produce a new and distinct occurrence when they come together, the conception I advocate takes these elements as components within a single process, terminating in that particular state of affairs we regard as the effect of the process. To be sure, the various elements in this process have their own histories, which may be entirely independent of one another; however, when seen as constituting elements that, together, are responsible for a particular effect, they form part of the process that terminated in that given effect. For example, in our earlier illustration of how an exceptionally good harvest was to be explained, we noted that in addition to the good growing weather it was necessary to take into account the labor of the farmers and their skills. Although the meteorological factors responsible for the favorable weather and the factors explaining the skills of those who raised the crops constitute two wholly independent sets of factors which had independent ancestries, on this occasion they combined to form one process: The weather and the skills together, during the growing season, led to this exceptionally fine crop.

In the foregoing example, it is obvious that what is seen as constituting a single occurrence may be relative to the effect to be explained. For example, the meteorological factors that were partly responsible for the fine crop form part of numerous other histories, that is, they may be seen as contributing not just to this one effect, but to other effects as well. The very same conditions favorable to the crop might, for example, have been extremely unfavorable for attracting tourists, and might therefore have been part of the story of why income was poor for one segment of the population of a region while at the same time it was extremely good for another. The actual weather can thus be a causal factor in different series of events, forming part of different occurrences; its role in any causal explanation will depend upon the specific nature of the effect one sets out to explain. Whatever has led to this particular effect (which is not itself a discrete event but simply the terminal state of a process) *is* the cause of that effect, and this cause is nothing other than the whole set of factors that entered into that process.[10]

If we then ask what temporal relations obtain between cause and effect, it is clear that the effect is the end point of a process, and the causal factors leading to the effect must precede it. However, the cause as a whole—that is, the whole set of factors that together make up this process—is not an event separate from the effect, and cannot, as a whole, be regarded as existing prior to it. When, for example, I move a heavy sofa from one part of the room to another, each phase of the process of pushing and hauling and tugging precedes the final coming-to-rest of the sofa in its new location, but until the sofa actually is in that location the process has not been concluded: The cause is not complete. Thus, an effect does not occur subsequent to its cause, but only subsequent to some of the occurrences that are involved in that cause; the cause is complete only when the effect occurs.

This view, I suggest, escapes the temporal paradoxes sometimes thought to inhere in the casual relationship. Not only does it escape the difficulty of how a cause can bring about an effect if it is precedent to that effect (and therefore is not occurring when the effect occurs); it also escapes the paradox that consists in holding that if the relation between two events, A and B, is a *necessary* relation, then we may as well say that the later event, B, was the cause of A as that A caused B, since the existence of either would entail the existence of the other. This paradox, of which much has recently been made,[11] need not arise when one recognizes that a cause and its effect are not two distinct events, but are to be differentiated as being

aspects of one and the same process. Since we explain the effect by
tracing out the concrete occurrences that led up to it, the temporal
direction of causal attributions is ineluctable: One cannot separate
cause from effect and speak of them as if the relation between them
were some abstract logical relation. Thus, this paradox as well as the
first temporal paradox—how a cause can bring about an effect if it is
precedent to that effect—will disappear when cause and effect are not
treated as if they constituted two events distinct and separate from
each other. Not only does the view of causation that I am defending
enable one to escape these apparent paradoxes, but, more important,
it allows us to make sense of the way in which causal explanation
occurs in any advanced science.

It has of course been argued by Russell, among others, that the
concept of causation is otiose in the sciences; however, these arguments rested on identifying causal explanations with the type of
shorthand explanation of any given occurrence that is commonly used
in everyday life, in which one picks out some antecedent occurrence
and identifies it as that which, because of its own nature, has the
power to produce this type of effect. When one refuses to view such
shorthand causal explanations as paradigms of what is involved when
seeking the cause of some particular occurrence, it can be seen that
whenever a scientist is called upon to explain what has occurred in
any given instance, he too uses a causal mode of explanation in which
a particular effect is viewed as the outcome of a complex process of
change.[12] It is especially apparent in scientific explanations that the
causal factors to which any effect is attributable are not separate,
antecedent events: The physicist in speaking as a physicist will not,
for example, explain the motion of a billiard ball simply in terms of
its having been struck by another ball; the impact, which to the naked
eye appears total and instantaneous, will be regarded as a process in
which a series of changes occurs within fields of force; what is taken
as the effect—the motion of the ball that has been struck—is the end
product of these distortions. Similarly, as we have seen, a physiological account of the state of a tubercular patient is to be explained as
the end result of a process, not as a state that followed the occurrence
of some earlier, quite different, isolable event. Thus, in the sciences as
well as in our more careful causal explanations in everyday life, what
is to be explained is not explained in terms of regularity of connection
between distinct types of events, but is accounted for by tracing the
elements within the particular process that ended in this effect. This
as we shall later see, makes it possible to bridge the gap between the

causal explanations given in everyday life and the sophisticated explanations of particular effects characteristic of the advanced sciences. Before showing that such a harmony does indeed exist, it will be necessary to discuss the way in which the concept of a law of nature is related to our analysis of the causal relationship.

II. CAUSAL EXPLANATIONS AND NATURAL LAWS

Causal explanations, as we have seen, are directed toward answering the question of what was responsible for some particular occurrence. A natural law, on the other hand, consists in the formulation of some invariant connection between properties or events of specified types. As we have already noted, in order to discover or confirm any such law one must deal with particular occurrences; it is also true, as we shall see, that established laws are important in our causal explanations of what has occurred in a particular case. Thus, causal analyses and the formulation of laws are connected enterprises, but how they are related, as well as how they differ, remains to be seen.

Unfortunately, the differences between the procedures required in giving causal explanations and in discovering and confirming laws have been concealed by the fact that paradigmatic examples of both processes have too often been drawn from shorthand causal explanations and from the crude lawlike generalizations that are characteristic not of the sciences but of everyday life. If one takes as the model of a causal explanation the fact that crops are good because of the weather, or that an electric light comes on because a switch has been flicked, there seems to be little difference between such an explanation and merely citing a general rule or law. The trouble, however, is that such causal accounts not only are very incomplete but permit of exceptions, as we have seen; therefore, the law that they are taken as exemplifying will not in fact state an invariant connection, but will be a crude generalization concerning what generally happens, or happens "under normal circumstances," and its application will depend upon introducing a vague *ceteris paribus* clause.

If, instead, a full-fledged causal analysis is chosen as an example, it immediately becomes clear that there is a radical difference between what such an analysis includes and what is involved in the formulation of a law. To give a causal analysis is to trace an ongoing process that terminated in the specific effect we wish to explain; this involves describing a particular set of interconnected occurrences. In formulating a law, on the other hand, one is concerned not with a particular effect, but with an effect of a specified type; the object is to show on what factor or factors an effect of this type always depends. One might, of course, assume that whenever an effect of a given type is present, some specific type of antecedent occurrence will also have been present, so that a law simply expresses the existence of a correlation between two types of occurrences. This is more or less characteristic of one of the ways in which we are inclined to formulate lawlike generalizations in everyday life: If an occurrence of some particular type is frequently observed to be associated with some type of effect, and if effects of that type have never been noticed in the absence of such occurrences, we are inclined to assume that there is a necessary connection between them, and we take the statement of that connection as the formulation of a law.

However, generalizations of this sort are not really comparable to the kinds of laws found in any advanced science. In the first place, such generalizations would be both too crude and too unreliable to count as laws. They are crude because they do not identify the kinds and degrees of resemblance that various occurrences must have if they are to bring about a given type of effect. They are unreliable because, as we have seen, in any actual case other conditions may also have to be present if a specific effect is to occur; as a consequence, a *ceteris paribus* clause must be introduced to buttress these common-sense generalizations. In any advanced science, however, no such clause is included when a law is stated: A law applies to all cases and not "under normal conditions" only. In the second place, and of more importance from a general theoretical standpoint, is the fact that these common-sense generalizations are formulated in terms of a relationship between specific types of *occurrences*. In the sciences, however, a law used in explaining any actual occurrence also applies to what would have occurred under other circumstances, had certain conditions been fulfilled. Thus, such laws deal with relationships that may be present without being manifest, and with factors that become manifest only under other conditions. Scientific laws have this range of applicability because they do not attempt to state connections between actual occurrences, but between properties characteristic of occurrences of given types. For example, in Boyle's law an attempt was made to relate the pressure and the volume of a gas, under any conditions, so that given a change in either factor a covariant change in the other would occur. Similarly, in Galileo's laws of falling bodies, or in Newton's gravitational law, the law aims to state a relationship not between actual occurrences, but between specific characteristics of certain types of objects or events. In other words, instead of seeking to find some one type of occurrence that is invariantly connected with a particular type of effect, a scientist will fractionate these occurrences into factors, seeking to establish what factor within such occurrences is connected with a factor invariantly present in the effect.

It is at this point that one can see why Hume's account of our generalizations from experience accords so poorly with the methods and the results of scientific inquiry, and why some form of analysis such as Galileo's method of resolution is necessary for the formulation of scientific laws. These laws express relationships among factors that may be present in occurrences of many different types; they are not confined to statements concerning invariant sequences. Consequently, one cannot maintain the distinction that has sometimes been drawn between "causal laws" and laws that serve to correlate two sets of properties, such as the length of a pendulum and its periodicity, or the chemical composition of a metal and its melting point.[13] To attempt to maintain such a distinction would almost surely involve denying that laws such as those of Boyle or of Galileo or of Newton were "causal laws." In this same connection, it becomes evident that once the Humean regularity view is abandoned, one can also abandon the notion that the specific factors responsible for a given effect must be occurrences antecedent to that effect. As Max Black has observed in discussing the causal relation, the assumption of temporal priority fails to square with examples such as the fact that "the moon's gravitational pull lasts as long as the tide it produces; difference of temperature registers throughout the period that thermometric expansion occurs; a catalyst continues to act during the chemical reaction it is influencing; and so on, for any number of similar cases."[14] Finally, we may again observe that if one spells out the laws involved in cases such as those Black mentions, these laws do not concern concrete types of occurrences, as Hume supposed. Rather, they express functional relationships between factors included within the situation. For example, an explanation of the causal relation between the moon and the tides will be formulated in terms of gravitational attraction, which is dependent upon relations of mass and of distance, rather than in terms of some antecedent event.

It is worthwhile to note once again that an appeal of this sort to specific properties or factors in a situation, as a means of explaining a specific type of effect, is not confined to the advanced sciences; it is also characteristic of explanations frequently given in everyday life. To explain why some objects float when dropped in a pond and others sink, we may appeal to what they are made of, or to their weight. Such explanatory generalizations, as we have already noted, are insufficiently accurate, since while we can in most cases count on wood to float, waterlogged wood will sink; and weight is not the decisive factor, as ships of large tonnage conclusively prove. Thus, these statements are no less inadequate when considered as statements of laws than are any cases in which we seek to establish an invariant sequence between some specific type of antecedent occurrence and a specific type of effect. Nevertheless, there is an important difference between these types of explanations, both of which are often given in everyday life, and it is to this difference that I should here like to call attention. One cannot readily move from an attempt to establish correlations between actual occurrences to a formulation of strict scientific laws, since in order to have a strictly invariant connection between some type of antecedent occurrence and some specific type of effect, we must define the nature of each more narrowly, and the law thereby becomes increasingly less general in its applicability. On the other hand, in more clearly specifying the properties on which some type of effect depends, in order to make sure that no exceptions arise, we move from restricted properties, such as that an object will float because it is made of wood, to more general ones, such as that it must not be "too heavy," and then to more accurate statements of functional dependence involving the concept of specific gravity; such a statement is even more general, as well as being more precise, since it is applicable under all conditions, and without respect to whatever other properties an object may possess. Thus, starting from a type of crude generalization that is no less characteristic of our explanatory generalizations in everyday life than are generalizations concerning sequences of events, we can move toward the formulation of laws that hold, without exception, in a wide variety of instances. Unfortunately, no such transition takes place so long as we search for laws that attempt to state invariant connections between one type of antecedent occurrence and some type of effect.

Having now seen that the laws on which reliance may be placed do not conform to the model of regularity-of-sequence, but state functional relationships between types of factors rather than between types of actual events, we must examine how laws concerning these functional relationships enter into concrete causal explanations of specific events.

Let us recall that when we seek to trace the cause of a given effect we are seeking to establish the elements that entered into the process that terminated in the effect we wish to explain. These elements are themselves occurrences that, when considered as leading to the effect, form a single unified strand. The question arises, however, as to what gives unity to any such strand: Why are just these occurrences, and not others, to be regarded as leading to the effect that is to be explained? One part of the answer to this question is obvious: In some cases these occurrences are merely phases within the process taken as a whole, as the positions and the motions of each billiard ball in a three-cushion shot are but parts of the occurrence we trace. However, in tracing the occurrences that together form the whole, we find that there are points at which they intersect, and at which they appear to affect one another. To explain how each is affected by the other, and therefore to explain what has occurred, we cannot merely describe each of the phases included within the process, but must look to the ways in which the parts of the process may be connected, thus forming one causal strand. For example, in the successful three-cushion shot, the phases of the process consisted in a series of occurrences without which the shot would not have been successful, but to explain what linked these occurrences to one another in a way that made them phases within one causal strand, appeal would have to be made to factors such as the momentum and the angle of incidence of impact and the like, which, at each successive juncture, determined the path of the cue ball. In an account such as this, the mortar that serves to make a single process out of what might otherwise be seen as only a successive series of occurrences is the relationship of functional dependence between some of the factors embedded in those occurrences. Thus, in explaining an effect as the outcome of a particular process we must not only describe the series of concrete occurrences that entered into the process, but must also take into account how each occurrence within that series was related to at least one of its other components. To do so, we must appeal to generalizations concerning how some aspect of the one was dependent upon some aspect of the other.

This is not only true with respect to an example such as that of a three-cushion shot in billiards, where we have the advantage of being able to appeal to well-established laws concerning motion, it also applies to cases in which our generalizations are loose and relatively unreliable. (To the extent that they have these characteristics, the causal explanations that depend upon them must also be regarded as open to challenge, and to subsequent correction.) For example, in the field of human relationships, if we seek to give a causal account of why two friends became estranged and suddenly turned into enemies, we shall have to trace a series of episodes during which there was growing tension between them, and we shall have to take into account the final climactic episode in which their entire relationship changed. The stages in this process will constitute our causal account, but at almost every juncture we shall have to explain the dynamics of these attitudinal changes by appealing to functional connections between specific factors present within the episodes, such as the fact that failure leads to envy, and that hatred arises out of injured pride. As one sees in Spinoza's account of the passions, it is possible to generalize with respect to functional relationships among our attitudes without referring to the specific occurrences in which these attitudes manifest themselves. Such generalizations permit us to trace connections between different states, and show in what ways the series of occurrences belong together as parts of a single process. Thus, such generalizations provide mortar for our causal accounts even though they do not provide the materials out of which such accounts are formed.

The generalizations that are used to formulate connections between two occurrences often refer directly to some features of those occurrences by means of which we would naturally describe them. Such, for example, was the case in the immediately preceding illustration, in which the connective relationships were characterized through using terms such as "envy" and "pride." In other cases we may formulate our generalizations in more precise, technical terms. While still referring to features that are directly identifiable in those occurrences, such terms often indicate factors in the occurrence that we do not ordinarily consider apart from one another. For example, in describing what happens when one billiard ball strikes another we may distinguish between momentum, the angle of incidence, the spin of the ball, etc., all of which refer to factors that are directly recognizable in what is observed, but which we consider separately only when called upon to give a closer, analytic account of what occurred. In such accounts, generalizations concerning these isolable factors are used in explaining the connection between the motion of one billiard ball and that of the other, thus serving as connective links in our causal explanation. Finally, there are generalizations that do not apply directly to what is observed in the case at hand, but explain the connections between observed features of the occurrence through reference to laws concerning what might be called "micro-occurrences," that is, to occurrences underlying what we describe as occurring. For example, in explaining what occurs in the collision of billiard balls, we need to understand the laws governing their elasticity, but these laws refer to their internal physical structure, not to any factors directly observable in the occurrence we describe. Similarly, the laws that serve to explain the connection between being shot through the heart and dying are physiological laws that relate the circulation of the blood and other vital processes, but these laws apply to micro-occurrences, not to the events we specify when we say that he was killed by a bullet that passed through his heart.[15]

It is important to note that when we use generalizations of any of these kinds as a means of explaining the linkage between specific occurrences, such generalizations do not in any sense serve as substitutes for the causal explanation we seek to give. For example, the physiological generalizations that serve to explain the connection between a person's being shot through the heart and his dying are generalizations that connect aspects of what occurs when a bullet passes through the heart and the micro-occurrences that constitute dying; in order to make use of such generalizations we must describe what, in this instance, occurred. It is for this reason that I have said that while the laws we use in our causal explanations provide mortar that may serve to connect factors that are present in these occurrences, they do not provide the materials out of which such accounts are formed.

This relationship may be further clarified in the following way. As we have seen, any law that is taken as formulating a necessary relationship will be phrased not in terms of relationships between specific types of actual occurrences, but in terms of relationships between factors that can be considered in abstraction from the specific occurrences in which they may be present. This being the case, one could not (so to speak) "reconstitute" any actual occurrence merely by knowing what laws were applicable to it: One would, on the contrary, have to be in a position to offer a concrete description of that particular occurrence before being able to apply these laws to it. This is of course acknowledged even by those who hold that adequate explanation always takes the form prescribed by the deductive-nomothetic model: They too insist that one must possess accurate knowledge of the relevant initial conditions in order to use a law in explaining (or in predicting) the specific effect we are to explain (or which we wish to predict). We are therefore forced to start our explanations from our descriptions of what is present in any given case. However, in explaining what occurs, it will not be sufficient merely to describe the original initial conditions; one must instead trace the successive occurrences brought about as these conditions change. For example, if a change in one brings about a change in the other because of some invariant connection between two aspects of the original conditions, then we must trace the consequences this change will have for other aspects of the conditions that were originally present: In most cases one does not move smoothly and without any intervening processes from a change in some one pair of conditions directly to the final effect. For example, in Carl Hempel's well-known illustration of the cracking of a radiator on a cold night,[16] one could not deduce the final effect from the freezing of the water alone: As Hempel recognized, the freezing of the water had to be connected with an expansion of its volume, and the coefficient of expansion had to be connected with the degree of pressure at which the radiator would crack. It is therefore misleading to speak as if a particular set of laws would be sufficient to enable us to explain (or predict) a given occurrence, once the original initial conditions were known. Instead, the laws must be applied *seriatim* to a sequence of changing conditions; and this is to say that a causal account must be given of the series of occurrences leading to the final effect. To be sure, at least some of the connections among these occurrences may be formulable in terms of such general laws as the freezing of water at a specific temperature, the expansion of water when it freezes, and the laws determining the bursting point of a container having the structural properties of this particular radiator, but these laws are not applied *all at once* to the initial conditions, as Hempel's account might seem to imply: They apply to a series of occurrences, and are thus instruments used in causal explanations and not surrogates for such explanations. Nothing could make this clearer than the fact that in explaining (or in predicting) a specific effect in terms of the deductive-nomothetic model we must not only take into account the boundary conditions that exist when the initial state obtains, but we must exclude changes in these boundary conditions as the series of events is taking place.[17]

It will be seen from all that has gone before that I hold our causal analyses to be primarily descriptive: They analyze an ongoing process into a series of occurrences terminating in a specific effect. Given these occurrences, and no others, we may say that it was necessary that the process should have terminated in this effect, but this is not to say that the process as it actually occurred was itself a necessary process. It is not to say that nothing could have interfered, after its initial state, to prevent the occurrence of what did in fact occur. It is a view of the latter sort that is best characterized as "determinism." What I wish to show is that determinism, if taken in this sense, is not a necessary consequence of holding that all processes can be analyzed in causal terms, nor of holding that there are necessary connections among the factors upon which such processes depend.

III. ON "DETERMINISM"

I do not deny that some processes are in fact determined, in the sense in which I am using that term. Any process that takes place under boundary conditions that exclude the influence of outside factors, and in which what occurs can be said to represent the self-transformation of a system according to some set of laws, is a process that can be called determined: Given the initial state of the system, nothing but this particular end result could occur.[18] Chemical reactions taking place under experimental conditions might serve as examples of deterministic processes when determinism is construed in this sense, and it is in this same sense that one can formulate the position of metaphysical determinism. That position, as one can recognize in Spinoza or Laplace, takes the universe as a whole to be a single system that undergoes a series of transformations according to one set of laws; whatever occurs in such a closed system had to occur, given the earlier state of the system and its laws. However, unless one is willing to assume from the outset that the universe can be said to be a single, unitary process, no particular instance of determinism should be construed as if it itself had been determined to occur. For example, while a chemical reaction that takes place under experimental conditions may be an instance of a completely determined process, there is no set of initial boundary conditions, and no one set of laws, from which it can be deduced that the experiment itself would be performed. Nevertheless, once we know that it actually was performed—and performed when and where and in the way in which it was—there is no reason to deny that the *effect* was determined, even though the event as a whole was not. There is no paradox in this position, since it is only what occurred after the experiment started that represents a transformation within a closed system; the planning of the experiment and the task of carrying it out might have been interfered with by any number of extraneous factors, and the event as a whole would not then have taken place when or where or how it actually did. Thus, if the occurrences in which one is interested do not take place under circumstances in which they are insulated against the effects of other occurrences in their environments, what occurs cannot be said to have been determined, so long as we are speaking from an empirical point of view, rather than assuming the truth of a comprehensive metaphysical determinism.

This does not of course mean that these effects may not have been necessary (in some sense of "necessary"), given the facts of what did actually occur. The problem is to characterize the necessity that is to be ascribed in cases in which we do not invoke a complete metaphysical determinism, and in which there is not that form of empirical determinism that characterizes the self-transformations that occur within a closed system. The first thing to be said is that this form of necessity is not to be regarded as an example of *logical* necessity. Hume offered reasons adequate to show that any causal necessity we ascribe to events is not equivalent to logical necessity. In addition, however, we may note that whenever we trace the cause of a specific effect we must take into account a multiplicity of other occurrences, and no one of these occurrences can, by itself, be taken to be a *sufficient* condition for the occurrence of the effect.[19] Therefore, no one of these occurrences can be said logically to entail the effect; rather, the effect follows from the contingent fact that each of these occurrences took place when and where it did. Nor can we show that this concatenation of occurrences was itself *logically* necessary. Therefore, it would be a mistake to view the necessity that links cause and effect as an instance of logical necessity.

Nor can we assume that there is, in all cases, a necessary relation between any one condition and the effect we seek to explain. This can be illustrated with reference to what has been called overdetermination. For example, if a man is executed by a firing squad, his death is attributable to the bullets penetrating his body; but if we assume that each of the bullets struck some vital organ, can we say that any one of the shots was a necessary condition of his death? Under these circumstances, his death would have ensued from any of the bullets that struck him, and, as a consequence, no one of them was a necessary condition of his death. As we shall now see, this issue is not restricted to cases of overdetermination, but is relevant to many other instances as well.

An example chosen from among those already discussed may be used to illustrate this point. Consider the case of a fire that destroyed an entire house with the exception of one wing, which had been constructed to be proof against fire. In such a case some of the specific occurrences and conditions that entered into the real and entire cause of the effect may be said to have been necessary for that particular result to have occurred, but others, when taken individually, should not be regarded as having been necessary even though they formed part of the set of conditions that, when taken together, were both necessary and sufficient to produce that effect.[20] For example, given all of the events constituting this fire, some may be so linked to the final effect that if they had not had the characteristics they actually had the effect would not have been just as it was: No other event would, under the same circumstances, have led to precisely this effect. On the other hand, some other events may have been essential to the occurrence of this effect only because of one particular characteristic they possessed, and any event sharing this special characteristic might therefore be said to have been substitutable for it without altering the effect that actually occurred. In our example, for instance, it is doubtful whether the final result would have been identical in character if the wing of the house had been saved because firemen put out the spreading fire, rather than because it was built to resist this sort of fire; an examination of the remains of the wing would almost surely give evidence as to which of these two alternatives had occurred. On the other hand, if a fire that is known to have started in an attic consumed an entire house, the same result could have been brought about whether the fire started due to faulty wiring or due to the spontaneous combustion of a pile of oily rags. So long as either source of heat was intense enough to ignite what was in immediate proximity to it, and so long as there were similar materials at hand to spread the flame, the fire would have spread rapidly from the attic through the rest of the house in an identical manner, regardless of its original source. In that case we should not be likely to use the concept of necessity in describing the relation between the original source and the final effect, even though the source was one of that set of conditions without which this specific effect would not have occurred. We would not do so because we recognize that some occurrences might be substitutable for others within any given set of circumstances. This does not, however, alter the fact that since we are dealing with what did actually eventuate—and not with what might have been true under another set of circumstances—it is legitimate to claim that the effect was a necessary consequence of what did actually occur.

On the basis of such examples we may say that the sense of "necessary" that is applicable to the causal relation here under consideration is a restricted or conditional one: *Given* the entire set of causal conditions that did occur (and no others), it was necessary that the effect should have occurred. This obviously does not entail that the event was determined either in the metaphysical sense or in the empirical sense in which I have used the concept of determinism. We are not, for example, committed to saying that, given the nature of the universe, it was determined that each of the conditions that occurred must have occurred just as it did, and when it did; nor are we claiming that what occurred in this instance was uninfluenced by external factors, and represented merely a necessary course of self-transformation occurring within a closed system. In other words, contingency may be acknowledged a role in all cases in which we explain an effect through tracing back the conditions upon which it depended, and yet we may nonetheless say that, whatever may have been the explanation of why just these conditions, and no others, occurred when they did, it was *necessary*—given their occurrence—that the effect that did in fact occur should have occurred.

Chapter Five

On What and Why
in History

It may at this point seem as if the two preceding chapters involved an unnecessary break in the argument of a book that is ostensibly concerned with historical knowledge. Yet, it will rapidly become clear that one cannot understand the ways in which historians explain the nature and the connections of events without first destroying the assumption that the causal relationship is a relationship between two separate and distinct events, one of which, by itself, may be regarded as having caused the other. Nor would it be possible to understand the important but auxiliary role that lawlike generalizations play in many (although not all) historical explanations, unless one has first separated the concept of causation from the concept of an explanatory law. Furthermore, it is important to distinguish between the notion of "necessity," which historians as well as laymen often use, and a belief in determinism. Thus, the argument of the two preceding chapters is directly relevant to questions that arise concerning the nature and implications of historical explanation. It is this that the present chapter is designed to show. I shall first consider the nature of explanation in what I have termed "general history"—rather than "special histories"—for it is there that what has been said receives its clearest exemplifications.

I

In a well-known dictum—memorable because it is so extreme— Michael Oakeshott said, "Change in history carries with it its own explanations."[1] By this he meant to indicate, as he makes clear two pages later, that "the only explanation of change relevant or possible in history is simply a complete account of change. History accounts *for* change by means of a full account *of* change. The relation *between* events is always other events, and it is established in history by a full relation *of* the events."

Various reasons led Oakeshott to adopt this position, and I shall not attempt to disentangle them and lay each of them bare.[2] What is of interest is that Oakeshott took for granted that his view entailed that the concept of causation had no applicability to the processes of history. This followed from the fact that he equated the concept of causation with a set of minimal conditions always associated with the occurrence of an event of a specific type;[3] that is, he was willing to accept the conventional view of causation, in which the cause-and-effect relationship is simply an individual instance of some observed regularity between two types of events. However, as we have seen, this view fits only some shorthand explanations in everyday life and some rudimentary scientific generalizations; it is inadequate with respect to those cases in which causes and effects are not perceived as distinct and separate events, and it is also inadequate with respect to the explanations characteristic of the advanced sciences, for in them an analysis of what has occurred in a specific case involves far more than an appeal to directly observed regularities. Once this is recognized, the cause of any particular effect is not to be equated with some specific prior event, but is to be construed as that set of conditions without which the effect would not have occurred as it did, when it did. Thus, the gap between historical description and causal explanation is not the unbridgeable gap Oakeshott took it to be.

A position in some ways similar to that of Oakeshott but developed independently of an idealist metaphysics is defended by Louis O. Mink. In discussing historical explanation, Mink holds that "the minimal description of historical practice is that the historian deals with complex events in terms of the interrelationship of their constituent events."[4] Thus, unlike narrativists such as Gallie, White, and Danto, who have emphasized narrative structure, Mink views historical explanation not in terms of linear sequences, but in terms of delineating how a process is formed out of the relations among its nonsimultaneous parts.[5] Although there are aspects of Mink's position with which I am not in sympathy, I find that his view on this particular issue is wholly sound. It is precisely the view that seems most adequate when a historian seeks to offer a causal explanation of any particular effect. Consider, for example, an illustration used by Gardiner, by Dray, and by Danto: the problem of explaining the decline in popularity of Louis XIV.[6] To explain such a change in the attitude of the people toward their king, one does not look to a set of antecedent conditions, but to the king's decisions and to the people's reactions to them; that is to say, the explanation in this case resides in tracing out the elements that entered into the process that led from a point at which the king was highly esteemed to the view held of him at his death. Similarly, to take an example from Michael Scriven, when the historian seeks to explain the rise of the City of London as a financial center, he appeals to changes included *within* that rise, which together account for it.[7] Since no one of these changes, taken by itself, was identical with the rise of the City's power, that rise (which one seeks to explain) is to be regarded as the effect of a concatenation of individual changes that, together, account for it. And this, of course, precisely fits the analysis of causation I offered in the preceding chapters. It is now necessary, however, to develop in greater detail the ways in which this analysis applies to the work of any historian who is dealing with some phase of general history.

In any general history, it will be recalled, the facts with which the historian deals are always seen as connected with the nature of a particular society and changes within it. Even when a historian is, say, writing the biography of a political figure, or of some representative man of his age, it is in relation to the society in which he played a role that the historian views the person whose life is of interest to him.[8] This does not entail that the biographer must relate his subject's life to every aspect of the society in which that subject lived: No historian need be committed to a concern with all aspects of societal life. What he finds to be of interest and worthy of study may simply be some one aspect of societal life, or some particular group of persons who occupy a special position within that society. While many general historians are interested in the long-run changes in a society, others may be primarily interested in studying various segments or aspects of the historical process in closer detail. At present, it is probably true that professional historians are apt to focus attention on special topics and issues, rather than to deal with the nature of a society considered as a whole and the changes that have occurred in it. This, however, does not involve an abandonment of interest in the nature of a society and the changes it has undergone: Any society will include a multiplicity of institutional structures, and in any complex society that extends over an appreciable territory there are likely to be regional differentiations and some degree of regional autonomy in its institutions. Since any of the institutions in a society, or any of its regional components, may serve as the subject matter for historical study, it is not incompatible with what I have termed general history for historians to restrict their studies to limited topics. These specialized studies belong within general history because they concern the nature and changes of specific institutions or of specific facets of the institutionalized life of a particular society.[9]

This clarification of what is here meant by general history leads to a second point it is important to recall from earlier chapters: Any historical study, of whatever type, has a particular subject under investigation, and it is with reference to that subject that the historian, in his account, includes some events and excludes others. The subjects that historians choose for investigation vary widely in scope as well as in kind, and any historian will, in general, be working on a particular scale, depending on what subject he has chosen as the central topic with which he is to deal. There will be many events that naturally belong within his account of the topic he has chosen, and which, even without investigation, he knows cannot be excluded from it. A political historian of the United States cannot, for example, fail to include the results of national elections during the period he has under consideration. An economic historian dealing with modern societies cannot exclude from consideration the industrial, agricultural, and demographic factors in the economy he is to consider, nor can he neglect its financial structures, its methods of exchange, its levels of consumption, and its foreign trade. Thus, in order to be a political historian or an economic historian, a person cannot be wholly naïve, without any prior conception of what features of societal life are likely to be of concern to him. History, like science, never starts completely *de novo*: The activity of being a historian, dealing with a particular subject, presupposes that one already has some knowledge of, and some interest in, the materials with which one is to deal. Nevertheless, a historian cannot stop with the familiar; in order to understand why the events of which he has knowledge occurred as they did, he must trace their connections with other events. Some of these events will be included within the ongoing process he wishes to explain, and thus he will simply be examining the event in greater detail so that he may discern its constituent elements; in other cases he will show how events that were not themselves part of that process entered into its nature by the impact they had on one or more of its constituent parts. In accounting for change, historians proceed in both of these ways. Yet, these ways are not ultimately different, since in either case what is of concern to the historian is accounting for a process in terms of changes within its parts, whether those changes were brought about by external forces or whether they developed without such influences, due to factors of adjustment and readjustment within the process itself.

Were one to assume that historians start to study and write history knowing nothing whatsoever about the past with which they are to be concerned—were they to start as Langlois and Seignobos assumed that they *should* start, with nothing but a scattering of isolated facts that fit into no context until historians synthesize them[10]—it would be next to impossible to explain how order is brought into the materials with which any historian must deal. However, a historian knows something about the nature of his own society through having grown up in it, and he will have learned through its culture something about its past; furthermore, in any society in which there is *inquiry* into the past, a historian will also know something about societies other than his own, and about their pasts. Although such information may initially be limited and often misleading, the development of historical inquiries will supplement and correct much that passed for historical knowledge at an earlier time. (And there is no reason to suppose that there ever will be a time when historical knowledge cannot be further extended both in range and in depth.) What is important to bear in mind is that such knowledge is never chaotic. From the beginning, in even the earliest historians, it is bound to have structure, since whatever events appear to be noteworthy within the life of a society, or in the relations between societies, will punctuate the flow of time, and the succession of these events will help define successive periods or phases in the history of the society with which a historian is concerned. Such a framework, once adopted, provides a context into which historians attempt to place further facts, and as historical interests broaden and change, the framework itself will in some respects change by virtue of the knowledge added to it.

Looked at in this way, whatever entity provides the subject matter of a historian's account is seen by him as belonging within some broader framework. At the same time, it is also seen as having some nature of its own, since any historian who elects to deal with a certain subject matter must have some knowledge concerning it, for he would otherwise have no interest either in finding out more about it, or in relating it to other events concerning which he already possesses some preliminary knowledge. This, I suppose, is obvious enough. What must not be overlooked is that this preliminary knowledge is itself *historical* knowledge, however primitive its level may be. It will of course be subject to correction as well as to expansion, but the knowledge a historian seeks concerning the events with which he deals is not wholly different in character from his preliminary knowledge concerning them: At any stage in his work, it is on the basis of some antecedent historical knowledge that he must build. And so, as I have suggested, historical inquiry never starts absolutely *de novo*.

Now, the events that a historian knows in a preliminary way pertaining to the subject matter in which he is interested form part of its history. Such events and the others of which he may learn and the connections among them that he seeks to establish are the history in which he is interested: To recount these events as they occurred and in their relationships to one another is—quite simply—to write the history he set himself to write. Even if one were to attribute to a nation, or to some other historical entity, a reality that is not exhausted by what occurred in its history—as we think of a person as something more than the sum of his actions and of what befell him— nevertheless, in presenting the *history* of a nation, that nation exists in the events themselves, and they—and nothing else—constitute its history. Similarly, when one is concerned not with the history of a nation taken as a whole, but with the nature and changes of some one of its facets, it is what happened within this facet of societal life that *is* the history with which the historian is concerned.

This is not to say, of course, that either a society or any facet of societal life develops in accordance with some inner dialectic of its own, without being influenced at various points by the impingement of events that otherwise form no part of its history. However, in impinging on it they enter its history. Their effect upon it becomes a part of that history even though other events of that type never again come into contact with that particular strand of history. The history of society, then, consists of a continuing strand of related events, the absence of any one of which would make a difference in the characteristics of what did in fact occur in the particular subject under investigation.[11]

One immediate objection may be anticipated. Surely, it might be said, a historian is not to be expected to include within his account everything that actually occurred within a society or occurred with respect to some facet of that society. No political historian need mention every town, nor need a business historian include in his account a consideration of every stock flotation, every bankruptcy, or every adjustment in tarriffs. Were this necessary, it is obvious that no such histories could ever be written. The objection, however, overlooks the fact that historians work to scale, and the scale on which they work is determined by how they define the subject matter with which they are to be concerned. As I have noted in using the analogy of map making, a historian can deal with his subject matter in the large, showing what series of events went into its formation, but he can then shift his attention to any one of these events and analyze the other, quite different series of events on which *it* depended: He need not know the minutiae contained within the complex process before he is able to pick out the macroscopic features of that process. To be sure, it is always possible that he may find, as he proceeds to analyze the subevents more carefully, that some of the relationships he originally believed to be present are open to serious question. However, when this does not turn out to be the case, he may be said to have explained the events with which he was originally concerned by showing that they resulted from the subevents included within them, as one explains other wholes by analyzing the relationships among the parts of which they are composed. In historical explanations, of course, one is dealing with a temporal whole, not with a whole, such as a watch, that is present all at once; but just as the explanation of how a watch runs depends upon showing the relationships among its parts, so one way of explaining a particular process is to bring to light the particular series of events out of which it was composed. (Cf. what has already been said concerning how a historian accounts for the outcome of a particular election, chapter 2, section 2.)

There is however, another way of dealing with the relation between whole and parts in general history. The life of a society need not be viewed primarily as a succession of phases or events, but in terms of the component structures that constitute the basic features of that society's organization. As I said in chapter 2, these two modes of viewing the relation of whole and part are not mutually exclusive, and in the end they must be used to supplement each other. Yet, for purposes of exposition I now turn to the second way of viewing the whole-part relationship: that which gives rise to the historian's interest in specific facets of societal organization rather than in the continuity present in any temporal segment of the society's life.

Once again we must note that the historian does not start from total ignorance, without knowledge of the institutional structures present in his own society: He has grown up in them, and has learned to react with respect to them, and is in fact brought up with an entire nomenclature relating to the organization of the society in which he lives. Gradually, of course, one's view of the nature and the interrelationships of institutional structures will change, and accumulated historical knowledge concerning the types of institutions found in other societies and the differences in the interrelationships among them will lead a historian to a far more sophisticated view of institutional possibilities than he would have possessed had he learned about societal structures only through his personal experience. Anthropology, sociology, economics, studies of comparative government, and the like place historians on the alert as to the diversity of the structures and the differences in their interrelationships that are to be found in different societies. It might be thought that psychology, too, has an indispensable role to play in this regard, pointing out the needs of men that must be satisfied in and through societies. Yet, a psychological approach to social institutions has in the main proved misleading, since any particular need may be fulfilled through different institutions and any one institution may help to satisfy different psychological needs. It was in fact one of the most disastrous—although one of the most natural—errors in the social sciences of an earlier generation to suppose that the structural elements in societal organization could best be understood through relating them directly to specific psychological needs.[12]

The original basis for our understanding of societal structures is, then, the experience of an individual in growing up in his society, and the enlargement of horizons that comes through a knowledge of other societies. Once again I must point out that this growth in sophistication comes to the historian through data that he and his fellow historians, and others, have gathered concerning various societies. In attempting to fit these data into their accounts, historians will often find themselves committed to further investigations as a means of resolving contradictions or for the sake of filling in gaps. They will do so by searching in materials they have previously overlooked for further relevant data. This does not commit historians to establishing generalizations concerning societal structures; what they are endeavoring to find are connections that may exist among these structures in whatever particular society is the object of their concern. While it is true that generalizations drawn from the social sciences are sometimes useful in this respect—and this is a fact to which we shall shortly return—it is important to note that a historian's knowledge of connections among institutional factors need not rest on any generalizations whatsoever: Such connections are often directly evident within the source materials with which historians deal. For example, if a political historian is dealing with changes in the political complexion of a particular region, the impact of economic changes for that region will be evident in many speeches in the legislature, in editorials in local newspapers, in campaign appeals, and in other materials with which one unavoidably deals in writing political history. Similarly, the same sorts of materials, which are readily available, usually permit historians to trace the immediate impact of some political decision on the economy, even though they may later have to rely on economic theory in order to trace the further repercussions that the decision had for the economy as a whole. The point is that the historian's account is structured by relationships that are clearly indicated in the materials with which he deals. These materials, independently of antecedent theories, often serve to direct his attention to the impact of other institutions on the particular facet of the society with which he has chosen to deal.

It is at this point that one can best see the complementary character of the two ways of viewing the relations of part and whole in understanding the history of any society. On the one hand, the history of a society is made up of a continuous series of events and can be studied longitudinally over time; on the other hand, a society has many facets, or specific institutional structures, whose changes are of interest to historians. These changes bring about changes in other aspects of the society, and so are important for tracing the basic longitudinal changes the society may have undergone. It also follows, however, that the history of any institution within a society cannot be isolated from what occurs in at least some of its other institutions, and thus the history of an institution must be seen in its context as part of the continuing life of the society as a whole. The complementarity of these approaches unifies the field of historical studies insofar as different historians deal with the same society in different ways, and it allows a fuller reconstruction of the nature and changes of particular societies than was the case when—in an earlier era— historians tended to be more exclusively concerned with viewing societies in terms of political institutions, seeking the basis of both continuity and change in the nature of these institutions. When viewed in that way, the problem of the explanation of continuing stability in spite of major political changes, and the problem of change itself, raised difficulties that a less restricted view of history avoids. It is with the problem of explanation and with the relation of "what" and "why" in general history that the next section of this chapter will be concerned.

II

As we have seen, Oakeshott believed that in order to explain what occurred in history, nothing is demanded beyond a more complete account of the nature of the changes that did occur; as he said, "History accounts *for* change by means of a full account *of* change." This suggests that there is no ultimate distinction to be drawn between what happened and why it happened, and this view is shared— though on other grounds—by Collingwood. So far as Oakeshott's position is concerned, it is less paradoxical than it initially appears. The paradox persists only so long as one assumes that what is to be explained is some single, isolated event, and not some continuous series of events. In order to explain the characteristics of such a series, one must refer to the elements that formed it, for it is they that made it precisely what it was. To be sure, as Oakeshott saw, one can always pursue the matter further, asking why these elements themselves were as they were. An answer to these further questions would involve a shift in scale, but not a shift in the method of analysis: In attempting to explain the occurrence of each event that went into the series, the historian would regard it as the terminal point in another process, tracing the elements that together made up that process. Once again, then, his explanation would have taken the form of tracing out a series of events that had actually occurred.

It will be my contention that the foregoing general remarks are equally applicable to historical accounts that are primarily sequential

in structure and to those whose primary aim is to explain some specific occurrence or state of affairs. Insofar as explanatory accounts
are concerned, we have, for example, seen that if one were asked to
explain some specific state of affairs such as the decline of popularity
of Louis XIV, or the rise of the financial influence of the City of
London, one would trace the series of events that, together, constituted that decline on the one hand, or that rise on the other. The
same situation obtains in any other form of explanatory history, in
which it is asked why a series of events had precisely this outcome,
and not another: One starts from a terminal state of affairs, and
analyzes the specific series of events that, in fact, led up to it. Similarly, in a sequential history, the understanding of how one state of
affairs led to another involves an attempt to trace the intervening
sequence of steps from the original position to whatever later conditions followed it. Thus, for both sequential and explanatory histories,
Oakeshott was correct in holding that the usual distinction between
what happened and why it happened tends to collapse; however, it is
by no means clear in his account how the events in any particular
series of occurrences are related to each other, so that it may be said
of them that they form a continuous series. I believe that this defi-
ciency in his analysis can be rectified by introducing two considerations that Oakeshott failed to introduce, largely because of his
metaphysical presuppositions.

The first of these considerations consists in a contention I attempted to establish in the preceding section, that the primary, or
initial, relationship between the events with which any historical account deals is a relationship of whole and part. The historian is
concerned with some specific subject matter, not with "history in
general"; given this subject matter, the data with which he works
guide him in seeing what parts belong together and what parts influence one another, and thus which specific events are to be treated as
components within some particular whole. In the second place, as I
have already suggested, there also are points at which theoretical
generalizations may be essential to the historian's understanding of
the relationships among events. For example, as I noted, the initial
impact of a political decision on the economy of a country may be
evident in the materials with which a particular historian necessarily
deals, but an understanding of the further economic repercussions of
that decision may presuppose an acquaintance with sophisticated
economic theories. A historian who lacks such knowledge may only
be in a position to deal with immediate consequences, and not be able

to explain the longer-run changes that the immediate consequences engendered, even though what happened at a later time may be important in the series of events with which he is concerned. What holds in such a case holds in many others, and much of the mortar in historical accounts is, as I shall now show, a function not of direct description but of generalizations concerning how various factors that may be present in many different occurrences affect the situations with which historians deal.

The most familiar of these generalizations concern the ways in which human beings may be expected to behave in various types of situations, and such generalizations are apt to be admitted as important for historical inquiries even by those who are most opposed to the introduction of generalizations of any other sort. The reason for this exception is that it is universally admitted that historians must rely on their "knowledge of human nature" in order to explain why individuals act as they do. The knowledge presupposed is not, however, a knowledge of how individuals always behave when they face situations of certain specific types. It is, instead, a knowledge of factors such as pride, loyalty, envy, courage, fear, a sense of rectitude, or greed, which may be evidenced in many different sorts of actions; also, it includes an awareness that emotions may affect a person's judgment, that persons may be influenced by what others do and say, and of other general factors that affect the behavior of individuals.

While this knowledge of human nature is general, being applicable to many different individuals in different situations, it does not consist in a set of generalizations as to how individuals will behave whenever they are confronted by particular sorts of situations. The inappropriateness of attempting to formulate such generalizations does not stem from any considerations concerning human freedom. It follows from the fact that human actions vary in accordance with the nature and strength of any specific individual's psychological traits, the situation in which he is placed, and how, at the time, he views that situation. It is therefore not possible to formulate simple generalizations, except of a very crude truncated type, that serve to connect situations of a given type with specific modes of individual action. Not only is this the case with respect to how *different* persons behave in different types of situation, it is also true of how the same person behaves under different circumstances. For example, a person whose actions are usually dominated by greed may on one occasion be moved by pity, and he will then behave charitably toward a person whom he would ordinarily cheat. His motivation cannot, however, be known—at least by others—until after he has acted; then one can draw inferences from his action as to how the situation probably appeared to him at the time. This, of course, is precisely what historians do when they interpret the actions of others; it is what they must do even if the agent has explained his own motivation in journals, letters, interviews, and books, for that evidence must also be interpreted in terms of the historian's "knowledge of human nature" if he is to assess its reliability.

One's use of this general knowledge may sometimes be misleading, and is often especially misleading when one attempts to interpret the actions of persons who lived in another age or in an unfamiliar cultural milieu. Nevertheless, the possibility of being misled should not be taken as discrediting the claim that through our own self-knowledge and through the observation of others we arrive at some measure of understanding of the capacities, the forms of reaction, the ways in which decisions are reached, and many of the other dispositional traits of persons that are general in both of two senses: They are widespread, and they are evinced in many different types of situations. In these two senses their generality resembles the generality of the concepts and relationships in an advanced science such as physics, for these are not only applicable to many instances but their applicability extends to instances that, from a descriptive point of view, are not all of one type.

At this point we are in a position to see how this general "knowledge of human nature" can serve as mortar in holding together some of the elements that enter into a strand of historical events. Given the fact that the actions of a specific person formed one element in a series of events, we may be puzzled as to why he acted as he did: for example, that he suddenly changed from being a strong supporter of some measure to voting in opposition to it. In such cases a legislator generally offers reasons to explain the change in his view, and the historian will have to seek to determine whether these were in fact the real reasons for the decision, or whether other reasons, such as promises or threats, may have been decisive. To decide between such alternatives a historian must of course know a great deal about the political situation at the time, but he must also use his general knowledge of human nature to interpret whether the reasons given for this particular decision are worthy of credence. Furthermore, if this legislator's change of mind occasioned changes in the voting behavior expected of others, the historian would again have to use his knowledge of the political situation at the time and his general knowledge of human nature to estimate what factors were present that induced the others to change their minds as well. Such interpretations are necessary if a historian is to explain why, on a particular occasion, a measure that was expected to pass was defeated; and what is true in a relatively simple case, such as this, is also true whenever historians must interpret the actions of the various protagonists in any historic decision.

Several important aspects of the foregoing claims must be explicitly mentioned. In the first place, a knowledge of human nature, taken by itself, is an insufficient basis for any historical explanation. As is also the case in the sciences, in order to use general laws in explaining any occurrence, one must possess knowledge of the initial conditions that were present. In the preceding illustrative example, these initial conditions would include both prior knowledge of the nature and functioning of political institutions at the time, and knowledge of the specific political situation in which the proposed measure was brought up for consideration: It is only because he possesses such knowledge that a historian is in a position to use his general knowledge of men's motivation to explain what occurred.

In the second place, it must be admitted that the general "knowledge of human nature" involved in historical explanations does not consist in clearly formulable laws comparable to laws formulated in any advanced science. This is not primarily because the factors involved are not dealt with quantitatively, as has often been assumed; a more basic reason is that the factors in terms of which we formulate generalizations concerning human nature have not been reached through equally rigorous abstractive analysis, and they are therefore less simple and less general than the fundamental concepts used in any advanced science. Nevertheless, because they remain closely tied to types of actions with which we are acquainted in everyday life historians can utilize them. Although it has been possible to develop a relatively advanced science of experimental psychology in some areas of human behavior, the results that have been obtained in these areas cannot be directly applied to explain the sorts of actions with which historians are concerned: The relevant initial conditions for their application are simply not known in such cases.[13]

In the third place, however, it is to be noted that the lack of rigor introduced into historical explanations by the absence of precisely formulated laws can be compensated for in ways that have no true parallel in the exact sciences. Although the scientist is necessarily concerned with particular cases when he formulates and tests his generalizations, the analysis of what happens in any single case of a given type is only incidental to his main purpose, which is to explain all cases of that type. The historian, on the other hand, attempts to explain the particular case, and he uses generalizations only incidentally for this purpose. The fact that his generalizations are loose does not prevent him from offering increasingly accurate and convincing accounts of what happened in any particular case, since once he has obtained guidance from a generalization he can look for further evidence either to support or to modify his use of it in the case at hand. He can do so because the occurrences with which he, as a general historian, deals form an indefinitely dense series: Having offered an explanation of the linkage between events at one level, he can pursue his inquiries in further detail, in order to verify the applicability of that generalization concerning human behavior to the particular case he seeks to explain. Such generalizations, then, do not have the explanatory power that their counterparts possess in the exact sciences, but they serve as useful tools in historical explanations, and are often seen to be wholly appropriate as a way of explaining the linkage between specific events within a particular historical process.[14]

What has here been said about generalizations that enter into the historian's "knowledge of human nature" applies also to the generalizations concerning institutional structures that enter into his account. To be sure, there are relatively precise generalizations in economics, and perhaps in other social sciences, which help to explain the linkage among different occurrences in an ongoing social process. However, in most cases the generalizations actually used by historians in seeking to explain the nature of and the changes in social organization are based on their acquaintance with their own and other societies, and even after studying anthropology, sociology, comparative political science, and a great deal of history, their generalizations remain loose in formulation; they therefore have greater heuristic than specifically explanatory value. I take this point to be important, and I shall therefore deal with it in some detail.[15]

One can, as we have seen, view the life of a society not in terms of a succession of phases or events, but in terms of the component structures that are the basic features of its organization. Among such components are its economic institutions for the production and distribution of goods; its systems of rules concerning kinship, family organization, and differentiation of function according to age and to sex; its legal and political structures; its religious institutions; and the like. It would seem that in any given situation any one of these components may act on one or more of the others, as in our society political decisions affect economic affairs, and economic changes not only lead to the enactment of new laws but may, for example, also have a direct impact on the organization of family life. Of course, any one of these components is itself complex and its various aspects affect one another, so that changes in some sector of political life will have repercussions on other aspects of the political structure, and any drastic changes in one part of an economy are likely to affect the whole. It is with such interrelationships that studies of government and the discipline of economics are largely concerned.

While the generalizations to be found in economics are both abstract and relatively precise, this is not the case with respect to most generalizations in the social sciences. The less abstract and less precise generalizations that historians can borrow from the other social sciences, or which they formulate in terms of their own knowledge of other societies, may nevertheless perform a useful heuristic function, just as do generalizations concerning human nature. Further investigation may prove these generalizations to be correct in a sufficient number of cases so that they can be regarded as offering reasonable hypotheses as to what may be true in further cases, each of which can then be examined in detail. For example, in discussions of alternative forms of government it is a commonplace that direct democracy can exist only where the population and the area to be governed are both of limited size; and that when the size of the population and of the territory grow, and the tasks of government become more complex, direct democracy must be supplemented by some representative form of government, if democratic procedures are to survive.[16] A generalization of this type, linking size and forms of government, is not precise, nor does it involve a high degree of abstraction in the types of factors it seeks to relate to one another; nonetheless, it is a common-sense generalization that seems to fit in many cases in which one deals with various forms of governance: not only state governance but governance in religious bodies, in union activities, and in many other institutions, such as universities. Nevertheless, such a generalization cannot be held to be a law of societal organization, not only because of its lack of precision, but because it cannot support a counterfactual conditional statement asserting that as size and area to be governed increase it becomes impossible to make decisions by voting except through some form of representative system. As a counterexample, one can imagine—though perhaps not without a shudder—a voting system based on modern technology in which a whole population can be polled on any issue by informing the citizens via television at announced times on what issues they are to vote and having an electronic voting-maching terminal available in each residence that allows each eligible person to vote once, but only once, on each issue. Thus, a generalization that seeks to link political forms with size cannot be taken to be a law of societal organization; it is only a generalization that seems to be accurate in many different types of cases, under the conditions that usually obtain in cases of these types. While not claiming necessity for such a generalization, it is reasonable to apply it to previously unexamined cases in order to see whether or not it leads to insight into changes in the system of governance that have occurred in whatever society or whatever particular institutions are under scrutiny. Such insight comes if investigation reveals that a representative system was in fact introduced to supplement or supplant direct governance in order to cope with new tasks, whether these arose through growth of population and an expansion of the territory to be governed, or whether changes in other institutions made it necessary to introduce governmental regulation into new areas of societal life.

There are, I believe, many generalizations of this sort that can be used in historical inquiries, such as those generalizations that seek to link forms of marriage—for example, polyandry and polygyny—with the ways in which a population gains its means of subsistence; or those that seek to interrelate various aspects of marriage in different societies, as Tylor attempted to link rules of residence and rules of descent,[17] or as Homans and Schneider in their discussion of the two types of unilateral cross-cousin marriage related these types to patrilineal and matrilineal kinship rules.[18] I would not wish to suggest that all such generalizations have been helpful in historical inquiries. In this connection one need merely think of generalizations that attempted to link forms of government with geography or climate to understand how misleading they can sometimes be. On the other hand, I also do not wish to suggest that all such generalizations fall into the class of those that are only of heuristic significance: Some may indeed come to be so precisely stated and well authenticated that they can be considered as sociological laws, and when conjoined with adequate knowledge of initial conditions can be used to explain the direction in which change has proceeded.[19] At present, however, it is at least doubtful that one can point to instances of such laws. It is, for example, extremely plausible to treat that most famous of all modern sociological generalizations, the Marxian doctrine of the relations between substructure and superstructure, as being a heuristic generalization only, rather than as being, in any strict sense, a law concerning societal changes. In fact, in Marx's preface to his *Introduction to the Critique of Political Economy* he speaks of his doctrine as having served as a guiding thread (*Leitfaden*) in his studies, which is not, of course, the same as holding it to be a sociological law. I do not wish to suggest that Marx did in fact regard it as a heuristic hypothesis only; on the contrary, I believe that he regarded it as a statement of a set of necessary relationships, even though he left it unclear as to how, if at all, these relationships can serve to explain all of those specific changes in the total organized life of a society with which historians must deal. In my opinion, one should not in fact regard "the Marxian hypothesis" as a law in the sense that it, together with a knowledge of the initial conditions that were present, would permit one to explain concrete events. Nonetheless, it can be extremely useful in a wide variety of instances of one treats it as a heuristic hypothesis only, using it in a search for new evidence concerning *some* of the factors involved in social change, without assuming it to be true of other instances in which no convincing evidence of its applicability has been found.

We are now in a position to understand how a series of events can be said to belong together as the related parts of a single process, and to do so because of their connections with one another. From what has been said it can be seen that the events with which a historian deals in tracing a process may belong together either because they are, quite simply, constitutive parts within that process, or because they have entered it through influencing one or more of these parts. In speaking of the constitutive parts of a series of events, I refer to the fact that when a historian seeks to understand the nature of and changes in a society, or in some aspect of that society, he is dealing with a complex whole, some of whose parts he already knows. It is these parts—and any others whose existence he uncovers—that are the parts of the whole, as the series of plays in a football game, or the four quarters into which the game is divided, constitute its parts. In a society, as we have seen, one can also regard its parts as being the organizational structures that, together, compose it, and this structural way of viewing the parts of a society is wholly compatible with viewing it as the sequence of events that together form its temporal history. In fact, as we have seen, these two ways of viewing any historical subject matter are not only compatible, but fuse in almost any historical inquiry. Thus, one can see that whenever a historian correctly analyzes the structures present in a society, or whenever he gives correct information as to the sequence of changes that it or any of its aspects has undergone, he has dealt with events that belong together because they are the parts of one continuing whole.

Such a whole is not formed merely because the historian has defined his subject matter in a certain way and has confined the scope of his inquiry to what occurred with respect to that particular subject matter in a certain place and over some restricted period of time. Rather, the events that he includes as belonging within the series of occurrences with which he is to deal are those between which he finds inherent connections because they have influenced one another. In the first instance, his awareness of such influences arises because he finds them explicitly indicated in the materials with which he must deal in his inquiry, as we have seen to be the case when anyone attempts to say, concretely, what actually occurred in the course of an election campaign. However, as we have now seen, what is evident in the first instance may be supplemented by the use of hypotheses drawn from the historian's knowledge of human nature and from his acquaintance with other cases. Such hypotheses—especially when he is puzzled by any turn of events—will lead him to look for evidence of connections that were not obvious in the original materials with which he dealt.[20] In this way, many hypotheses that are neither precise nor well confirmed may serve to suggest where a historian is to look for relations that may exist between various factors effecting the course of events. If he finds evidence of such relations, he will have established in more detail an explanation of how it was that a particular series of events came to the conclusion it did. And, of course, should there be any cases to which any precise and well-confirmed psychological, economic, or sociological law could be applied, such a law would serve to cement the relationship between the events that were involved. At present, it does seem that at least those relationships that the discipline of economics is able to trace can be important for historians in precisely this way.

Changes may be brought about in a society not only because some of its structures undergo change and affect its other parts, but also because of external events. For example, a drought or an earthquake may influence life in a particular society, and the fact of its occurrence will then enter into the society's history, but the event itself cannot be said to belong within that history in the sense of being one of its constituent parts. Entirely parallel examples, though ones that have sometimes led to confusion, are cases in which what occurs in one society influences what occurs in another, as a war or a depression in one country may affect the economy of another. In these cases, too, the fact that there has been such a war or depression will properly enter any historical account of the affected country; yet the war or the depression cannot therefore be said to have been a part of that country's own history since it itself was not at war, nor did it itself suffer an economic depression at that time.[21] The influence of any such external events on the history of a specific society, or on any of its institutions, can be traced by historians in exactly the same ways as they trace internal changes: for example, by examining evidence that relates to how people at that time regarded these events, and by means of evidence as to whether their perceptions of the consequences of these events were or were not sound, and, in addition, on the basis of evidence as to the short-run effects that these perceptions themselves may have had on the situation. Also, of course, external events such as a drought may act directly on the size of a population, just as an invasion may overthrow an autonomous state. The further consequences of any such events will not depend primarily upon how the situation was perceived by the people affected; the society and its institutions will not have changed due to internal factors (*pace* Hegel and Toynbee), but through external factors that intervened in its ongoing life.

The collection of all such evidence, the marshaling of it in a convincing fashion, and a willingness to search for further evidence that may alter the picture that earlier evidence seemed to suggest comprise the task of any individual historian. His knowledge of the views held by his predecessors on the basis of the evidence that was available to them will both help and challenge him, as will any generalizations concerning either human nature or societal organization that are new in his generation or that have been newly revived from the past. All of this raises questions as to how much the rewriting of history permits one to say that history is a discipline in which reliable knowledge accumulates, or whether it is a field in which particular sets of beliefs about the past are merely supplanted by others, with none proving, in the long run, to have been more worthy of trust than those that had gone before.

We shall deal with that question, which is the question of objectivity in historical knowledge, in succeeding chapters; at this point we must conclude our discussion of historical understanding by examining how "what" and "why" are related to each other in special histories, and also in those historical studies whose structure is neither sequential nor explanatory, but is basically interpretive in nature.

III

Unlike sequential and explanatory forms of general history, special histories do not have continuing entities, such as a society or some facet of its structure, as objects of investigation. Instead, they deal with specific aspects of human culture, such as forms of technology and literary or artistic styles, which often spread across the boundaries of societies, following a course of their own. Also, the subjects with which special histories are concerned may have an intermittent existence, as one can see in following the influence exerted by a literary or philosophic figure, or the influence of a political or social ideal.

In all special histories the historian's conception of the cultural element with which he is to deal is of fundamental importance: What constitutes "literature" or what characterizes "Gothic architecture" or what is included under "technology" will determine what is to be taken into account in the history he proposes to write. This is not the case in general histories that are either sequential or explanatory.[22] Even when historians confine themselves to examining particular aspects of societal life, choosing to investigate political changes or changes in the economic institutions or in the educational system of a specific society over a certain period of time, they will be dealing with complex structures in which the relationships among the parts are not dependent upon the historian's initial conception of that aspect of societal life. Whatever antecedent assumptions a historian may bring to his materials, he will find that if he is to describe the functioning of some particular structure in social life, he must relate it to various other structures, and in doing so he may be forced to revise his conception of the nature of the institutions with which he was attempting to deal. In special histories, on the other hand, if a particular series of works falls outside the definition of literature or of Gothic architecture or of technology that a historian has adopted, he will not be compelled to include them in his history, even though others—working with other definitions—will do so. Thus, the manner in which a historian uses general concepts to bring order into the materials with which he is to deal plays a primary role in special histories. Whewell, in another connection, referred to this use of concepts as "colligation," and a number of recent writers have applied that term to what they take to be the fundamental characteristic of *all* historical writing. That thesis is not, however, my present concern. (For a criticism of the notion of colligation as applied to general history, see chapter 6, section 3.) What I here wish to point out is the very marked degree to which general conceptions or theories concerning some type of subject matter or some human activity define and limit the tasks that special historians set themselves.

Take, for example, the case of literature. Not all printed works will be classed as literature, but only those that conform to a particular view of what separates literature from other forms of expression or communication. Similarly, "technology" is usually not taken as a term that includes all of the instruments that men make and use, but refers to the ways in which tools are used to satisfy the basic needs of men living in a particular society. Consequently, while fishhooks and canoes, and the ways in which they are used, are considered to be aspects of the technology of *some* societies, they are not so considered in ours. Of course, there is much room for disagreement with respect to whether or not certain objects or certain activities resemble one another in their functions or aims. Such disagreements will obviously limit the extent to which different special historians dealing with what is ostensibly the same subject matter will present complementary or conflicting accounts. With that problem we shall later have to deal. At this point, what must be examined are the respective roles of description and explanation in special histories, and we shall find that in such histories—in contrast to general histories—there is no tendency for description and explanation to coalesce.

In special histories, whether they be histories of some form of art or art movement, of philosophical doctrines or schools, of science or of technological innovations, one fundamental task for the historian is to describe the nature of the objects that enter into his history. He must understand and be able to present to his readers the salient characteristics of those works of art, doctrines, or discoveries with which the history deals. In addition, of course, he will attempt to show how these works may have been related to one another, and to certain traditions in which they stand. Accounts of the latter sort play a large role in any form of special history, and I do not wish to minimize them. What I wish to emphasize, however, is the extent to which descriptive analyses of individual works enter into every special history. Such descriptions almost inevitably include an important element of evaluation, and the evaluation of any work will in part depend upon the historian's conception of the aims and the functions of such works, and of the genre to which they belong.[23] This is not to say that these evaluations are necessarily bound to the conventions dominant in the historian's own cultural milieu: Historians are in fact able to recognize that the arts, for example, have different aims and perform different functions in different periods; consequently, their evaluations will not be tied to what art means in their own culture, but will take into account the relative success or failure of different works with respect to the period in which they were produced. Supervenient upon such evaluations, a work may also be viewed by the historian in terms of its ability to evoke admiration as a work of art on the part of those whose views of the aims and functions of art are not limited to those of the artist's own time. The ability to transcend one period, evoking admiration at other times (although not necessarily in all times), is what makes a work a classic, whether it be in the arts, in philosophy, or in science. Such classics, of course, play an important role in special histories, but they do not usurp the stage so long as the historian is engaged in historical inquiry, rather than in a specifically critical enterprise, for even a classic must be understood in relation to other works of the time and cannot be totally lifted out of its context and understood *sub specie aeternitatis*.

This is not to say that any work of art, of philosophy, or of science is wholly embedded in the society in which it is produced, for the components of human culture may pursue an itinerant existence and, in general, they have a sporadic rather than an uninterrupted influence within the culture of those societies in which they successively appear.[24] Thus, to understand a work in relation to its time, one must be alert to the cultural milieu in which it made its appearance, and this includes not merely the culture indigenous to that society but whatever cultural traditions are available to those who created the works the historian seeks to understand.

Naturally, no work can be understood merely in terms of that which has been passed along to its creator, or creators, by what others have already done. Works of art, philosophic arguments and systems, theological doctrines, scientific discoveries, and technological innovations are the work of individuals, and in addition to the available cultural heritage—which individuals absorb differently, and to which they may react in different ways—the personality, intelligence, and other predispositions of an individual, as well as what he experiences, will shape the aims and the nature of his work. It is here that we come to the problem of explanation in special histories.

In order to offer an explanation of the characteristics of a particular work or set of works, the historian must go outside the work itself. He must in the first place relate it to the cultural tradition in which it stands, tracing whatever influences may have been brought to bear on it. Yet, as we have noted, almost any single work will also bear some impress of its maker, and the historian who is concerned with offering an explanation of what may be more or less unique in such a work will have to attempt to relate it, insofar as he can, to the talents, limitations, interests, and experience of the person who made it. In addition, of course, any cultural product is apt to reflect some characteristics of the society in which it was created, and both the similarities to be found in a series of works produced in a given society and the discontinuities in works produced by different generations within that society will often be explicable only in terms of changes in various aspects of the society itself. Such changes often affect the ideological content of literature, philosophy, the arts, or religion, and even changes in style may be explicable only in terms of changes in technology or through changes in social stratification and social ideals. Therefore, the historian concerned with some aspect of culture must not only appeal to influences spreading through a cultural tradition when he attempts to trace changes that his subject matter has undergone; he must also view that subject matter in terms of societal change. In philosophy, religion, the arts, and also in the sciences, this task is usually far more difficult, and also more controversial, than attempts to trace the spread of specific cultural influences within a given field. As C. S. Lewis said in discussing influences on English literature in the sixteenth century: "Thus far we have been concerned with ideas, and ideas have an effect on literature which can be traced, often with great probability, and sometimes with certainty. When we turn to social, political, and economic conditions, we are in a very different situation. No one doubts that these things affect a man's writing at least as much as his ideas do: but the influence is very much harder to identify."[25] Nonetheless, no historian can neglect such influences, and in some fields, such as technological innovations and technological decline, they often are of primary significance.[26] Consequently, as we earlier had occasion to stress, special historical inquiries cannot at all points be wholly autonomous but need to draw upon the results of general histories.

We are now in a position to draw a sharper contrast between special and general histories than we have previously done, for the difference between them is not only one between a history dealing with a society, or with some aspect of its structure, and a history dealing with some phase of human culture; there is also a difference between the types of explanations to be found in them. In special histories, as we have just seen, the explanation of the characteristics to be found in one or more works is through recourse to something lying outside these works themselves, for example, through an appeal to certain cultural traditions, or to the talent and temperament and unique experience of the person who made them, or to the impact of societal change. In general histories, on the other hand, the explanation of what it was that happened is given through deeper penetration into what did actually happen, just as Oakeshott and others have maintained. Even when an earthquake or an invasion drastically alters the nature of a society, it is because the *society's* economy has been altered or the *society's* political autonomy has been overthrown that the effect has come about. When one seeks to explain *how* its economy was altered by, say, an earthquake, or *how* it was deprived of its political autonomy through an invasion, one gives further descriptions of these events: One traces the different ways in which the earthquake disrupted the economy, or one traces the outcomes of the battles that followed the invasion and the peace treaty that brought the war to a close. In all of this one has remained within the framework of the ongoing processes that make up the life of a society. On the other hand, the elements that make up some strand of cultural history are individual works, or aspects of these work. They are not components within an ongoing process; they constitute a series only because of their resemblances to one another, and these resemblances are due partly to the fact that they have influenced one another. Therefore, when some outside influence affects the characteristics of such a series of works—as a change in economic needs affects technology, or political change affects literature, or new scientific conceptions affect philosophy—the explanation of how such a change has been brought about is not given by probing deeper into the materials of the special history with which one is concerned: One must explain it by relating it to the ways in which, at the time, the individuals who worked within these areas were themselves affected by changes around them to which they responded. Thus, it is on the basis of specialized biographical investigations, through a knowledge of other forms of special history, and also through a knowledge of general history that the special historian is best able to offer concrete explanations of the changes in the cultural materials with which he deals.[27]

From what has been said it follows that the role of explanation in special histories does not consist in further, closer description of what has in fact occurred in an ongoing process, but is one of accounting for new influences and for changes of direction in that series of works the special historian has under consideration. Because the explanatory aspect of special histories differs from their descriptive aspects, it is not surprising to find many cases in which a historian has adequately and sensitively traced the nature of and changes in, say, a series of works of art, but in which one would be forced to reject the explanation he offers for the features that he finds they possess in common, or for the transformations in those features in the course of the movement he traced. For example, the fact that one historian may account for similarities and changes in style through appealing to "a spirit of the age" should not be taken as justified by the adequacy of his descriptions, nor should their adequacy be impugned by those who—quite properly, as I believe—would reject that type of explanation of these features. Yet, in the field of general histories the events that explain what occurred are themselves part of the series of occurrences, and a false explanation is simply one that has misrepresented what did occur.

Turning now to histories that are primarily interpretive in structure, rather than primarily sequential or explanatory, it may be said that the historian aims to present a description of what he finds to be the dominant physiognomic characteristics of a period, and the same would hold true had he chosen to present an interpretation not of a period but of some person, or of some aspect of culture within a given period, such as an artistic style. However, in what follows, I shall be directly concerned only with interpretive accounts that deal with a society, rather than with an individual or with some aspect of culture within a period, although what will be said will be so phrased as also to apply to them, *mutatis mutandis*.

The possibility of writing general interpretive history presupposes, of course, a very substantial store of prior knowledge concerning the society with which the historian is to deal, and that store of knowledge cannot be confined to any one strand in the society's history, but must include knowledge of various facets of societal and cultural life at the time. Given such prior knowledge, the role of colligation—that is, of bringing various aspects of life together under some concept or general theme—becomes highly important. Unlike special histories, where the historian works with some prior concept of what constitutes "literature" or "Gothic architecture" or "technology" or "philosophy," an interpretive account of a society purports to extract its unifying concept or theme from an examination of the characteristics that were most fundamental, and therefore most pervasive, in the particular society with which it deals. Therefore, as we have previously noted with respect to interpretive histories, the adequacy of an interpretive account can in fact be measured against the evidence it marshals, and against the points at which its basic colligatory theme has led the historian to overlook other evidence. Furthermore, it is usually the case that buried within an interpretive account there are some explanatory assumptions that the historian takes to be indicative of which elements in the society accounted for the origin and spread of the theme that pervaded its parts. This is not to say that it is the primary purpose of interpretive histories to offer explanatory accounts of the relationships among the various aspects of the society with whose nature they are concerned: Their primary task is descriptive, portraying the distinctive features common to the various aspects of a society within the particular period with which they deal. Nevertheless, such common features do not arise simultaneously in all aspects of societal and cultural life, and the locus of what is taken to be their primary source, or sources, will reveal the explanatory assumptions on the basis of which the interpretive historian has in this case seen fit to proceed. Such assumptions are open to criticism: They must be squared with the results of explanatory investigations that others concerned with the same society have produced, or they must prove to be more convincing because they include a wealth of evidence that the explanatory accounts did in fact overlook. The latter is not often likely to be the case and therefore, as we earlier noted, interpretive accounts are not usually granted precedence of authority over the other forms of general history.

There is, however, one way in which an interpretive historian's thematic approach may permit him to fend off some forms of criticism. This defense lies in the manner in which he characterizes the period with which he has chosen to deal. As we have seen, every periodization of history involves a choice as to which aspects of societal or cultural life are to be taken as defining the period under consideration; what are regarded as major changes in these aspects are then taken as signalizing the beginning and the end of the period. Since different aspects of societal and cultural life do not necessarily change in a synchronous fashion, the themes that seem pervasive in some aspects of society or of cultural life during a given span of years may not be present in other aspects during that same span of time.

Thus, it is possible to write very different but nonconflicting interpretive histories dealing with the same society during a particular period of time, so long as it is made clear to which areas of life the interpretation is believed to apply. Misunderstandings on this issue are apt to arise only if an interpretive historian assumes that there is some single overriding and all-embracing unity in the age with which he deals, but that assumption is not plausible when it is recognized that every periodization of history depends upon the historian's selection of some aspect of life, rather than any other, as being of primary concern to him. The unity of a period may in this respect be very striking, but one should not assume that all other aspects of societal and cultural life will share in that unity.[28]

IV

I trust that it is now clear that historical studies are far more diverse than is usually assumed, and that this diversity is to some extent reflected in differences between the modes of explanation to be found in them. As a consequence, one need not assume that the methods employed by a first-rate economic historian, with his ability to use abstract generalizations drawn from the discipline of economics, have any exact counterparts in political history, nor that the methods of gathering and validating information that a political historian may use are likely to have exact counterparts in literary history. As we have seen, there is even a difference in the manner in which the concept of causation is applied in those cases in which emphasis is laid on explaining changes in societal life and in those other cases in which one attempts to account for change in some strand of culture. All this is apt to be overlooked by those who fail to anatomize the tasks that different historians set themselves in conducting their investigations, or who neglect the differences among the materials with which different historians deal.

To choose merely one example, it is now generally assumed that the primary subject matter of historians is to be found in human actions, though this assumption would not be so widely held were it not coupled with "methodological individualism"—the view that when a historian or social scientist refers to "an institution" he is referring in a quick and easy way only to some type of customary or rule-governed behavior on the part of most individuals who live in contact with one another at a given time and in a given place.[29] This view, as I have elsewhere argued, is fallacious; its present currency rests in large part on the assumption that it provided the only alternative to the views of those nineteenth-century sociologists and philosophers of history who held that societies change in accordance with a necessary law of development, and that the actions of individuals are effective in history only when they are in accord with those larger, impersonal forces that bring about social change.[30] That assumption is unwarranted. A society need not be merely a network of interpersonal relations in order for us to believe that the choices of individuals may profoundly affect historical change. Nevertheless, no one would hold that all choices of all individuals do so, and this basic fact is overlooked by those who assume that the primary subject matter of historians is to be found in human action. Different individuals play different roles in a society, and the roles that any one individual can play will depend upon the institutional structure of that society. The extent to which the choices of any individual carry over into action, and the extent to which they then have an effect on the course of affairs, will depend upon the institutional setting within which that individual acts and upon his place in that setting. Until the historian understands these institutions and the possibilities for action that they allow at any one time, he will not be in a position to explain societal change.

Nor is it possible to understand most types of cultural change solely in terms of the choices of individuals. The architectural or literary historian who traces changes in style and even the historian of technology can often appeal to the ends men seek as forming some part of an explanation of changes that have taken place. However, when one attempts to explain both continuity and change, such choices cannot be isolated from, nor be regarded as more important than the cultural and societal matrix in which they are made. The introduction of new models of composition through new contacts with other cultures, the availability of new building materials, the impact of new scientific discoveries, or changes in class structure are as important to the rise of new forms of expression or the creation of radically new inventions as is anything that is directly attributable to the ends men seek. Thus, in the realm of special histories, no less than in general history, the causal explanation of a series of events inescapably involves an appeal to a multiplicity of factors, and the distinction between what is "the cause" and what are "the conditions" breaks down. With it must go the attempt to hold that explanations of societal or cultural change must "in the last analysis" rest on an understanding of the motivations of men.

One reason why there is great reluctance to abandon the view that historical explanations are ultimately to be couched in terms of the specific choices and underlying purposes of individual men is that it seems easier to offer explanations of historical events in these terms than in any others. We know, for example, that traits of character such as pride and envy are widespread, we know how they are apt to dominate the lives and warp the judgment of some men, and we recognize the consequences that often follow when men are placed in circumstances of uninhibited power, of deprivation, or of psychological stress. Thus, it would seem that if historical causation were essentially a matter of actions purposefully undertaken, it would pose no problems with which we are not already quite familiar on the level of common sense.

Yet, historical causation *does* pose problems, and the experienced historian will not give the same sorts of explanation of historical change as are given by most journalistic interpreters of current events and as are commonly accepted by those who have had no training in the close analysis of the circumstances of social and cultural life. The most fundamental difference between the explanations of continuity and change that are given by historians and those with which others may remain content involves the breakdown of the single-factor view of causation with which we often operate on the level of common sense. This breakdown involves abandoning any firm distinction between "the cause" of an event and those accompanying "conditions" without which the event would not have occurred as it did and when it did. So long as one seeks to draw such a distinction when dealing with any of the facts of societal or cultural change one will not be able to offer an adequate explanation of what has occurred. There will be no specific type of event that always precedes a political revolution or a change in architectural style, as the Humean model of causal explanation would apparently have us assume. Nor will the analysis of Hart and Honoré serve better, since in the complex occurrences with which historians deal we shall not be able to isolate any factor as "the cause," as they use that term: There will not be any one single factor with respect to which the case in hand differs from what usually, or normally, occurs. Nor is it satisfactory to draw a distinction between cause and conditions in the way in which Olafson attempted to do. Relying heavily on Hart and Honoré, he sought to isolate the *decisive* element in explaining what has occurred in history, and found that element always to be some human decision.[31] However, as we have indicated, the effectiveness of human decisions in bringing about societal stability or change depends upon the institutional roles of the individuals making these decisions and the extent to which other institutional factors affect the implementation of these decisions. Thus, historical explanation demands the type of conception of the causal relationship that I have attempted to establish as valid in all cases in which we wish to offer a concrete explanation of a particular event or series of events.

To hold, as I have held, that the cause of an effect is the actual series of events that terminated in that specific effect is not paradoxical. It appears paradoxical only if one thinks of "an event" as some quasi-instantaneous happening, separated in time and space from those other events to which it may be said to be causally related. This, of course, is a natural enough way of looking at events if we identify an event solely with respect to the *sort* of event it is, and are not concerned with it as a concrete occurrence. However, when looked at as a specific occurrence and not as an event of a particular type, any event is seen as part of some continuing process, rather than as an isolated unit. Even in the sciences, as we have seen, when a scientist is concerned to analyze a particular case, such as the death of a person, what is to be explained is that which has been brought about in the course of a process. In order to fill in the gaps in any such process, tracing its continuity, the scientist cannot remain on the level of explanation with which he started, but must seek the connections within the process in terms of an analysis of the micro-events on which it was based. And this, too, as we have seen, is characteristic of the procedures of historians who explain connections by laying bare the further subevents that, together, brought about what occurred.

Yet, as we have seen, this type of causal explanation applies only when one is dealing with changes occurring within some ongoing process, as is the case when, in general history, the historian is concerned with changes in the nature of a society or in some aspect of its societal structure. On the other hand, when special historians deal with the influences responsible for changes in some strand of human culture, they must look to what may have affected those persons who were the innovators of change. These influences may have come from contacts with innovations in other societies, from a cross-fertilization between different cultural strands, from the impact of changes in the structure of the society in which the innovations arose, or from all of these and, in addition, whatever factors in the innovator's own personality throw light on his innovative tendencies and on why they took the shape they did. In all of this, one cannot separate "cause" from "mere conditions" and give a single-factor explanation of cultural change. Every cultural innovation takes place against a background of what is already familiar, and the characteristics of this background will affect even the most innovative personalities in one way or another; it is the task of historians of culture—in whatever field they may work—to uncover this background so that they may understand both continuing traditions and change. It is only the layman who lacks that background who will see a single innovative personality, or view a single discovery, as "*the* cause" of movements in the arts, or in the sciences or technology, or in philosophy. Historians, on the other hand, when they deal with problems of tradition and change take into account not only dominant creative personalities but the whole complex pattern of influences that form cultural stands.[32]

The temptation to adopt a simplistic view of historical causation is, of course, strong when one sudden change is seen following immediately upon another, just as the rapid succession of two quasi-instantaneous events in everyday life leads us to think of one as the sole or true cause that brought about the other. Yet, as we have noted in the case of flicking a switch and having a light come on, experience shows that the relationship is by no means simple: A whole set of conditions must be present for the flicking of the switch to initiate the process whose terminus is the light's coming on. In history, too, one may be misled by a pairing of two changes in rapid succession, but the historian who has learned to analyze societal change and is aware of the complexities involved in cultural changes will not be thus misled.

But are there, one may ask, any further parallels between causal attributions in history and in every day life? Two remain to be mentioned. In the first place, as we have seen, in our direct experience we often directly see—or believe that we see—causal connections, such as the transference of motion in the Michotte experiments, or the relationship between the movements of a person's hand when he is writing and the chalk marks on the blackboard that seem to flow from these movements. The clearest of such cases, as I have suggested, involve not only spatial and temporal continuities but the qualitative similarity between cause and effect that Duncker designated "correspondence." Within the materials with which both general historians and cultural historians deal, some parallels to these factors are to be found; but in these cases, as in the case of perception, the strong impression of the existence of a causal relationship that one immediately understands may prove to be misleading. To choose merely a single type of example, in the case of special histories one may have the strong impression of an uninterrupted stylistic continuity in a sequence of literary or artistic works, but investigation may prove this to be merely an artifact of selection: There may have been no possibility of influence between one work and the others. On the other hand, of course, stylistic similarities often do suggest influence, and the special historian may be able to trace the fact that there were either direct or indirect influences to account for these similarities in style. Cases of this sort clearly parallel instances, such as the collision between two billiard balls, where the initial perception of causal relations is not only capable of withstanding objections, but in which analysis show that there was a continuous series of finer-scale events that together constituted an ongoing process. Similarly, in the case of general history, the historian concerned with what appears to be a mounting crisis, leading to a revolution or a war, may not be deceived by the sense of mounting apprehension and alarm in the documents with which he deals, but will be able to trace the interplay of those factors that were responsible for the alarm and also for the revolution or the war that actually took place.

On the other hand, we did note with respect to our everyday causal beliefs that it is often the case that similarity in the patterning of diverse elements, such as one finds in the awareness of a gathering storm, sometimes leads to the belief that while each of these elements is not itself a causal agency, it is an expression of some single basic underlying force—the gathering storm itself. This is a further point at which it is useful to draw an analogy between causal attributions in everyday experience and causal attributions in either general histories or histories of cultural change. When one finds a pattern of resembling qualities in the various aspects of culture in any period, it is easy to interpret them as expressions of the spirit of the age. The resemblances may also carry over into at least some aspects of societal organization, as when cultural revolutions in various arts, in science, and in religion seem to be paralleled by revolutionary breaks in political traditions or drastic realignments in class structure in that age. It is then easy to appeal to some basic spiritual change that manifests itself in all of these forms and is responsible for them. Many general histories that are primarily interpretive in structure have done precisely that. Yet, as we have repeatedly noted, it is unlikely that all aspects of societal life and all phases of culture will change in a synchronous fashion; once this is recognized, the degree of unity to be found in any age becomes not an explanatory principle but something that is itself to be explained. Thus, the problem shifts —as it must also shift in similar cases in everyday life—from an attempt to explain the parts through an appeal to that whole to which they ostensibly belong; instead, it will be seen that the explanation of the whole will depend upon understanding the connections that exist in the patterning of its parts.

PART THREE

OBJECTIVITY

Chapter Six

Objectivity and
Its Limits

There should by this time be no doubt that in the field of historical studies there is great variety in the materials studied and that different historians often set themselves quite different tasks when dealing with these materials. Therefore, when one raises the question of the extent to which historical knowledge can be *objective*, and what the limits of such objectivity may be, one cannot expect a single answer that will be equally applicable to all types of historical inquiry. Instead, we shall have to consider the answers that are likely to be most adequate in the various sorts of inquiry with which historians have been chiefly concerned. First, however, it will be useful to consider some of the different ways in which the concept of objectivity has been used.

I

When the question of the objectivity of historical knowledge is raised, the issue is one concerning the accuracy or reliability of that knowledge; but not all uses of the concept of objectivity are equally concerned with this problem, which has to do with the truth of what is actually affirmed or denied in the judgments we make. Instead, the concept is often used in ways that do not refer directly to the content of a particular judgment, but call attention instead to the conditions under which that judgment was made and by which it may have been influenced. It is in this sense that we say that a person has been objective if he has tried not to let self-interest or fear or anger influence his judgment. Similarly, a person may be said to be objective if he is not prejudiced for or against specific individuals because of their class, their nationality, their religion, or their race. A person's judgments may also be regarded as objective if he does not exaggerate the virtues of those to whom he is attached, nor exaggerate the failings of those who may have injured him. In all such cases, "objectivity" has to do with keeping personal considerations, sentiments, and emotions from warping one's judgment, whatever may be the object one is judging. While these forms of objectivity often have a bearing on the truth or falsity of a person's beliefs, it may turn out that a person has judged truly even when he has not, in this sense, been objective; and he may have judged falsely even though he has. Therefore, when the concept of objectivity is used in this sense, it should not be tied too closely to the question of the truth or falsity of that which is believed. Similarly, the criterion of objectivity may be applied in assessing moral judgments: We challenge the validity of a moral judgment when it seems to spring from self-interest, bias, or special emotional ties to those who are judged. This attempt to purge moral judgments of subjectivity is characteristic of what has been called "the moral point of view," and it is a recognized element in all moral theories, whether they are classified as cognitive or as noncognitive. Since, according to noncognitivists, truth and falsity are not applicable to moral judgments, it is once again clear that the concepts of objectivity and subjectivity are sometimes applied with reference to the conditions under which a judgment is made and are not necessarily tied to the question of whether what is asserted is taken as true or as false.[1] Furthermore, we may note that the concept of objectivity is often used with reference to the way in which a person conducts himself in a particular situation, suppressing prejudices, sentiments, or personal inclinations, and in these cases, too, we are not primarily concerned with the truth or falsity of his beliefs. For example, we may hold that a judge did or did not display objectivity in the way in which he conducted himself in court, or in his charge to the jury; similarly, a teacher may or may not be objective in his assignment of grades. In such cases "objectivity" is clearly not used with reference to what one may justifiably claim that one knows.

These facts have not, however, been recognized in most discussions of the problem of historical knowledge. Many controversies have arisen, and have been needlessly prolonged, because it has been assumed that the basic issue is one concerning "objectivity," taken in this sense. Thus, it has been supposed that the truth claims of any historical account must be assessed in terms of the extent to which the historian's work has been insulated from all personal considerations, sentiments, or emotions connected with the events he attempts to understand and depict. This has been unfortunate, since "objectivity"—when interpreted in this sense—does not provide any test of whether or not a statement or set of statements is true or false, either in history or elsewhere.

There is a further, quite different way in which the concept of objectivity is frequently used, but it, too, lacks any necessary connection with the question of the reliability of our knowledge. What is referred to as objective, in this second sense, does not have to do with whether our beliefs are free from the influence of our likes and dislikes, of self-interest, or of our emotions; instead, it involves a contrast between what is attributed to the knower and what exists whether or not it is known. Taking the distinction between that which is "objective" and that which is "subjective" in this sense, philosophers have often included within the subjective all that falls within the realm of human *experience*, as distinct from whatever—if anything—exists independently of being experienced. Not infrequently this has led them to identify the subjective with "the mental." These particular uses of the subjective-objective distinction are more often found in philosophic discussions than in other contexts, but it is also the case that in everyday life we commonly distinguish between what is subjective in the sense of being "ours," and what is objective in the sense that it is independent of us. For example, the tickle in our nostrils before we sneeze, the soreness of our muscles after unaccustomed exercise, the throbbing of an injured finger, the shooting pain of a headache are all experienced as subjective, as belonging peculiarly to us. In these cases we localize what is experienced as being within our own bodies. These, then, are "subjective" states, and we do not regard them as having existence independently of our experiencing them. Similarly, we regard our thoughts, dreams, and memory images as subjective, rather than as existing independently of us. With respect to the latter instances, we are not even aware of any bodily conditions upon which they presumably depend; thus we are apt to take them as the clearest examples of that which is subjective, and only subjective. On the other hand, *what* we see or touch we take to be independent of us. In philosophy, however, there has been a long-standing tradition holding that all that is available to us as a foundation for knowledge is the data of consciousness, taken as subjective states. Most phenomenalists and many idealists belong within this tradition. Those who reject phenomenalism and reject subjective forms of argument in favor of idealism take the opposed view, which is also adopted by most laymen with respect to the foundations of human knowledge: They assign priority to what we immediately identify with the objective pole of our experience.

Fortunately, this epistemological question need not be debated here. What is important to note is that discussions of historical knowledge have sometimes become entangled by it. This is evident, for example, in Croce. His insistence that all history is contemporary history rested on his view that artifacts and documents, considered as objective facts, are without significance until the historian who examines them brings them to life through his imaginative re-creation of them. Thus, for him, none of the data with which historians deal are ultimately independent of the subjects by whom they are known. A similar emphasis on subjectivity, in this sense, is to be found in Collingwood's treatment of what constitutes historical facts. Unlike facts concerning nature, it is the "inner side" of events, not their outer, objective forms of expression, that is of primary importance to the historian, who—according to Collingwood—must grasp this inner core through thinking the thoughts that were responsible for what occurred.

On the other hand, many who have discussed the problem of historical knowledge would not accept any such emphasis on the subjective, insofar as the basic materials for historical construction are concerned. For example, although Charles A. Beard frequently cited Croce as a source and an ally of his theory, Beard regarded the artifacts, documents, and many atomic facts concerning the past as objectively given. It was only when he discussed how the historian makes use of such facts in constructing a historical account that

Beard approaches a Crocean position; it was his claim that the way in which a historian synthesizes these facts is a reflection of his experience and is not to be construed as a reflection of independent, objective relationships among the facts themselves. Thus, even a theory that assumes that the ultimate data for any historical account are objectively given may nonetheless claim that any historian's way of relating these facts to one another will be "subjective," rather than depending on the nature of the facts themselves.

It may seem as if the question of what is "subjective" and what is "objective," taken in the sense of what is contributed by the subject through his own experience, and what is independent of that experience, would be the basic issue concerning the objectivity of historical knowledge. This, however, is not the case. In *every* field of knowledge the background and experience of the investigator will affect his investigations. For example, it is only because of his background and experience that a scientist discerns the problems with which he is to deal; furthermore, whatever solutions he proposes will have been suggested to him through what he already knows, or believes that he knows. In spite of this, the scientist's experience, interpreted as a subjective fact concerning *him*, is never taken as adequate testimony for the truth or falsity of his interpretation of the events and relationships he claims to have established. In short, whenever we claim knowledge of anything other than of our own immediate experience there is an appeal to that which is regarded as being independent of that experience. This is true not only with respect to our knowledge of nature, as some have been inclined to hold; it is true also of our knowledge of others, and of how they experience the world. In claiming that we know the beliefs or intentions or ideals of other persons, we are claiming to know something other than what we ourselves are experiencing. Thus, whenever the objectivity of some form of knowledge is being discussed, the contrast between the "subjective" and the "objective"—in the present sense of these terms—is irrelevant. Even though subjective facts concerning the experience of any investigator may help to explain how some of his judgments came to be made, they will fail to settle any questions concerning the accuracy and reliability of what these judgments affirm or deny.

In addition to the two senses of the concept of objectivity with which we have so far been concerned, there is a third way in which it is often used. It is this sense that is directly relevant to our problem.

A judgment can be said to be objective not merely because it was not due to self-interest, prejudice, or the like, and not merely because it refers to events and relationships that existed independently of the experience of the person judging, but because we regard its truth as excluding the possibility that its denial can also be true. The objectivity of a judgment, taken in this sense, constitutes a basic principle that is presupposed whenever we seek to establish the reliability of our judgments concerning matters of fact, including facts concerning those forms of direct experience that are interpreted as being subjective rather than objective. This principle is obviously related to the so-called laws of thought, and when applied to the problem of knowledge it may be stated quite simply as follows: Our knowledge is objective if, and only if, it is the case that when two persons make contradictory statements concerning the same subject matter, at least one of them must be mistaken. It then becomes necessary to say, in any particular area of discourse, how one is to establish which of the contradictory statements *is* mistaken, or to adduce reasons for holding that both are to be rejected. As we have seen, this cannot be decided on the basis of the attitudes, emotions, predispositions, or prejudices of the person or persons responsible for one or another of the contradictory judgments. Nor can a decision be reached by citing those elements in a given historian's background and experience that influenced whatever judgments he may have made, since all historians, as well as all scientists, judges, or other persons, are influenced by their backgrounds and experience. Whatever test must be used must in all cases be directly applied to *what* is being affirmed or denied, not to whatever real or supposed influences may have led to that affirmation or denial. When this is recognized, at least some of the conventional arguments for historical relativism, and against the objectivity of historical knowledge, lose much of their force.

In what follows I shall attempt to show that when one clears away the preceding misunderstandings, the interlocking connections among the data with which historians are concerned permit us to hold that the cumulative results achieved through their individual inquiries can, in most cases, be regarded as establishing knowledge that is objective in this third sense of that term. To be sure, there are innumerable individual cases in which this contention appears open to challenge, but in many such cases, as we shall see, conflicts arise because the referents of the two sets of judgments have not been spelled out with sufficient care. In such cases, the two conflicting judgments may not in fact be contradictory, and as soon as the defect has been remedied both judgments can be accepted without violating the principle of objectivity. Nevertheless, as we shall also see, there are cases in which the opposing judgments do contradict each other, and a decision concerning the truth or falsity of one or the other cannot be reached unless one can appeal to some well-authenticated general theory that lends its support to one rather than to the other.

II

In what follows, I shall not initially be concerned with any differences that may exist between general and special histories insofar as the problem of objectivity is concerned; instead, I shall first examine questions that arise in any form of historical inquiry, whether its dominant structural form is sequential, explanatory, or interpretive, and regardless of the subject matter with which it deals. The most obvious of these general questions, and the one with which it is simplest to deal, is the question of how, if at all, the fact that different historical accounts deal with events of different dimensions, rather than examine all events on the same scale, is related to the issue of objectivity. A second, analogous question arises because different historical accounts often deal with different facets of the same events, and this may seem to raise questions concerning their objectivity. Our answers to these questions will help lay the groundwork for a consideration of the more difficult questions with which, in subsequent sections, we shall be concerned.

To take up first the issues arising with respect to differences in scale, it will be recalled that I used that notion to refer not only to differences in the time span covered in different historical accounts, but also to differences in how restricted or how extensive the subject under investigation may have been. Thus, I not only contrasted the scale of a history of the United States with a history confined to the events in the Civil War period, but I also contrasted a history of the United States with a history of one of its states or one of its municipalities. At first glance, there may seem to be a fundamental difference between the problems that arise when one uses the concept of scale in these two ways, one of which is temporal while the other is, so to speak, geographical. It would seem that every event of historical interest falling within the Civil War period is also an event belonging to the history of the United States, although not every event that happened in Georgia, or in Atlanta, can equally well be said to belong within *United States* history—however important it may have been in the political life of Georgia, or for the economic development of Atlanta. Nevertheless, no ultimate distinction of this kind can be drawn. As I have indicated in first introducing the concept of differences in scale, one does not expect maps drawn on different scales to convey the same information: If they did, there would be no reason for a shift in scale. And this holds no less when we are dealing with shifts in the time span covered in a historical account than it does when we shift attention from any other more extensive subject to some subject that is, in a sense, included within it.

Consider the latter sort of case first. That which a political historian dealing with a particular state wishes to trace will be changes in *its* political life, not in the political life of the United States. Changes in the latter may drastically affect changes in the life of any or all state governments, as when various powers become concentrated in the federal government; and there also are times at which what occurs in the political life of a particular state may greatly influence what occurs on the level of the federal government, as is the case when an issue arising in one particular state has an impact on the issues or the outcome of a national election. Nevertheless, a historical study that has as its subject matter the political life of a state is not a study of the history of the United States, and a study of changes in the politics and economic conditions in one municipality within a state is not to be confused with a history of that state. This, I should suppose, would be entirely clear. It is equally true, however, that a history of each of the states does not serve as a history of the United States, and a series of local histories does not constitute any state's history. The fact that histories of these types interlock at many points and that studies of the one must often rely on studies of the other should not lead us to confuse them: In each case the specific subject matter is different, and this holds true whether the histories are primarily sequential, explanatory, or interpretive.

Precisely the same situation holds with respect to histories that differ in time scale. A historian dealing with the Civil War period must trace the political, military, and economic events occurring within that period; he must understand and follow their consequences during the Civil War itself. Naturally, some of these events will have had further, long-run consequences; others will not, and in that case only their immediate impact on the course of the war will be of importance. When, however, a specific event such as Lincoln's Emancipation Proclamation has relevance to what happened in subsequent periods of American history, that event will find a place in histories that use a different time scale. These other histories, which

are not histories of the Civil War itself, need not go back and trace
the various causes of the event whose subsequent influence they are
tracing, nor need they describe its original context in detail, both of
which a Civil War historian would be expected to do: It will be
sufficient for them to consider it, and its consequences, in the framework of the longer time span with which they are concerned.

Putting the matter more generally, the facts with which historians
are concerned when they work on different scales are not "the same
facts," even though they relate to the same actual occurrences. There
is nothing odd about this. Take, for example, almost any important
episode in a person's life. One may view such an episode in either of
two ways: One may describe it and analyze it, treating it as a particularly memorable, self-contained episode, or one can view that same
episode in a larger context, as a turning point in that person's life.
When one views such an episode in these different ways, which features appear as most significant may be quite different, since the same
episode is being viewed in different contexts. Relativists are apt to
seize on this fact as establishing the contention that any historical
account is dominated by the historian's own interests, which lead him
to view an event in one context rather than in another. The existence
of the influence of one's interests on the context in which one happens, or chooses, to view an occurrence is indisputable. What must
not be overlooked, however, is the fact that these different approaches are not in the least contradictory, since the truth of each is
compatible with the truth of the other. To be sure, if any historian
were to assume that his account could capture *everything* that occurred with respect to his subject—if he were to assume that his
written work could replicate in all detail the actual occurrence itself,
making a historical work equivalent to what Beard termed "history-as-
actuality"—then the existence of multiple histories dealing with the
same occurrences would entail their being contradictory. Yet, I know
of no historian who can be said to have been guilty of such a fool-
hardy assumption. It would involve confusing a written work with
those events to which the work refers. To be sure, some historians
have been misled by some philosophers, and have assumed that when
a document refers to a fact concerning an occurrence it can be taken
to be true, and not a vicious abstraction, only if it refers at the same
time to all aspects of that occurrence. This, however, is simply to
confuse what is a fact concerning an occurrence with that occurrence
itself. While it is truly a fact—based on testimony there is no reason
to doubt—that Charles A. Beard died on September 2, 1948, one

need know neither the causes nor the circumstances of his death for that to be a fact, even though it is the case that when any death occurs there are causes that brought it about, and brought it about at one place rather than another, and with or without others in attendance. While it is sometimes important to investigate such causes and circumstances, the fact that death did occur on that date will not be altered, whatever may be the outcome of these further investigations.

A similar but somewhat more complex situation obtains when we turn our attention from differences in the scale of the events with which different historians deal to differences in the *facets* of the events that may occupy their attention.

In some cases it is fairly obvious that two different historical accounts that deal with different facets of the same occurrences are more likely to supplement one another than to clash. For example, a military historian's account of a war and a political historian's account of the war period can be expected to mesh, since political decisions are frequently linked with military successes or failures, and military successes or failures may depend upon political decisions. To be sure, these historians—like others—may disagree with respect to some points that each discusses, but this will not be because they are dealing with different facets of the same occurrences; nor should we assume that the judgments of one are more reliable and more in conformity with all of the evidence simply because he is concerned with one of these facets rather than with the other. In this case, as in others, the evidence cited, along with other evidence that might be cited or that might be discovered, is the basis on which the controversy is to be resolved. What is important to note is not the existence of any such disagreements but the fact that neither the political nor the military historian can adequately cultivate his own specialty without relying on data and interpretations with which the other is primarily concerned. What holds in this obvious case holds also, in greater or lesser degree, in other cases—even, as we have seen, with respect to the ways in which a special history of, say, Dutch painting relates to the political and social history of the Netherlands during that period. If one thinks of the different facets of a society and the elements entering into its culture as different perspectival views of one very complex object, the advantage of multiplying the perspectives from which one views that object becomes obvious. This is analogous to the fact that if one is to learn the true shape of a mountain one must be able to see it from many angles, since no one perspectival view will, by itself, reveal its dimensions and its contours. So it is with multifaceted materials with which general historians, at least, are required to deal.

Trouble develops, of course, when a historian contends that one perspectival view is more important than any of the others because he believes that facet of societal life to be more basic, or more revealing, than any other. Such claims may be made with respect to specific societies: that in *this* society, in *this* period, certain events—economic or political or religious—had a preponderating role in shaping the society and the changes it underwent. It is in fact almost inescapable for those concerned with general history to make assumptions of this sort as to which of the facets of a particular society were of greatest significance in ensuring its stability or in bringing about change in it. It need not, however, be assumed that there was only *one* such facet, rather than several, that played a crucial role in these respects. While different historians will often disagree on such questions, there exists the possibility of going far toward the resolution of their disputes through the examination of evidence as to how events that were primarily of one type influenced events of other types, and the extent to which the latter were influenced by the former.[2] While such disputes may not be readily resolved to the satisfaction of the disputants, the fact that unresolved differences of opinion are to be found in this area should not lead one to accept a relativistic conclusion, any more, say, than unresolved disputes between medical practitioners concerning the causes of an illness and disputes as to how best to treat it should lead one to hold that in medicine there are no criteria on the basis of which such disputes can in principle be settled. In such cases we do not hold that each practitioner, given his background, interests, and preconceptions, is equally entitled to his own view as to the relative importance of the factors that are admittedly present in the situation concerning which they disagree; instead, we assume that there are ways in which further knowledge can lead to a resolution of the issue.

While adequate in many simpler cases, this answer may break down when the issue does not concern which of several facets is of primary importance in a specific society at a particular time, but involves a theory that in all societies, at all times, certain facets are basic while all others are dependent upon them. Theories of this type are predicated upon a view of the nature of a society and upon beliefs concerning the factors responsible for societal and cultural change. In the history of sociological theory there are many examples of such theories, and many philosophers of history who would not consider themselves sociologists also represent the tendency to generalize in this fashion. In either case it is important to examine how general theories influence attempts to understand historical events and what relevance they have for the problem of objectivity.

III

It may safely be said that there is no universally agreed upon meaning of the term "theory" such that all philosophers of science will distinguish in the same way between what they regard as a law and what they regard as a theory. Insofar as my own use of the term "law" is concerned, the reader will recall that I held that a law formulates an invariant functional relationship between factors present in a variety of concrete occurrences (chapter 5, section 2). No one, I take it, would regard such a characterization as a correct formulation of what we designate as a theory. Nor is a theory simply a generalization from a set of experimental laws, since the acceptance of a theory may precede the discovery of those observations and laws that serve as partial confirmatory evidence for it. Furthermore, it is to be noted that direct observations and experimental findings may in many cases be explained through appealing to different theories; therefore, no theory is rigidly entailed by some particular set of data. Speaking generally, though nontechnically, a theory (as I shall use that term) is a widely applicable hypothesis that serves as an explanatory framework through which a variety of observations and— ideally—a variety of laws can be connected with one another. The unifying function of a theory depends upon the theorist's ability to show that the basic concepts and assumptions of that theory can be applied to a wide variety of phenomena and can usefully serve to connect a diverse set of apparently independent laws.

In the physical sciences, the particulate theory of matter is one example of a theory, taken in this sense, for it is applicable to a host of observations and serves to connect a wide variety of experimental laws that are not known to be deducible from any one more general law. In the biological sciences, on the other hand, there were no already well-established laws that Darwin's theory was called upon to connect, but there were many apparently independent phenomena that he was able to bring together in a single explanatory system. He accomplished this by first assuming that in any new generation some

individuals will possess characteristics not possessed by their ances-
tors, and by assuming that there is a selective process operative in
nature as well as under domestication. On the basis of these assumptions, and by using the concepts of a "struggle for existence" and "the
survival of the fittest," his theory served to connect many observed
facts concerning the distribution of plants and of animals; it was also
able to account for the existence of similarities and of differences
between apparently different species; it also offered a consistent interpretation of the fossil record.

Similarly, historians and social scientists have repeatedly sought to
establish connections among broad ranges of historical facts by
means of theories concerning societal organization and the factors
responsible for societal change.[3] Marxism is one example of such a
theory; so too were the evolutionary doctrines of Comte and of Spencer, various forms of functionalist theory in anthropology, and the
philosophies of history of Vico, Spengler, and Toynbee. In fact there
are so many such theories, most of which are mutually inconsistent,
and so few of which have seriously sought confirmation through an
examination of a sufficiently broad survey of available data, that
historians are likely to hold that no general theories of societal organization and change have a proper place in historical inquiries.
This, however, is a misguided claim. Historical inquiries do not ever
proceed without at least an implicit acceptance by the historian of
one or another set of theoretical commitments—as Werner Sombart
remarked, "No theory, no history."[4] Among such commitments will
be those that characterize the historian's view of the nature of societies and of the factors affecting social stability and change. For
example, some historians envision social institutions as reflections of
the concrete aims and ideal goals of those who share in the ongoing
life of a society, and they therefore seek explanations of stability and
change in the values and choices of individual persons. Others—
usually termed "holists"—deny that the aims of individuals determine the institutions under which they live; instead, they regard
institutions as developing and changing to meet the needs of the
society in which they are embedded, regardless of the goals that
individuals may wish to attain. Such differences in the basic conceptions of a society (to which, of course, there are alternatives) will
deeply affect the sorts of inquiries that different historians are likely
to undertake, and also the ways in which they explain what has taken
place in the past. So, too, will differences in their views regarding the
degree to which various aspects of life in a society form a single

integrated whole. Some historians expect a very high degree of free play in the institutional and cultural life of any society, whereas others expect that changes in some one institution, or in some aspect of culture, will invariably be correlated with changes in all others. Some historians will not, of course, hold either of these extreme views. They will work within a different theoretical framework, believing that different societies display different degrees of unity in their organization and that no one society need at all times display the same degree of unity. Not all of the relevant theories one might cite are as general as these. I have used them as illustrations to show that even though historians usually look with grave suspicion on the utility of the more specific theories that have been formulated by social scientists to explain societal organization and change, they cannot themselves escape taking a stand with respect to some general theoretical issues concerning the nature of societies and the factors involved in societal change. To this extent at least, there is justification for Sombart's dictum "No theory, no history."

The question now arises as to whether the presence of such theories necessarily limits the degree of objectivity to be found in any historical work. The answer will depend upon the extent to which the theory informing a historical work is itself capable of being tested for its truth. If the general theory one accepted were to depend upon one's attitude toward the world, as the economist J. C. R. Dow claimed in reviewing a book concerned with the work of J. M. Keynes,[5] it would not be plausible to maintain that objectivity is attainable. On the other hand, even if a general theory cannot be confirmed through showing that a particular set of facts is deducible from it and not from any of its rivals, it may still be possible to show that the total weight of the evidence favors one general theory rather than another; and this is all that one can expect by way of confirmation for a general theory (as distinct from an experimental law), even in the natural sciences.

In most forms of general history—to which I shall for the moment continue to confine myself—it is indeed possible to marshal convincing evidence in favor of, or against, some general theories. When the theories are as broad as those concerning the roles of individuals and of institutions in fostering stability and change, a comparison of different situations in a wide variety of different societies would surely show that neither extreme view can be rendered plausible by the evidence. In this case, as in the question of the unity of a society, practicing historians would be inclined to take the middle road. Here, too, they are apt to think that they are not espousing any theory at all, simply because their theory does not propose that whatever is true of one society at one time must also be true of all societies at all times. What it *does* propose—and what permits one to consider it as a theory—is the view that in all societies at all times one must be prepared to take into account *both* institutional factors and the actions of individuals if one is to understand stability or change. Similarly, the view that the nature and changes of one institution often have repercussions on other institutions is a theory that offers historians guidance in their attempts to explain many of the events they are called upon to explain. If a historian doubts that this constitutes a theory—holding that it is merely common sense—he need only consider the extent to which earlier general histories of nations were written primarily—and sometimes almost exclusively—in terms of political life. Implicit in those histories was a theory of societal organization, whether it was articulated or not, according to which the institutions of government were the most basic feature in the society, and societal change could be understood almost without reference to changes in any other institutions, except for the role played by religious differences in political life. The fact that this politically oriented theory has now broken down does not mean that an older form of history has merely been supplanted by a new and different form. There has been an advance. Political history is still written, and is very well written, but since it is now recognized to be merely one form of historical writing, dealing with only one facet of societal life, historians are more alert to the possible effects of other institutions on government, and the explanations of political change that they are in a position to offer have proved to be richer and deeper than those previously offered when "society" was equated with "the state." For those acquainted with the relevant data from anthropology, or for those interested in the Middle Ages, it can scarcely be doubted that it is a mistake to assume that at all times and in all places political events should be allowed to occupy center stage whenever a historian seeks to explain either stability or change. Thus, theories that were once very much taken for granted are given up when historians extend the range of their interests to include evidence previously unknown or neglected.

To be sure, some theories may be dogmatically held and be very resistant to change, especially if they are connected with metaphysical commitments or with basic political-ethical convictions. It is then that they reflect what J. C. R. Dow labeled "rival attitudes toward the

world." Yet even the most basic attitudes toward the world are sometimes drastically altered because of an accumulation of new data that
they are unable to absorb. Unfortunately, many general theories of
society and social change have defended themselves against this possibility by defining as relevant only such data as conform to their
initial interpretive scheme. Among philosophers of history, for example, it has commonly been the case that the only facts or periods
or even geographic areas considered to be relevant to the truth of the
theory are those that illustrate whatever grand design the philosopher
of history takes to be paramount in importance; all else is dismissed
as insignificant "in the long run." This tendency is clearly evident in
Hegel, but it is no less true of Comte and of Spencer, who held the
discipline of history, as practiced by historians, in contempt.[6] Marxist theory has often (and sometimes with justice) been condemned
for the same fault, although some formulations of that theory involve
an attempt to bring it into line with a wider range of facts than Marx
himself was able to take into account. Even in the case of an interpretive history, where the theme of the study dictates what materials are
to be included and at what points the main emphasis is to fall, it is
possible (as I have already suggested in chapter 2, section 3) to
assess its adequacy by checking its interpretation against further
ranges of fact. Thus, while I acknowledge that there often are limits
to objectivity in theory-dominated works, it is not true that the impact of a general theory, or point of view, makes it impossible, in
principle, to justify or to refute an interpretation of the past.

When, however, we turn from any form of general history to special histories, and consider the question of objectivity with respect to
them, the problem becomes more complicated. Not only will the
special historian, like the general historian, be forced to make certain
theoretical assumptions concerning the factors that induce societal
and cultural change, but his work will also presuppose some characterization of the particular subject matter with which his special history is to be concerned. For example, an art historian's work
presupposes at least an implicit theory of what separates art from non-
art. Similarly, underlying any history of philosophy there will be at
least a tacit definition of philosophy that serves to justify labeling
some persons as philosophers, but withholding that designation from
others who may to some extent share their intellectual, moral, and
religious concerns. We have already noted that the same situation
obtains with respect to the problem of what constitutes "literature."

Sometimes the definition of a concept such as "literature" derives from a general theory of the arts; in other cases it represents a program or a tradition to which the particular literary historian (knowingly or not) tends to adhere. In neither case can such disputes be readily resolved, even in principle. In this field, therefore, there is some reason to doubt that objectivity can be attained. This point is worthy of further comment.

Insofar as the definition of what, for example, constitutes "literature" rests on a general theory of the arts, the major difficulty lies in the fact that the particular instances usually used as evidence for or against such a theory are not neutral facts whose relevance is beyond dispute. When there is a dispute that is fundamental, involving two different general theories of the arts, each disputant will be inclined to reject the counterexamples that his opponent will be most inclined to cite, precisely because his definition of his subject matter differs from the one his opponent accepts. Thus, if the evidence upon which one draws in support of a general theory of the arts is confined to the particular instances that the theory attempts to interpret, the quarrel between rival theories cannot be resolved: Each will in the end be arguing circularly for his own theory.[7] What holds with respect to the difficulty of establishing objectivity in the field of literary history, because of its dependence on a general theory, also holds, *mutatis mutandis*, in all other forms of special history. Thus, we have here approached the possible limits of objectivity in one form of historical inquiry.

In those cases in which different definitions of literature are not primarily dependent upon the acceptance of one or another general theory, but rest upon familiarity with an interest in different traditions, or upon commitments to different programs as to what is worthy of encouragement and what is not, the limits of objectivity are also reached. In such cases, so long as each of the opposed historians maintains his position, each will be writing a history that is biased by the nature of the works with which he is already best acquainted and of those that he prefers. When one takes into account the fact that literary forms and modes of expression have undergone radical changes over time, one can appreciate how pervasive such biases among literary historians are likely to be: A literary history written at one time, in the light of the then known past, will almost certainly differ in orientation from one written with full awareness of the changes in genre and in style that subsequently occurred. What is in this respect true of literary historians is no less true of those concerned with other forms of special history, such as the history of philosophy, of science, or of art.

It may seem that the factors I have mentioned as limiting objectivity in special histories would necessarily limit the objectivity of any general history as well. Such an argument might be constructed along the following lines. Just as a literary historian's definition of the special subject matter with which he is concerned determines the content of his work, so the general historian selects certain types of event with which he chooses to deal and constructs his account to include events of this type, while excluding others. And just as the literary historian is limited by the tradition in which he stands, or by programmatic aims as to what is and what is not of importance in literature, so the general historian tends to be confined within one or another historical tradition, or to be influenced by one or another programmatic aim. Finally, it might be argued, the field of general history has undergone many radical changes in its style and in its concerns, and much of it now differs profoundly from historical works that were produced in Greece or Rome, in the Renaissance, or even in the Enlightenment; to expect these different ways of writing history to yield compatible results is simply quixotic.

However, it is mistaken to draw this parallel between general histories and special histories. It will be recalled that I emphasized the fact that general histories have as their subject matter particular societies, which are continuing entities existing in a region over a particular period of time, whereas the subject matter of any special history is a class of resembling cultural products, many of which are related through strands of influence but which do not comprise a unitary ongoing entity, as does a society (cf. chapter 1, section 3). As a consequence of this difference, a general historian cannot exercise the same freedom in delimiting what will and will not enter into his account. He must take a society as it is, analyzing it in terms of connections that exist among its component parts. Thus, even though a general historian may define his task as one in which he will deal directly with only one facet of a society and not with the society as a whole, he is not thereby set free of constraints as to what must be included within his account: He will have to recognize whatever other factors may have directly affected the changes with which he seeks to deal. When, on the other hand, a special historian defines *his* subject matter, he does not necessarily place himself under the same types of constraints. He may, for example, decide to deal with a certain body of works produced by some writers, but not others, setting himself the task of tracing the similarities and differences in their interests and styles, and comparing them with respect to the esteem in which they were held. He may or may not choose to account for whatever similarities or differences he finds among them, or in their popularity; one cannot say that given the task he has set himself, he is obligated to do so. Thus, the criteria we use when estimating the work of a special historian may shift according to the sort of task he has set himself; we can demand that he do well whatever he has set himself to do, but we cannot criticize him for not having done something else. In the case of a general historian, however, the situation is different. He purports to understand and depict what was in fact true of some society, or true of some aspect of it; the scale on which he has chosen to work will of itself determine what he should include—as well as what he need not include—in his account. If, for example, his account purports to deal with some segment of the political history of a nation, and if he did not take into account the impact of some religious or economic changes on the changes that occurred in the political life of the period, we do not say that he need not have done so; we hold that his account stands in need of correction, even though we may still admire his ability on other grounds. In short, even though we recognize that different general histories reflect different assumptions, we demand a reconciliation of their differences, rather than accepting both. On the other hand, in the field of special histories, we demand a reconciliation only of differences among accounts that proceed on the basis of the same assumptions, or on the basis of assumptions that are compatible with each other. Unfortunately, it is often the case that different historians of literature, or different cultural historians generally, proceed on the basis of incompatible assumptions, and when this occurs a limit of objectivity has been reached: In comparing two such accounts, we cannot say that at least one of the ways in which the past was depicted must be rejected. It will be recalled that it is precisely in this sense—and not in any other—that the concept of objectivity is being used in this discussion.

The contrast just drawn between the objectivity to be expected in general histories and what may be said of the unresolved differences between different special histories has a bearing on recent discussions of the role of colligation in history. The term "colligation" was apparently first used in a specifically philosophic context by William

Whewell in his discussions of method in the natural sciences; it was W. H .Walsh who first introduced it into discussions of historiography.[8] Whewell had characterized colligation in saying, "Facts are bound together by the aid of suitable Conceptions. This part of the formation of our knowledge I have called the Colligation of Facts: and we may apply this term to every case in which, by an act of the intellect, we establish a precise connexion among the phenomena which are presented to our senses."[9] In his use of the term, Whewell was referring to the step in scientific method that he regarded as intervening between the establishment of facts and our inferences to hypotheses: Colligation involved bringing appropriate concepts to bear on what had been observed. Thus, it was a step preliminary to the formation of the hypotheses that were to explain what had been observed. Walsh, on the other hand, does not use the concept of colligation to apply to a step preliminary to explanation; he views it as the way in which historians transform their data into "significant narratives" that do not stand in need of further explanation. He says: "Different historical events can be regarded as going together to constitute a single historical process, a whole in which they are all parts and in which they belong together in a specially intimate way. And the first aim of the historian, when he is asked to explain some event or other, is to see it as part of such a process, to locate it in its context by mentioning other events with which it is bound up."[10] According to Walsh, it is through the introduction of "dominant concepts and leading ideas" that the historian moves from a merely "plain narrative" of *what* happened to a "significant narrative" in which we are able to see *why* it happened, that is, to see it as a part within a larger intelligible whole.[11] Whether this position leads to a subjectivistic or to an objectivistic position depends, of course, on the factors that determine the nature of these intelligible wholes. On Walsh's view, the concepts by means of which the historian colligates his facts are concepts such as "the Industrial Revolution" or "the Enlightenment," which he claims are "arbitrary and not natural units."[12] Thus, according to Walsh, it is the historian's own choice of concepts, rather than the data with which he works, that underlies the kinds of explanations he offers of the events with which he deals. This in itself is sufficient to undermine any claim to the objectivity of historical knowledge.[13]

On the basis of what has already been said concerning the role that definitions play in delimiting the materials with which historians of "art" or "literature" or "philosophy" deal, there would be much to be said for Walsh's emphasis on the importance of colligation—and the lack of objectivity it introduces—were he concerned only with what occurs within the realm of special histories. This, however, is not his concern: He is attempting to deal with all forms of historical explanation. Even were we to grant—as he assumes[14]—that in history generally we are always concerned with human actions and that human actions are always to be interpreted teleologically, historians are not free to use whatever concepts they choose in order to arrange these data into significant wholes. As I have repeatedly attempted to show, once a historian has chosen a subject matter and a working scale, it is in the first instance the data that inquiry reveals, rather than the historian's own initial concepts, that serve to control the structured connections of the facts within his account. Wherever his selection of facts appears to be dependent upon his initial conception of what the whole must be like, rather than being confirmed through inquiry, his reconstruction of the past may be considered interesting as revealing his own mind and as mirroring his own times; but that does not mean that it will be accepted by those who are primarily interested not in him, but in the events his work sought to depict and explain.

A similar contrast can be drawn between the objectivity to be expected in general histories and the limitations on objectivity in special histories if one considers the ways in which periodization affects each form of historical inquiry. In both cases the historian periodizes the past in terms of events he regards as marking the beginning and the end of a particularly significant development. The general historian may mark off periods in terms of the reign of a ruler or a dynasty, or in terms of what he regards as the beginning and the end of some significant economic development within a society or group of societies, or he may do so in terms of the rise and decline of a nation or an alliance of nations. Similarly, in the field of special histories periods are marked off in terms of, say, a dominant style in literature or a style that is held to characterize various forms of art at the time; or a period may be marked off in terms of the acceptance and subsequent rejection of a set of presuppositions in philosophy, or in the background, development, and final acceptance of a series of epoch-making scientific discoveries. For example, one thinks of Romanticism or of the Baroque, of Rationalism, of seventeenth- and eighteenth-century Empiricism, or of the Scientific Revolution as terms sometimes used to characterize periods in literature, in the arts, in philosophy, and in the sciences. Where general histories and spe-

cial histories differ with respect to periodization is not in their delimitation of a period by means of significant events in the field with
which they are concerned; this is common to both. Where they differ
is in the impact of their periodization on what their accounts will
include and exclude. In a general history the periodization may rest
on political events, on economic changes, or on a view of changes in
the relations among nations over a particular span of time, but whatever dictates the choice of these events as marking off a period will
not justify the historian in excluding other types of events that
brought about changes in society during that time. On the other hand,
when a historian writing a special history has characterized a period
in terms of the development of a style or in terms of a common set of
philosophic presuppositions or in terms of the development and acceptance of a new set of scientific concepts, methods, and paradigms,
what he is obliged to include within his survey of that period are only
those other works that share a common denominator with the works
that have given rise to his periodization. However, the works produced within a particular period, even within a suitably defined
geographical area, are not apt to be characterized by any simple
homogeneity in conception or execution, even when one confines
one's attention to those that are clearly comparable in intent and in
function. Disparities in taste and the influence of regional and class
interests are evident whenever one looks closely at the total range of
these works, even when there is one overriding style that generally
dominates the period.[15] This is not only true with respect to literature and the arts, but also clearly applies to philosophy as well. For
example, it is unmistakable that there was a continuing scholastic
tradition both in England and on the Continent throughout the period in which Descartes, Spinoza, and Leibniz, as well as Boyle and
Locke, provided the innovations that mark the new Rationalism and
the beginnings of modern Empiricism.

The difference between general histories and special histories with
respect to problems of periodization is symptomatic of the basic difference between them: General histories have as their subject matter
entities having a continuous existence, and special histories do not.
Therefore, as we have already noted with respect to histories of literature, and as now also appears with respect to periodizations in special
histories, unity is introduced by a principle of exclusion that permits a
historian to consider only certain works, and not others, on the basis
of his evaluation of their importance when they are considered as
representative of the type of cultural activity with which he is con-

cerned. No matter how intimate the connections among these works may be, it is not their relationships that are decisive in singling them out for attention; if it were, the historian would also have to trace all of their other influences, and not be content with how they influenced works that, on his view, were also important. Since different historians will adopt different views, based on different theories or evaluative criteria, one cannot expect a resolution of the differences between alternative special histories, each of which may be excellent so long as one adopts *its* point of view, but each of which will prove unsatisfactory if one does not. Thus, in this field, one cannot expect objectivity in historical knowledge.

One final contrast may be drawn between general histories and special histories insofar as the problem of objectivity is concerned. While different general histories may deal with different facets of a society and need not make use of identical scales, any one such history will dovetail with others, and a cumulative, consistent record of past societies can be built up. Similarly, different biographies of the same person—though starting with varying interests, and stressing different aspects of that person's character and career—will, when taken together, yield a more trustworthy interpretation than will any single biography that seeks to interpret his achievements and failures solely with reference to one of many alternative points of view. What holds of biography also holds of interpretations of the literary, philosophic, or scientific work of any specific person with whom a special historian of literature, philosophy, or science may be concerned. While many interpretations of classic figures in these fields are possible—and some prove to be extremely stimulating even when they are obviously one-sided—in the end an attempt must be made to achieve an interpretation of that person's work in terms of its author, its contemporary context, and the cultural traditions to which it belongs. While preferences and personal background will tend to dictate what any one interpreter will see and will stress, it is necessary when dealing with the life and work of a particular individual to take diverse points of view into account and to offer a nonidiosyncratic interpretation of the person with whom one is concerned. Nor is this impossible, even when one is dealing with writers, painters, scientists, or philosophers. Therefore, what precludes objectivity in some forms of cultural studies is not the character of the materials with which they deal, however value-laden these materials may be. Rather, it is the fact that if a historian of culture is not dealing with the life and work of one person, or with some limited group of persons, but is seeking to trace a continuous history of some form of cultural life, the principle by means of which he chooses and organizes the specific materials with which he is to deal represents merely one among many possible principles. In the field of general history, the same factor of relatively free selection is not to be found. It is to establish this point, and to conclude this discussion of objectivity, that we next turn.

Chapter Seven

Objectivity, Causation,
and Laws

The problem of objectivity in historical knowledge turns on the question of what controls the work of historians once they have set themselves some specific topic to investigate. Any number of different reasons may be cited to explain why particular historians chose to investigate the topics they did. Such reasons are to be sought in biographical data concerning their backgrounds, training, and predilections, as well as in the topics that were of interest in the milieus to which they belonged. Furthermore, both the nature of their choices and the ways in which they carried them out are bound to have been dependent, to some extent, on the historical knowledge available at the time. Questions concerning these factors, both in particular cases and in general, are of importance to historians of historiography, but they are not directly relevant to the question of objectivity with which we are here concerned. Our problem is whether it is the case that when two historians disagree in their interpretations or explanations of the very same events, at least one must be held to be mistaken. The fact that different historians are motivated in different ways to undertake whatever investigations they pursue would be relevant to the question of objectivity only if the connections they trace among the events with which they are concerned were primarily artifacts of what originally determined their choice of their subject matter. Disagreements would then be expected, and would be ineradicable in principle: Any historian seeking to justify one account against others could be accused of being predisposed to favor that account because of his own interests and background. On the other hand, if historians are constrained by the nature of the materials with which they must work, and if the connections they trace did in fact exist in the events to which these materials refer, then it is to be expected that different historical accounts can be used to supplement and correct one another; a belief in the objectivity of historical knowledge could therefore be maintained. Nor would this conclusion be undermined by the fact that every historical account is partially conditioned by what may have been the state of historical knowledge in its own time. That new knowledge develops and new modes of treating the past arise does not of itself prove that there is no compatibility between the old and the new. Once again it remains possible that these differing accounts could be used to supplement or to correct one another, and a belief in the objectivity of historical knowledge could be maintained. That this is true with respect to general histories, what has already been said and what follows should serve to make clear.

It will be recalled that general histories are concerned with the nature and changes of particular societies, or with the nature and changes of specific aspects of their structure. The dominant approach in some general histories, as we have seen, is sequential; others seek to account for a particular state of affairs by examining the events on which it depended; still others seek to interpret and portray the nature of society through examining its various facets and noting their interplay. While these represent three basically different forms of organization in historical accounts, every account will at one point or another have to include elements that typify the other approaches. We have already seen that some degree of objectivity can be ascribed to interpretive histories, based on the extent to which the basic interpretive theme employed seems to illuminate a wide range of materials in addition to those the interpretive historian cited in favor of his interpretation.[1] Furthermore, that discussion should have made it clear that the adequacy of interpretive histories was dependent upon the accuracy of the sequential and explanatory accounts on which they were dependent. I shall therefore now turn to examine the degree of objectivity that can be credited to such accounts, first considering those that are sequential rather than explanatory in their basic, over-all structure.

Any sequential account has as its focus of interest some chain of events; the historian seeks to depict the nature of the successive links in that chain and their connections with one another. This is as true of sequential accounts that fall within the realm of special histories as it is of sequential general histories; however, it is only with the latter that I am now concerned. In a general history the series of events with which the historian deals are events that occurred with respect to some entity that had a continuing existence, and the historian (as we have noted in Chapter 6) must already possess some knowledge of that entity and of some of its changes in order to have become interested—for whatever reason—in investigating the course of its history. What leads the historian, given such an interest and some tentative and preliminary knowledge, to include certain events within his account and to exclude others? As has just been remarked, the answer to this question is crucial to any discussion of the problem of objectivity.

In the first place, when the historian selects the subject with which his inquiry is to be concerned, he will already be in possession of various documents and reports referring to what occurred with re-spect to that subject at various times. This supplies a chronological framework. Other documents and reports that he gathers referring to his chosen subject will generally fit easily into this same framework, though occasionally they will suggest a need for adjustment in it. In any case, the mere chronological sequence of what occurred with respect to a given subject provides a basic skeletal structure for the historian's account. To be sure, the materials he gathers, all of which treat of the same subject, will differ with respect to scale, some of them treating larger segments of that subject's history whereas others bear evidence as to some brief episode only. These documents and reports fall naturally into place when, for example, some tell of the course of a war and others provide eyewitness accounts of one of its battles. In general, any such sorting of documents will initially pro-ceed easily and without hitch, and may proceed without the histori-an's being acutely aware of what he is doing. Thus, in the accumulation of materials with which the historian is subsequently to work there already is an order, and that order is both temporal and analytic: The materials refer to a sequence of events that are not only linearly ordered but some of which possess a structured relationship to others, since some are known to be component subevents of others. As the historian proceeds in his attempt to gather further materials concerning his subject, this structure becomes more and more clearly ordered, rather than becoming more amorphous because of the wealth of accumulated data.

To be sure, among the documents and reports that the historian accumulates there will be contradictions as to what actually occurred. When such contradictions appear they do not usually undermine the basic structure of the account that has been building; they often contradict only specific items that a historian has previously accepted, and do not force a change in the general outline of the account. This occurs when the conflict in his materials leads to the substitution of one element for another. Although this will affect the account—perhaps even altering its interpretation of some other events in a radical manner—it will not involve a total dismantling of the chronological and analytic structure in the series of events taken as a whole. This is true not only with respect to the efforts of an individual historian, it is true of the collective enterprise of historians generally. Those dealing with the same events may find themselves forced to offer quite different interpretations of those events, but these differences do not totally alter the basic structure that previous historians have found to be present in the same events.[2]

Nor does the fact that different historians are primarily interested in different facets of a society necessarily cast doubt on the degree of objectivity attainable in sequential general histories. An adequate understanding of the nature and changes of a society could not be achieved if all historians focused their attention on only one aspect of the life of that society. This will become more evident when we consider the explanatory form of general histories, but it is relevant to mention it now since we have already noted that all sequential accounts will also include segments that are primarily explanatory in nature. The fact that different historians focus attention on different aspects of a society and construct different histories in doing so would undermine the objectivity of historical knowledge only if these accounts were contradictory. Yet they need not be. Any society includes within itself many different institutions, and any adequate account of the nature of that society must therefore be based on a knowledge of these institutions and the changes that have taken place in them. Since no one historian can be expected to investigate the history of each of these institutional factors in detail, a proliferation of histories of the same society, seen from different points of view, is to be expected. Conflict among them is engendered only insofar as general theories of the relative importance of different institutions intervene, with different historians tending to explain all other changes in a society in terms of some one or some few institutional factors. When this occurs, claims to objectivity must be relinquished unless there are ways to assess the truth of the alternative theories themselves. This is not always impossible, as the argument of the last chapter attempted to show.

There is, however, another difficulty that arises because different sequential histories of the same subject concentrate on different aspects of it. This difficulty consists in the fact that such histories are not likely to periodize their accounts in the same way: What appears as the beginning or end of a significant epoch in one may be seen as merely incidental in another. Such disparities in periodization were already noted in chapter 1, but their relevance to the question of objectivity must now be discussed.

Were there only one way in which the past could be correctly divided into successive periods, then the existence of the many different periodizations that one in fact finds in the works of different historians would, of course, entail a lack of objectivity in historical knowledge. However, the manner in which a historian periodizes history depends upon the facet of social life with which he is concerned. In the course of events there are indeed points at which new developments take hold in a society and points at which their dominant role comes to an end. Even though one can always find related antecedents for these developments, and even though one can expect a lingering influence to remain, there often are major turning points that can be said to mark off a period in some particular aspect of the life of a society or a connected group of societies. It is therefore natural that histories written with a particular aspect of a society in the forefront of attention should treat of the past as if it were punctuated by these events. Yet, when one takes a view of the society as a whole, in all of its several aspects, any period shorter than that marked by its origin and its ultimate collapse (if such points are to be found) will appear as relative to the historian's focus of interest since, as a whole, the society functions as a continuing entity.

The problem is similar to "the problem of generations," which is in fact one form that the problem of periodization sometimes assumes. Strictly speaking, there cannot be "generations" in a society, though there are in families. Every day new individuals are born and others die, and the stream of life does not start and stop at the boundaries of what a historian—for example, a literary or social historian—regards as a generation. Yet there is good reason for historians to speak of generations, marking them off in terms of a sudden change in dominant interests or in style, since such changes link a group of persons and separate them off from those who preceded them. However, these lines of demarcation apply only to one or a few common characteristics: Many other aspects in the life of a group of persons are apt to be continuous with what went before. Were a historian to be concerned with other facets of life in a particular society—say, with its science instead of its literature, or its entrepreneurial system instead of its politics—periods and generations would be differently delimited; it would then be only on the basis of some theory as to which aspect of societal life was to be considered primary that one of these ways of dividing history would be given priority over the others. In the absence of an established theory of this sort, each periodization must be seen as relative to a particular point of view.

This would seem to undermine the objectivity of periodizations, but once it is recognized on what they are based, the variety of ways in which histories are periodized should not be regarded as contradictory: Their focuses of interest may be different, but the relationships among the events that they describe may be the same.

The situation with respect to periodization is comparable to that which arises whenever the past is regarded from an ethnocentric point of view. A sequential history constructed to depict the past of western European societal and cultural life will leave out much that would be relevant to the history of, say, Indonesian society. Though some common antecedents will appear in both, there is no single sequential stream of historical change to which both belong. Thus, it is illegitimate to speak as if there were a single sequential "world history," as many philosophers of history and some social evolutionists have done. Those who have viewed the whole human past as if it were a single sequential process have done so because they have been interested primarily in tracing out the antecedents of their present historical position, rather than concerned with other strands of development.[3] Abandoning an ethnocentric approach of this sort does not entail that inquiries into the past that are conducted from two disparate points of view lack objectivity. Each may be wholly compatible with the other since each will be concerned with much that is of no concern to the other, and even when the same set of events, such as colonial expansion, appears in both, it will often be in relation to different antecedents and different consequences.

I shall now take it for granted that the objectivity of historical knowledge is not to be impugned simply because different historians who are concerned with the nature of a particular society not only work on very different scales, but may choose to deal with different aspects of that society. As a consequence of such choices, their periodization of changes in that society can be expected to differ; once the reason for these differences is understood, one can hold that the periodization of history is relative to a point of view even though a knowledge of the relationships that obtained within any period can be objective. It remains to show, however, that objective knowledge can in fact be obtained in sequential general histories.

A basic clue to the solution of this problem has already been suggested in earlier chapters when, contrary to common belief, it was held that the connections with which historians are concerned are not primarily linear, but are part-whole relationships where the wholes are processes and the parts are events included within these processes (see, for example, chapter 2, section 2, and chapter 5, section 1). Which events are to be included is not a matter left to the historian's free choice. Were he to possess a series of documents that stated only bare facts, such as "Washington crossed the Delaware at McKonkey's Ferry, near Trenton, on December 25, 1776," he would not know what to do with them; without further knowledge he would not be able to construct a historical account that included them. To interpret any such statement as referring to a fact that can be of concern to a historian, it must be brought into contact with other materials that serve to place it in some societal context, and in this case what would be involved is relating it to the Revolutionary War, of which it was part. This is not, however, merely a matter of including it in a class of maneuvers: The date at which it occurred will bring it into a sequence of battles, sieges, advances, and retreats, and these are connections that must be established by further documentation. Such connections are not in any respect relative to the historian's own point of view.

I am not here raising the question of *why* Washington crossed the Delaware at that time; to do so would demand an explanatory account of his choice among various strategies, and it is not with the explanatory segments of sequential histories that I am now concerned. What I wish to point out is simply that if a historian were to start from documents that merely stated single atomic facts, he could proceed only through a search for other documents that also referred to these facts, and which placed them in context as parts of some ongoing whole. However, historians always have other prior accounts that help to interpret whatever new documents they find, and so they proceed by enlarging and correcting prior accounts through showing in greater detail the nature of those events upon which the process of concern to them depended.

The search for such events is by no means blind. The materials with which historians work are not restricted to documents that merely report isolated atomic facts: Such materials are apt to contain explicit references to at least some other events upon which that process depended. These clues must be supplemented by a search for further documentation as to what occurred with respect to the events already reported, and in this search the historian will be guided by his knowledge of the structure both of his own society and of other societies—in particular by the knowledge he has already obtained concerning the society with which he is specifically concerned. The result is that, over the long run, a series of historical inquiries builds up an ever denser network of accounts referring to the events that occurred in a society during a given span of time. While the focus of interest of these individual accounts will vary, and while historians may disagree as to which of these events were of greatest importance, knowledge will grow concerning the actual structure of the societies that have been studied, and changes that they have undergone will have been traced.

When a sequential historical account concerned with general history traces a series of changes that ended in a particular state of affairs, it provides a legitimate answer to the question, "What brought about or caused that state of affairs?" Such an answer differs, of course, from explanations that cite some single event as the cause of whatever state of affairs one wishes to account for. While the latter may be a convenient enough shorthand answer if enough other factors are taken for granted, it should be evident from our previous discussions that such answers involve gross oversimplifications. A war, for example, can be said to have been won or lost in a single battle only if one has already taken into account the other events that made it impossible for the loser to fight on. Thus, it is not one battle only, but a series of changes in the relative strength of the opposing forces that is needed to account for the fact that one side was forced to surrender to the other. Similarly, as we saw in chapter 5, section 1, the loss of popularity of a king or the rise of a new economic power is a state of affairs to be explained through recounting the series of successive changes that led to it. What gives objectivity to such causal accounts is the fact that, in history, documentation is essential to the acceptance of any account, and whatever connections are traced in a series of events must be shown to be supported by all relevant evidence. Where lacunae are present in the evidence historians must search for further evidence; and wherever there is evidence contrary to a given account, that evidence must either be discredited or be proved compatible with all the other evidence at hand.

The question of objectivity becomes more acute when we turn from sequential to explanatory accounts. There is, as we have seen, a sense in which a sequential historical account offers an explanation of what has occured, for it traces a series of events that led to some particular terminal state of affairs. Such explanations appear adequate so long as the events forming the series are regarded as parts of a single ongoing process, as the speeches and television commercials in an electoral campaign are parts of that campaign. Questions arise, however, when it is necessary to explain these parts themselves, since what led up to them will not in all cases be included within the original series. In an electoral campaign, for example, a particular speech or set of commercials may have to be explained by tracing the impact of some previously unassociated event, such as a revolution in a neighboring country, upon the course of the campaign. Whatever changes in the campaign were brought about by that event will subsequently be seen as part of the history of the campaign, and belong to it. Nevertheless, to explain the change that occurred at that point involves going outside the course of events that were included in the campaign. For this reason, although a history may be primarily sequential in structure, there will be many points at which it will include investigations that break the pattern of sequential exposition. Consequently, questions concerning the objectivity of accounts that have an explanatory structure are not only important in their own right, but affect the reliance that can be placed on most sequential accounts in the field of general history.

It will be recalled that the difference between the structure of a sequential form of historical account and an account that is primarily explanatory in structure is that a sequential account is concerned with a single ongoing process, whereas an explanatory account starts from any state of affairs, and not from what is regarded as the end point of a continuous process; it then seeks to discover what other events, taken together, account for this occurrence. Such accounts may trace the background of some of these events in a sequential manner, but their primary focus of interest will be on how events with different antecedent histories yield the result they do when they come together.

Given such a problem, the historian will in the first place examine whatever direct evidence there is to show that some of these independently originating events had an impact on others. Such evidence can sometimes be found in the ways participants themselves connect some events with others, as a candidate in a campaign may connect a revolution in a neighboring country with the need for a change in the policies of his own country. The historian weighing the impact of the revolution on the actual course of the campaign will then have to estimate the effectiveness of the candidate's claim, and this he will do by gathering evidence from editorials, opinion polls, and the like, and by estimating in the same way how effective the responses of the opposition were. While there will always be room for disagreement in weighing the evidence, there is nothing to suggest that any such disagreements warrant a skepticism more radical than would lead us to say it is often very difficult to be certain how important one or another factor was in bringing about a result. This measure of doubt does not provide a good reason for distinguishing between history and other forms of inquiry insofar as their ability to attain objective knowledge is concerned. As is also true in other fields, there will be great variations from case to case as to the amount of direct evidence one can gather regarding the impact of one event on another; in some cases there is little room for debate, though in others there may be major differences of opinion.

In addition to any direct evidence that can be found regarding the impact of one event on other events, historians rely on generalizations that are lawlike in character. This has been denied by many who were dissatisfied with Carl Hempel's classic paper on "The Function of General Laws in History," but that paper, as I indicated, went far beyond the issue with which we are here concerned.[4] Hempel not only argued that generalizations have a place in historical investigations—which is what I shall argue—but he claimed that all historical explanations require deductive inferences based on these generalizations. One need not go so far in order to show that generalizations are presupposed in many historical accounts. In order to indicate that this is the case, I shall briefly examine W. H. Dray's well-known example of an engine seizure, which he used in criticizing Hempel's covering-law model of explanation.[5]

In his illustration, Dray has an automobile mechanic explain to him what caused an engine seizure through tracing a series of states of affairs in which a leak on the underside of the oil reservoir permitted all oil to escape, and therefore the oil pump could not deliver oil to the cylinders, and the motion of the pistons against the dry cylinders caused them to expand and therefore to lock; the engine could not then continue to run. Dray contends that this "trouble tracing," which enables one "to envisage a continuous series of happenings," does not leave out any essential factors, and provides a parallel to historical explanations. Unfortunately, however, this illustration presupposes an acquaintance with generalizations at almost every connecting link in the chain. It presupposes that one knows that a substance such as oil will leak out, because of gravity, if there is a hole on the underside of the reservoir, that friction causes metals to become hot, that metals expand when heated, and so forth. Without an acceptance of these facts, which are lawlike generalizations and not statements concerning the particular sequence of events involved in the seizure, the seizure would not have been explained. Thus, this case differs from others, such as my examples of election campaigns, in which the relationships of part and whole are explicitly contained in the documents with which the historian works.

I do not use Dray's example to disparage his continuous series model of explanation in those cases in which it does apply, but only to illustrate that there may well be other cases in which lawlike generalizations have an important role to play in historical explanations.[6] Economic generalizations probably provide the least controversial cases in which historians can use lawlike generalizations in order to show the relationship between one event and another. (On the role of economic generalizations, see chapter 2, section 2.) However, some generalizations suggested by anthropologists, political scientists, and sociologists may at least direct the attention of historians to factors they might otherwise overlook in their explanations of what has occurred (see chapter 5, section 2, for examples). While it is true that most of these generalizations are formulated with less precision than generalizations in economics, and while even the latter are probably more restricted with respect to their applicability at different times and places than are generalizations in the natural sciences, I do not believe these to be the only reasons they are looked upon with suspicion. There also is a tendency among most humanistically inclined historians to deny that lawlike generalizations can, or should, be applied to human events. Widespread as such a tendency has been, it rests on assuming that to believe that laws are applicable in human affairs is tantamount to believing that determinism is true. As we have seen, this is a wholly erroneous assumption. In fact, it rests on a misunderstanding of the role of laws in any form of scientific explanation, and this misunderstanding appears to me to be the basic reason why most historians are reluctant to admit that lawlike generalizations may be important in their discipline.

A law, it will be recalled, is a statement concerning an invariant relation between two or more factors that may be present in many different occurrences of diverse types. In order to use such a law to explain occurrences produced by the elements present in a particular state of affairs, one must possess accurate knowledge of the nature of the initial conditions present in that state of affairs; one must also know the boundary conditions—that is, what, if anything, that is not a part of the initial conditions will have an impact on the ensuing process before the event in question occurs. Thus, laws *by themselves* do not enable one to predict events that will later occur, either in history or in the natural or social sciences. Furthermore, because these laws concern the relations between certain types of factors, they are applicable only to situations in which factors of these types are present. Therefore, if there are lawlike generalizations in the social sciences, a historian can make use of them only when the situations with which he is concerned contain factors of that specific sort, just as one can use Boyle's law only when one is dealing with the behavior of gases. For example, any generalizations concerning rules of descent as correlated with matrilocal or patrilocal residence have no applicability in our society, where there are no such residence rules; nor would any generalizations concerning the consequences of cross-cousin marriages be of use to historians of the United States, since cross-cousin marriages do not represent any norm governing acceptable social behavior. On the other hand, not only economic generalizations but generalizations such as "the iron law of oligarchy" and generalizations concerning the tendency of Americans to "vote their pocketbooks" may help to explain many of the events with which historians of the United States are concerned.

To be sure, not all situations in which one might expect to find "the iron law of oligarchy" exemplified will conform to one's expectations; nor does the outcome of every election prove that the voters have "voted their pocketbooks." This should not occasion surprise, and it does not of itself disprove that these are legitimate lawlike generalizations. Objects do not fall to the earth as one might expect on the basis of Galileo's laws of falling bodies alone, since wind currents and the resistance of the air may significantly affect the fall of some objects, although not the fall of all others. Similarly, in times of war or impending war people may not "vote their pocketbooks," and there may also be many individual situations that mitigate the effects of "the iron law of oligarchy." These generalizations—if authenticated—would no more be refuted by such apparent exceptions than the effects of air currents refute Galileo's laws. Assuming for the moment that there is sufficient evidence to make "the iron law of oligarchy" plausible as a law concerning the distribution of power, it will present the historian with a twofold opportunity: first, to trace the degree to which some evidence is explained by it; and second, to seek evidence that explains why, in a particular case, the results were not what one would have predicted, given the initial conditions and the law. Similarly, when a historian accepts the generalization that people tend to "vote their pocketbooks" he will look for evidence among various classes of voters that they did so vote, but he will also search for evidence as to what factors, in this case, served to offset that tendency and led to a result other than that which he would have predicted, given the economic situation and his acceptance of the law.

It is my contention that even when historians dealing with general history deny the applicability of generalizations in their inquiries, they make tacit use of them just the same. This is obviously true insofar as they presuppose general knowledge of the ways in which different types of individuals may be expected to respond to different types of situations; without presupposing such knowledge a historian could never interpret many of the materials upon which he attempts to build a reconstruction of what occurred in, say, Greece or Rome. To be sure, there is danger in using generalizations of this type since one is inclined to assume that whatever classifications of individuals and of situations one regards as natural within one's own society will apply equally to other societies, and this need not be true. The process of correcting errors proceeds in the same way here as in any other field. When there are continuing discrepancies between what the generalization would lead one to expect and what actually occurred, one must either change one's analysis of the initial conditions present in these cases, or must alter the generalization itself. In the field of social theory, both have repeatedly occurred. In some cases the system of classifying individuals and types of situations has had to be altered, as our conceptions of what is to count as "religion" or "a family" have altered as acquaintance with nonliterate societies has grown; in other cases, what has been corrected were the generalizations themselves, as when knowledge of other societies has made it clear that one cannot assume any inherent connection between material rewards and willingness on the part of a population to engage productively in arduous work. As in other fields, it is only through continuous attention to evidence that the generalizations historians use are discarded, refined, or confirmed.

In explanatory historical accounts—and also in explanatory segments of sequential or interpretive histories—the function of generalizations is to help explain why two or more independent series of events that intersect at a particular place and time produce the results they do. To illustrate this function I shall first choose an obvious example. Suppose that a steep rise occurred in grain prices on the Chicago commodities exchange, and one seeks an explanation of that fact. The generalization that shortages send prices up suggests itself; and since what is traded are grain futures, an anticipation of shortages can be held responsible for the rise in prices. Thus, an economic generalization, plus a comprehension of what the exchange is dealing in, offers an explanation, but one too lacking in specific detail to be satisfactory. For a more satisfactory explanation one must discover what accounted for the anticipation of shortages, and here generalizations are not likely to help. Rumors of bad crops in one or more major producing areas could be the explanation, but so could the likelihood of a war, which would interfere with the production of grain. Although such causal accounts of why a shortage was expected may not rely on generalizations, at least one generalization was essential in the explanation: It had to be assumed that there is a direct relationship between shortages, whatever their causes, and a rise in prices. Without that knowledge, the explanation of the rise in prices would collapse. Thus, in a historical investigation that is explanatory in form, rather than merely sequential, one can expect to find some generalization, but what is also needed is knowledge of the concrete nature of the situation, and of how one is to account for the presence in the situation of those specific factors that the generalization employs. In this case the generalization was concerned with the connection between prices and supply. Knowledge of the relevant factors in the situation included knowledge that trading is based on anticipation of the next harvest, and knowledge of the current price of grain which had been governed by previous supplies. What was in this case needed for the generalization to yield a concrete explanation of the rise in prices was to account for the anticipation of a future shortage; this part of the explanation did not directly rely on any further generalization, but on an analysis of what led to the beliefs that drove prices up. Because it is necessary for a historian to know and describe the conditions initially present, and to account for the presence of whatever new factor has been introduced into that situation, and because these are matters that chiefly occupy one's attention in reading his account, the importance of generalization for his analysis is too easily overlooked. Yet, as the previous simple example shows, the use of a generalization is often crucial.

A less obvious case that can serve to illustrate the same point would be the following. A historian knows from census reports that over a period of two decades there has been a marked decline in the population of rural areas and an increase in the population of urban areas, and he wishes to explain why this shift has occurred. Migration from the rural areas to the cities would provide one obvious explanation, but others are also possible; one might be a marked difference in the birthrates of the areas, and another would be a marked difference in their death rates. These possibilities could presumably be ruled out by choosing a sample of rural and urban counties and examining their birth and death statistics to see whether there have been significant differential changes in the number of births and deaths that were recorded. However, a historian would not be likely in the first instance to take this approach, not because it might not be relevant, but because his background knowledge of the factors that cause major shifts in the number of births and of deaths in a given population would not seem to fit with any differences in conditions in rural areas and in cities that would be sufficient to account for the shift that has occurred. Thus, lawlike generalizations concerning the factors capable of influencing rates of birth and rates of death within *any* society will be used by historians to rule out some types of explanation as likely ways of accounting for a pattern of historical change. In addition, the historian's prior knowledge of the frequency with which shifts in population have occurred because people have moved in large numbers from one place to another would naturally lead him to investigate migration as the explanation of this population change. Where would he be able to gather evidence to show that this did in fact provide the explanation for which he is looking? In a large-scale and nationwide shift in population from rural to urban areas, any attempt to rely solely upon an interviewing technique would be bound to fail. Thus, a direct collection of data would not in this case be able to provide an explanation of what occurred. To be sure, a sampling of persons who are known to have migrated from one region to another—either in other instances or in the case under consideration —could reveal the kinds of factors that lead to migrations; for example, that people migrate for economic reasons, and that they also sometimes do so because they feel themselves to be politically or socially oppressed and expect a better life elsewhere. Thus, at least two lawlike generalizations could be formulated, one concerning the correlation between economic factors and migration and the other between oppression and migration, and the historian might look to see which, if either, applies to the situation he wishes to explain.[7] This would involve analyzing the conditions actually prevalent in the rural areas and in the urban areas with which he is concerned, in order to see whether either of these generalizations is applicable, or whether both are. Having reached a tentative decision, sample interviews could be used to confirm his hypothesis, or could lead him to revise it in one way or another. (For example, interviews might show that economic motives were dominant, even though an examination of actual economic conditions might show that no important discrepancies existed at that time between opportunities in rural and urban areas.) What is important, however, is the role of generalizations in such accounts. The evidence obtained by interviews and by comparative studies of conditions in the areas concerned is of course important for the historian in authenticating, through factual detail, the manner in which he has accounted for the change; without having used generalizations, however, he would not in such cases have been able even to make a start toward offering an account of what he wanted to explain.

It is to be noted that the lawlike generalizations that have been mentioned are different from the sort of lawlike statements usually brought under attack when the problem is discussed by those who reject the possibility that there are explanatory laws applicable to history. The types of laws that I have cited do not attempt to formulate invariant connections between actual occurrences of specific sorts, such that given any event of type a, another event of type b will always follow.[8] Instead, they concern relationships between factors that may be present in any number of situations of different types; the invariant connections they attempt to formulate concern the functional relationships between these factors, not connections between particular sorts of occurrences.[9] What occurs cannot then be said to occur simply because an occurrence of another type preceded it. Instead, what follows will depend upon the precise nature of the situation and the fact that when one of two correlated factors changes, the other will change as well. Since both are present in the same situation, the situation will have changed from what it originally was.

The foregoing analysis should suffice to show that lawlike generalizations play an important role in historical accounts when these are explanatory in their overall structure. It should also suffice to make clear that the use of such generalizations does not supplant the need for tracing a sequence of events if a concrete explanation is to be given of the changes that have occurred. This is evident in the fact that when a historian relies on a generalization to account for a change, he must also show what prior events led up to a change in one of the factors with which his generalization is concerned. Thus, the use of lawlike generalizations in history cannot be held to supplant sequential historical accounts, as Hempel believed they should.

Although any explanatory account will involve a sequential mode of explanation as well as the use of generalizations, and many accounts that are sequential in structure will, at places, make use of lawlike generalizations to explain what occurred, there nevertheless remain fundamental differences between historical accounts that are primarily explanatory and those that are primarily sequential in structure. As I pointed out in chapter 2, sequential accounts are concerned with some central subject and their structure is directed by an attempt to trace its course over time. While they may include mention of many events other than those that form part of the history of their central subject, they do so only because these events impinged on it, altering its course. The primary concern of a historian will remain the one continuing strand of history that he set out to trace. In special histories, as we have seen, such central subjects will not be continuing entities, but will depend upon the historian's characterization of the class of objects with which he wishes to deal. In general histories, on the other hand, the central subject will be a society or some facet of a society, or it may be an individual's life or some aspect of his life. This accounts for the difference in the objectivity that can be attributed to general histories as opposed to special histories when both are sequential in structure. When a historian sets out to deal with a particular society or with some individual or with some facet of the history of either, he cannot pick and choose what evidence is relevant to his task: Neither the nature of a society nor the life of an individual is something that is altered by one's characterization of it. To be sure, every historian works on some scale, and when he is dealing with events on one scale he need not include in his account all that would have to be included were he working on another. This does not signify, however, that he has been free to choose what is relevant to his account; his freedom has been exercised in choosing the subject he has chosen and choosing the scale on which he is to work, but once these choices have been made his freedom to reject evidence disappears because the events with which he deals possess a structure of their own.

It is because societies have a structure and are not merely an agglomeration of events that historical accounts concerned with general history can provide satisfactory explanations even when they only trace a continuous sequence of events. This is possible because those events are related to one another not merely with reference to the temporal order in which they occurred, but also as phases or as component parts of a single continuous whole.[10]

In an explanatory account, on the other hand, the historian's attention is directed to a single state of affairs, not to a continuous process. What he seeks to establish is what prior events were responsible for that state of affairs; thus, he starts backward in time and then follows the results of these prior events until they have terminated in the particular state of affairs that he has set out to explain. To be sure, his backward search is not endless, for once having found the particular set of events that brought about the state of affairs he is to explain, he need not ask what was responsible for these events themselves. To ask those questions would lead to further explanatory accounts, but these accounts would not be part of the explanation with which he was originally concerned.

In addition to the difference in the direction in which historians proceed in sequential and explanatory accounts, there is another difference we have also noted: that in explanatory accounts there may be included many different types of event that have no relation to one another save for the fact that, having come together at a particular place and time, they were jointly responsible for the particular state of affairs that the historian wishes to explain. The events that serve to explain this result are not in such cases parts of one continuous process; therefore historical change must to that extent be regarded as subject to many contingencies, rather than as developing in a determined manner through self-transformations within a closed system.

Neither of these features casts doubt on the objectivity of historical inquiries that are explanatory in structure. To be sure, if it were true that when a historian attempted to explain a particular state of affairs he had to start out from a position of total ignorance, he would not know where to look for the likely antecedents of that state of affairs, and he would have no tentative hypotheses concerning how any two factors in a social situation are likely to be related. In history, however, as in science, one never starts *de novo*. In most cases the historian has at his disposal prior sequential accounts that include reference to the state of affairs in which he is interested; he thus knows something about the stream of events in which it was embedded, and therefore about the events preceding it. When, however, it appears to him that these preceding events do not adequately explain the state of affairs in which he is interested, he will be led to offer an explanatory account of it. In doing so, he will be looking for other contributing factors, and here he will be guided by the sorts of hypotheses historians have used in other cases, and by his own conjectures as to the kinds of factors that can be expected to bring about a result of this kind. This reliance on the accumulated experience of historians with respect to what sorts of factors are likely to account for a particular kind of result parallels what one finds in the sciences. So too does the fact that individual historians must also rely on their own insight with respect to what may be important in a particular case, and they may thereby discover relationships between factors of which their predecessors were generally unaware.

In addition to accumulated experience and novel insights, general theories provide still another source for the hypotheses historians use in explaining particular states of affairs. As we have noted, historians often deny that they make use of any general theory in their actual practice, but this is usually because they take too restricted a view of what comprises a theory, identifying it with some general proposition stating that all historical events are to be explained in terms of some single factor, such as the modes of production, or the view that the basis of all human action is a drive for power. Supposedly, such theories can be directly applied to the events with which historians are concerned, providing explanations for them. On the other hand, as we have seen, there also are more general theories concerning the ways in which one is to conceive of a society and of societal change, and these are not intended to explain particular historical events any more than the particulate theory of matter can directly explain specific physical phenomena. Theories of this sort leave room for a great variety of concrete hypotheses that historians may use in their explanatory inquiries. Nonetheless, they control the direction in which a historian looks when he attempts to formulate these more specific hypotheses. Thus, a general theory, plus a knowledge of the initial conditions and the type of event that occurred, will channel a historian's search for a lawlike generalization, leading him to cast aside some types of hypotheses and to test others. This need not have a distorting effect on explanatory inquiries, undermining their objectivity, so long as the validity of the hypothesis is tested in terms of all available relevant evidence, not only in this case but in others in which similar factors are to be found.

This point can be illustrated with reference to those explanatory accounts that appear within special histories. Special histories, it will be recalled, have a sequential structure; however, like any other sequential histories they are likely to include many explanatory segments. In a history of literature, for example, an attempt may be made to account for a specific change in style, and in doing so a literary historian may call attention to political and social changes, to literary influences coming from abroad, or to the impact of changes in religion or philosophy or in one of the arts. While the acceptance of some specific theory, such as some form of Marxist theory of the arts, has sometimes led literary historians to explain these changes in terms of a single, dominant factor, the explanations of a literary historian may derive from a more flexible theory, which holds that cultural change must in all cases be assumed to be related to a number of different factors, all of which are to be found in each and every society. For example, he may hold—as a matter of general theory— that every aspect of the culture present in any society is always related to its own traditions as well as to at least some of the other aspects of the culture found in that society, and that it is also always influenced by the structure of the society as a whole. Usually such theories are only tacitly held, but they exert an important influence on how a special history of some aspect of culture will proceed. To be sure, so long as one is constructing only a sequential account of what occurred, general theories of this type are of only limited use; they simply suggest some of the quarters in which a historian is to look in order to gather materials relevant to his sequential account. However, as soon as the evidence suggests that what has occurred in the sequence apparently cannot be explained in terms of what has gone before, he must look to events outside that sequence. Here his general theory of the types of factors that can explain cultural change will suggest hypotheses as to what other occurrences might help to explain the change that took place. There is no reason to think that the same hypotheses will be adequate to deal with all different forms of cultural change, but the type of general theory with which we are here concerned (in contradistinction, say, to Marxist theory) would not demand that such be the case. It would merely suggest types of factors that might be correlated with one another in explanations of cultural change, leaving it to investigations in different fields—such as histories of literature in the modern period, or histories of philosophy or of technology—to formulate concrete hypotheses that help to explain the various specific changes with which they are concerned.

The foregoing remarks not only show that general theory is of use in the explanatory segments of special histories that are predominantly sequential in structure, but they also serve to suggest that one can claim objectivity for these particular segments of special histories. Objectivity may be claimed for them since the hypotheses on which they proceed, which were suggested by general theory, are subject to the same check against evidence as is the case in any other explanatory account. As we have seen, this objectivity cannot be claimed for any special history taken as a whole, since different cultural historians define the subject matter with which they are concerned in different ways, and what is included in each will therefore be somewhat different from what is included in others. However, as soon as an effort is made to explain whatever changes have come about within a series—however that series has been defined—the need for evidence will provide a check on the explanatory hypotheses that were used, and the possibility of objective knowledge reemerges.

In short, a claim for the objectivity of historical knowledge rests, in the first instance, on the fact that historians must supply evidence for the statements they make. This fact would not of itself establish objectivity were it not that the events with which historians usually deal fit snugly together, so that one historical account can lend support to another, or their failure to fit will be obvious and, as a consequence, at least one will have to be modified or abandoned. In the case of special histories, however, where historians can structure their materials to conform with their own definitions of what is to belong, or not belong, in their accounts, objectivity will not be attainable in the history as a whole, but only in its explanatory portions. In these portions, when a historian is, for example, attempting to trace individual influences or account for basic changes in the character of the works with which he has chosen to deal, what constitutes relevant evidence is no longer subject to redefinition by him: Having once defined the materials with which he is to deal, he will have to follow where the evidence leads. The fact that in approaching the problem of explaining what occurred he may bring to bear specific hypotheses or more general theories that he is already inclined to accept does not vitiate the claim that such explanations can be characterized as objective, as I am using that term. The hypotheses or theories must themselves be supported by prior evidence, and must be shown to be applicable in this instance by evidence that can be gathered in support of the explanation that follows from them. When in such cases historians disagree, these disagreements in weighing evidence do not entail that historical knowledge is *not* objective, any more than the parallel situation in, say, psychology or biology would lead to that conclusion.

A relativist might object that all this is well and good, but that it is merely a consequence of the way in which objectivity was defined. What purpose does it serve, he might ask, if one can claim that historical knowledge is *in principle* objective and that if two historians disagree at least one must be wrong, when all the time we know that *in practice* historians disagree, and disagree because their accounts are *not* objective in either of the other two senses that the term "objective" may have (chapter 6, section 1)? To this we must now, in conclusion, reply.

With respect to the claim that historical accounts are not objective, in the first of the senses of "objective" that I distinguished, it must be recalled that there is a great difference between two questions that have sometimes been confused: (a) the reasons why a historian may have elected to write about some particular subject matter, and (b) the reasons why he explained that subject matter as he did. It is necessary to draw this distinction not only with respect to the problem of how a historian's interests and values affect his work, but also because confusion has sometimes arisen regarding the sense in which explanations are context-determined. As I argued in chapter 3, section 2, and chapter 4, section 1, the questions individuals ask and the kinds of answers they expect to receive are in fact context-determined. Nevertheless, when one is called upon to assess the adequacy of an explanation, one must do so with respect to its relation to the evidence upon which it rests and on the basis of its relation to other evidence supplied by independent accounts. The adequacy of a material explanation is not assessed with respect to whatever may have led this particular historian to offer the explanation he gave. This obvious point is easily overlooked if the works of one or two historians are considered apart from the accounts of the same subject matter that have been built up over several generations. Through a continual accumulation and sifting of evidence, general agreement is actually reached concerning much of what occurred in the past; however, when specific works are individually considered, their differences, rather than their similarities, are likely to strike one as their most interesting characteristics. This fixation of attention on differences will lead one to overlook the existence of the more general framework of historical knowledge into which each of these differing accounts may actually fit. To be sure, the advancement of historical knowledge is not smoothly continuous; there are many unexpected new starts as new issues arise out of chance discoveries and out of new interests, but these sudden shifts can occur only because there already is an accepted background of knowledge that they may challenge at points, but without which whatever is new in them would lack meaning.[11]

It is also possible to indicate, in an equally brief form, a good reason to reject the belief that historical accounts cannot be objective in the second of the senses of "objective" that I have distinguished. That belief rests on the assumption that the order and connection of the events in a historical account is not a characteristic of the events themselves, but that they depend upon the way in which the historian organizes his facts. This assumption rests, however, on a confusion between the events themselves and the evidence for those events with which a historian must deal. Such evidence can come to him in any order. Furthermore, the kind of evidence available concerning two events, or concerning two aspects of the same event, may be quite different, and neither bit of evidence may contain any reference to the other. This does not mean, however, that what is referred to in one bit of evidence was in fact independent of that which was referred to in the other. There is no mystery in how such relationships can be established even when each bit of evidence, if taken by itself, fails to reveal a connection between one event and the other. Each may refer to an event that occurred at a particular place and time, and the historian who has access to both will then find that he is dealing with successive occurrences, or with what are different facets of the same occurrence. These are not relationships that he makes; they are relationships he has found on the basis of evidence. To push beyond this merely skeletal knowledge and find out just how two successive occurrences or two facets of the same occurrence may have been related poses a further problem, but it, too, is to be solved by means of evidence. A historian may, for example, look for such further evidence in statements made by persons who participated in these events, or in the reports of others. He may also form a hypothesis, based on other cases, as to how the events were related, but the applicability of such a hypothesis to the case at hand will then have to be checked by still further evidence, or will at least have to be made plausible by a failure to find any disconfirming evidence. That historical accounts grow in this way is not implausible when one notes that the evidence with which historians most frequently deal is of a sort that refers not to one event only, but to an event in its context: to a battle in a war, a speech in a campaign, the formation of an alliance between two nations against the threat of a common enemy. Thus, it is on the basis of the evidence with which he works that a historian is led to consider events as belonging together to form a series of related occurrences—a whole series of battles or of speeches or of political decisions leading to an alliance. Thus, the only basis on which it might be claimed that historical accounts are subjective in the sense that the relations they trace depend upon the historian himself is undermined. Once evidence is being gathered, it is this evidence itself that imposes structure on any historian's account so long as he holds close to that evidence.

Given these facts, we may also dismiss the argument often used by Charles A. Beard, among others, that history cannot be objective because the historian must select from among a welter of facts, deciding what to include and what to exclude. The resulting account, it is claimed, reflects whatever subjective factors control the historian's choices, rather than whatever objective connections may have originally existed among the events themselves. This argument is, however, convincing only if one overlooks the fact that within the materials with which historians work there are distinctions of scale and of the facets of the particular events with which they deal. Thus, it is not true that the sortal principles historians use in classifying evidence are merely subjective. Bearing these distinctions in mind, one may hold that a basic structure is imposed on a historical account by the evidence on which it rests; the existence of lacunae in that evidence, and the new questions that are present in it, direct the historian's attention to the need for further evidence of a specific kind. That this should be the case is not mysterious. Whatever is taken as evidence points beyond itself. Just as combinations of colors may be said to call attention to themselves, or lines lead us to follow a design, so the previously available evidence will often be seen as having gaps within it, or as being suggestive of a new direction in which other evidence may be found. Thus, whatever evidence is originally available to a historian will not be an inchoate mass, and the more evidence there is, the less choice he will have as to the alternative ways in which he may reasonably structure his account.

It should now be apparent that there is a close connection between the view of causation I earlier defended and the defense of objectivity I have now proposed. I argued that an adequate causal explanation does not consist in some rubric asserting that an event of one type is regularly followed by an event of another type. Historians do not try to explain what occurs in this manner; they are interested in particular events, not in all events of a given type. In fact, they are often especially interested in events that do not conform to what might have been expected on the basis of what occurred in other cases. When they wish to explain any event, whether it might or might not have been expected, they attempt to determine on what conditions its occurrence actually depended, and this involves analyzing the concrete relations between it, its context, and a series of prior events with which it was directly connected. It is on the basis of the connections inherent in the evidence with which historians work that they can propose concrete causal analyses of the events with which they deal. Consequently, the more evidence a historian possesses concerning what occurred in a society at a particular time, the less arbitrary and perfunctory his assertions of causal connections can be. It is not, then, on the basis of general laws that causal connections are authenticated; it is on the basis of evidence as to what actually occurred. Lawlike generalizations are at some points useful in establishing the sort of covert connection that existed between two events, but in most instances the connection among events is an open relationship, directly attested to by the evidence itself. To be sure, historians must exercise critical reserve in accepting the assertions of participants as to the true causal connections among events. However, what serves to correct the assertions of participants is not a general skepticism based on the claim that such assertions always represent some form of bias: They can be corrected only by more evidence showing that it was indeed bias that led to the assertions made.

It should not occasion surprise to have someone argue that historical accounts should be judged on the basis of evidence, yet this claim will undoubtedly be viewed as an extreme example of simpleminded-ness. One has heard so much concerning the subjective factors that enter into historical accounts that one now almost forgets that the creativity of a historian is shown in how he handles evidence and where he has had the insight to look for new evidence; it is not that he has told an old story in a new way and that his telling of it has made it seem of greater interest than it previously was. History as a discipline is not a form of art, and what each historian accomplishes he does not accomplish alone, as an individual: The significance of any historical inquiry, like the research of any scientist, depends directly upon what others have already done or will be enabled to do because of his work. This is even true in the case of special histories, since even though they cannot lay claim to the same degree of objectivity as is to be found in any form of general history, we have seen that at many points they depend upon the work of those concerned with the nature of and changes within societies, and that their inquiries can contribute to the knowledge that general historians seek. When one takes into account the interplay of general and special histories, and the fact that although sequential, explanatory, and interpretive inquiries are diverse in form they cannot exist in complete isolation from one another, the anatomy of historical knowledge reveals a unity of purpose and a unity of method: to understand the concrete nature of societies, the changes they have undergone, and the cultural products they have produced.

Appendix A

HUME

There have been many attacks on the atomistic sensationalism which was characteristic of British Empiricists in general and which provides an indispensable element in Hume's analysis of causation. While I share the views of some who have criticized Hume on these grounds, I do not believe that one need mount a wholesale attack on his psychological and epistemological assumptions in order to show that his argument contains a flaw that vitiates the attempt to prove that we do not—and cannot—ever directly perceive a connection between causes and their effects. It is necessary to expose this flaw so that my phenomenological account of those cases in which we believe we perceive such a connection cannot be dismissed simply because it fails to conform with Hume's position regarding the nature of sense experience.[1]

In discussing Hume's analysis of causation, it is important to distinguish between two different problems with which he was concerned: (a) whether we can justifiably claim that the relation between a cause and its effect is a *necessary* relation, and (b) on what basis we are led to identify one event as the cause of another. These problems clearly are not the same, but they were not strictly separated in his argument, since his answer to the second provided one important argument in favor of his answer to the first. It is only with the second that I shall here be concerned. With respect to the first, I am entirely willing to acknowledge that if we construe the term "necessary" in the strict sense in which Hume construed it, we have no grounds on which to establish the claim that the connection between a cause and its effect is a *necessary* connection: Were the world different from what it is, even the most reliable of our present causal attributions might turn out to be incorrect. This does not of course entail that if the term "necessary" were taken in some other sense, causal relations might not be "necessary" relations. It is not, however, with Hume's position regarding causal necessity that I am here concerned; rather, I address myself to the question of how, according to Hume, we come to identify one event as the cause of another. What I wish to show is that the position he adopted rests on an assumption that is factually false, and can be thought to be true only if one disregards his own distinction between "impressions" and "ideas."

A basic axiom on which his analysis of causation rests is his often repeated statement that what is distinguishable is separable. Throughout his epistemological analyses he applied this axiom to simple impressions, which he took to be the ultimate building blocks of all knowledge of matters of fact; thus, he held that any impressions that are distinguishable are in principle separable. He then used this axiom to show that we can never directly experience the connection between cause and effect: Since our impressions of what constitute the cause are distinguishable from our impressions of what constitute the effect, each is therefore separable from the other and any connectivity between them disappears. Hume therefore offered a psychological account of our conviction that we do experience a connection between a cause and its effect. He did so by appealing to the influence that constant conjunctions exercise upon our minds. While his positive account of our belief in causal relations is in many cases plausible, his basic axiom concerning the distinguishable and the separable led him to suppose that the same account would be applicable in all cases whatsoever. It is this that I wish to challenge, and I shall do so by criticizing the manner in which Hume put his axiom to work.

In examining his doctrine that all simple impressions are distinct and separable, we must keep in mind that what is at issue is how this doctrine applies to *impressions* (that is, to direct sense experience), and not how it applies to *ideas*. Whatever may be the difficulties in Hume's account of the difference between impressions and ideas (and I believe them to be many),[2] when he is analyzing our beliefs in the relation of cause and effect he is primarily concerned with our beliefs as to how objects that are experienced as contiguous in space and time are connected. To be sure, on some occasions—as when we receive a letter from a friend—we take it that there was a causal connection between some directly experienced object (the letter) and another object not now immediately experienced (my friend, who is abroad); but we form such a connection between impressions and ideas only because of prior experiences in which what we now recall was actually present to us along with an object of the same type as the one we now hold in our hand.[3] Thus, any conception of a causal connection must in all cases be ultimately based on the spatial and temporal relationships of directly experienced *impressions*, not on a relationship among our *ideas*.

Attention can be drawn to this point in another way. The reader need merely recall that, according to Hume, spatial contiguity as well as temporal succession is involved in the relation of cause and effect, but while it is clear that we know what it means to say of two *objects* that they are contiguous in space, it makes no sense to say of two successive *ideas* (say, of two memory images) that they are spatially contiguous, except in the derivative sense that the objects of which they are the images were themselves originally experienced as contiguous. Therefore, Hume's analysis of the causal relation must be interpreted as applying to impressions as they are directly given, and not to those simulacra of our original impressions that are our ideas.

This point is of fundamental importance in evaluating Hume's use of the axiom that "whatever is distinguishable is separable" as it relates to causation, since if he is to show that we can have no impression of any causal connection he must apply this axiom to *impressions*, and not to ideas. Yet, can it be so applied? If, for example, I am inspecting a cream-colored rectangle—say, a small sample of wallpaper—I can distinguish the shape from the color, but *as impressions* the shape and the color of a small patch are not separable. In order to separate them I must picture each of them in my mind's eye—this color merely as color, this shape merely as shape; but in doing so, I am transforming them from directly experienced impressions into ideas. This is true not only with respect to the simultaneously given qualities of simple objects, but also where succession is involved. For example, in Michotte's experiments on the perception of causation,[4] if I see one form moving slowly toward another, and I see them in contact and then continuing in motion together, I can *imagine* the motion of the first without that of the second, and I can *imagine* the motion of the second without that of the first, but I do not *see* this. The movements I saw had distinguishable aspects, for I did see two objects, but I did not at the time see these objects as having separate and independent motions. In other words, it is false to assume with respect to perception that what can be distinguished is separable, so long as we are speaking of what is given, and are not speaking of how what has been given might be analyzed after having been transformed from a set of impressions into a set of ideas.

In fact, Hume's atomistic sensationalism does not rest on a consideration of the given, but on an analysis of how we may decompose what is given when we reflectively consider it not as a set of impressions but as a set of ideas. For this reason, his analysis of our causal beliefs holds only in those cases in which the casual connections we find in experience depend upon observed regularities of sequence, and has nothing to say concerning other cases such as those discussed in section 1 of chapter 3.

Appendix B

HART AND HONORÉ

There are three counts on which I shall express my disagreement with the position developed by Hart and Honoré in the opening chapters of *Causation in the Law.*[1] First, I find that the way in which they have set up a contrast between an interest in the particular and an interest in the general is seriously misleading with respect to both historical knowledge and scientific explanation. Second, their views with respect to common-sense causal explanations are also misleading. Third, they are mistaken in assuming that the notion of causation they attribute to lawyers is also applicable to the explanations given by historians. My argument with respect to each of these points will raise a number of separate issues with respect to which I find the views of Hart and Honoré unsatisfactory. I trust that in attempting to compress my discussion of their views into this brief appendix I shall not be guilty of misinterpreting them.

(1) As I made clear at the outset, I accept the well-known distinction between the nomothetic interests of scientists and the idiographic interests of historians, but this is not to say that I accept (a) the contrast Hart and Honoré draw between the historian's interest in the particular and the scientist's interest in the general, or (b) their assumptions concerning the type of explanation that is characteristic of the sciences.

(a) Hart and Honoré open their discussion of the particular and the general in saying: "The lawyer and the historian are both primarily concerned to make causal statements about *particulars*, to establish that on some particular occasion some particular occurrence was the effect or consequence of some other particular occurrence. The causal statements characteristic of these disciplines are of the form 'This man's death on this date was caused by this blow.' "[2] This, however, is an impoverished view of the historian's interest in the particular: His aim is not merely to connect two events in linear, causal sequence, but to discover and to depict, in concrete detail, a whole set of events concerning a given subject matter, and to trace a variety of connections among them. Thus, in the example used by Hart and Honoré, the historian would be interested in how it was that these men came to meet when they did, what their previous relations had been, and what, in this particular situation, had led one to strike the other. An idiographic interest is not merely an interest in some particular event, but in understanding and depicting that particular event in its context.

Nor are Hart and Honoré more fortunate in characterizing the interests of scientists. In the first place, they fail to point out that if scientists were not originally interested in explaining particular events they would not be led to formulate generalizations in order to explain events of that type. In the second place, it is only through analyzing the specific conditions under which particular events of a given type occur that they can confirm their generalizations.

For these reasons, the contrast drawn by Hart and Honoré is misleading: It is not that scientists fail to be interested in particular events that sets them apart from historians; rather, it is a question of how historians are concerned with the particular, and in what ways particular events are of interest to scientists. This difference is brought out by the contrast between idiographic and nomothetic interests; it is not, however, made clear by the simple dichotomy of an interest in the particular versus an interest in the general.

(b) An even more fundamental difficulty arises in connection with

the view of Hart and Honoré concerning the nature of scientific explanation. It is their view that in the sciences a causal explanation
takes the form of exemplifying "some generalization asserting that
kinds or classes of events are invariably connected."[3] In short, insofar as the sciences are concerned, Hart and Honoré are content to
accept some form of the Humean regularity view. Yet, if we take any
advanced science as a model, we find that the laws that are most
characteristic of scientific explanations are formulated in terms of
specific *factors*, such as pressure and volume, or mass and distance,
which serve as variables in a wide variety of cases of very different
types; they are *not* statements to the effect that the occurrence of
some specific type of event is invariably connected with the occurrence of some other specific type of event, as Hart and Honoré,
following Hume, would have us believe. To be sure, some generalizations or laws illustrate Hume's view of causation in that they explicitly refer to instances of a given type, and to the conditions under
which such instances occur. For example, "litmus paper turns red
when immersed in acid," or "at sea level, water will boil at 212°
Fahrenheit." Nevertheless, the generalizations or laws that have this
form are usually regarded as calling for further explanation, and such
explanations are usually couched in terms of the specific factors into
which these occurrences can be analyzed. The factors that are taken
as providing the more adequate explanations are not confined to
objects or events of a particular type, but are present in a variety of
instances that differ markedly in their other characteristics. In fact,
generalizations such as those about litmus paper turning red or water
boiling when heated to a certain degree are not at all typical of the
advanced sciences; they are in some respects more similar to common-
sense explanations, such as "ice will melt at ordinary room temperature," or "porcelain cups break if they are dropped." They do, however, differ from these common-sense generalizations in one
important respect: They are assumed not to admit of exceptions,
whereas many common-sense explanations are regarded as adequate
even though they do not hold in absolutely all cases, but only state
what usually, or normally, occurs.

Hart and Honoré place great emphasis on this particular difference
between common-sense explanations and scientific generalizations,
and that is as it should be. They fail, however, to challenge Hume's
view on other points, except insofar as they are concerned (as they
are) with cases of interpersonal transactions. In short, they are willing to accept Hume's view of scientific explanation as being con-

cerned with the relations between specific *types* of events; it is this that led them to hold that the sciences are interested only in the general, and not in the particular. Furthermore, since they do not challenge Hume's claim that one cannot in any case perceive a connection between cause and effect, they have to hold that causal attributions in all cases presuppose some background of observed regularities as to what follows what. Therefore, on their view, the main difference between common-sense explanations and scientific explanations resides in the fact that in our common-sense explanations we focus on what was odd about a particular case that did not behave as one would have expected it to behave; we then settle on whatever abnormal feature was present in this situation, designating it as the cause of what occurred. While many causal attributions in everyday life do conform to this model, not all do so. This leads me to my second line of criticism of the views of Hart and Honoré.

(2) There are two reasons why their analysis of our common-sense view of causation is not in all cases adequate. First, as I attempted to show in chapter 3, there are many cases in which we do directly experience a causal relationship that is not to be accounted for in terms of past experience, yet Hart and Honoré's use of the distinction between what is normal and what is abnormal presupposes that all causal attributions rest on our knowledge of what has occurred in other cases. In the second place, their analysis does not take into account those cases in which we *do* say that one event caused another when there is complete regularity of succession between these events, without any deviation from what we take as normal and what we expected. In the third place, throughout their discussion of causation, Hart and Honoré presuppose that it is in all cases valid to distinguish between the cause of an event and whatever other *conditions* were necessary for that cause to have had the effect that it did. While we sometimes do draw a distinction between "cause" and "conditions," and while such a distinction may perhaps be of the utmost importance for affixing responsibility in the law, one should not lightly assume that the same distinction can be drawn in all other contexts. As I repeatedly try to show in chapter 4, it is actually false to hold that we draw this distinction in all cases of causal explanation that arise either in science or in everyday life. This is especially true in history.

(3) I do not believe it unfair to say that although Hart and Honoré repeatedly link the historian's conception of causation with causation in the law, any careful examination of what interests historians, and

of what they actually do, is singularly lacking. In the only passage in which this topic is explicitly discussed (pp. 58–59) one is led to believe that when historians use causal notions in an *explanatory* way their purpose is confined to giving an explanation of "some puzzling or unusual occurrence." Yet, historical explanation is surely not thus confined. What is of greater interest to Hart and Honoré than causal explanation in history or the law is the *attributive* use of causal notions, that is, the fixing of responsibility for what occurred. It is with this use of the causal concept that the passage in question is primarily concerned. Now, it is assuredly true that historians, like practitioners in the law, do make these attributive causal judgments, assigning responsibility to individuals, or to particular circumstances, for having brought about (that is, "caused") certain events. For example, in *Americans Interpret Their Civil War*,[4] Thomas J. Pressly surveyed one particular set of judgments, namely those that showed changing opinions as to what factor, or type of factor, was most basic in leading to the Civil War. However, several points should be noted with respect to this example, for they are of wider applicability.[5] In the first place, Pressly's account is *not* an account of the Civil War itself, nor is it a detailed study of the differing accounts of the background and the outbreak of the war that each of the authors whom he studied actually gave. Rather, it discusses these accounts from a single point of view, abstracting from each what its author took to be the most basic factor leading to the war. Thus, quite legitimately, Pressly was concerned only with the most general attributive causal judgments to be found in a number of representative writers; it was not his aim to assess the detailed treatments these writers had given of all of the other factors that might have been involved in the outbreak of the war. However, if a historian is to be in a position to make general attributive judgments concerning what was "most basic" with respect to the Civil War, he must first know—or believe that he knows—the nature of a great many facts concerning slavery, the abolition movement, the aims and actions of various political figures, the state of feeling in different parts of the country at different times, and the like. If he is to be considered a reputable historian, it will be on the basis of his reading of all such facts that he will have put forward his attributive causal judgment. In gathering these facts and in tracing their concatenations, the historian is not engaged in a further series of *attributive* causal judgments, nor is he engaged in explanatory causal judgments if by this is meant that what he is seeking to account for are puzzling or unusual occurrences: He is engaged in attempting to discover *what happened*. Similarly, before a case goes to trial, inquiry into matters of fact must be made by the lawyers; and it is only after such inquiries have been made that one can argue in court where responsibility lies.[6] On this analogy, it may be said that although it is not uncommon for historians to be concerned with attributive causal judgments similar to those Hart and Honoré discuss with reference to the law, this cannot be the first or primary task of the historian. Furthermore, it is a task that can be avoided by historians, even though it is unavoidable for judges. Historians need not sit as judges. It is therefore my contention that, contrary to the view of Hart and Honoré, there is no close analogy between what historians do, and what is done by lawyers arguing in court or by judges when they decide a case. Nonetheless I admit that it is unfortunately true that laymen, being neither historians nor lawyers, often think it within their powers to make attributive causal judgments concerning what has occurred in history when they have not first investigated the facts.

For all these reasons I find it necessary to disagree with the enormously influential analysis of causation we owe to Hart and Honoré.

NOTES

CHAPTER ONE

1. Wilhelm Windelband, Präludien (5th ed.; Tübingen: J. C. B. Mohr, 1915), 2: 144–45.

2. The conflation of these distinct questions is apparent in the first two sentences of Hempel's paper, which read as follows: "It is a rather widely held opinion that history, in contradistinction to the so-called physical sciences, is concerned with the description of particular events of the past rather than with the search for general laws which might govern these events. As a characterization of the type of problem in which some historians are mainly interested, this view probably can not be denied; as a statement of the theoretical function of general laws in scientific historical research, it is certainly unacceptable." For Hempel's criticism of my claim that the primary aim of the historian lies "not in the formulation of laws of which the particular case is an instance, but in the description of the events in their actual determining relationships to each other," see the footnote to section 7.4 of his paper, in which the two issues are again identified.

Hempel's paper was originally published in the *Journal of Philosophy* in 1942; it is reprinted in his *Aspects of Scientific Explanation* (New York: Free Press, 1965).

3. For a general discussion of the problem of explaining cultural traits in terms of diffusion or in terms of independent origins, as well as for a discussion of the phenomenon of convergence among cultural traits, the reader can consult A. A. Goldenweiser, *Anthropology* (New York: Crofts, 1937), chaps. 28, 29.

On the other hand, those who wish a concrete example in which relatively sophisticated generalizations play a part in the actual work of a historian can consult H. R. Trevor-Roper's essay "The European Witch-craze in the Sixteenth and Seventeenth Centuries," which was originally published in his *Religion, the Reformation and Social Change* (London: Macmillan, 1967). Whether or not one agrees with his interpretation, Trevor-Roper's interest was that of a historian but his method included the undisguised use of a number of sociological and psychological hypotheses.

4. I here paraphrase the position of Charles A. Beard in "Written History as an Act of Faith"; a similar position was adopted by Carl L. Becker in "What Are Historical Facts," and elsewhere. These essays are readily available in Hans Meyerhoff, ed., *The Philosophy of History in Our Time* (Garden City, N.Y.: Doubleday Anchor, 1959). (For the relevant passages, see pp. 140 and 124, respectively.) The same point of view had earlier been espoused by James Harvey Robinson in his essay, "The New History" (1912), where he said: "In its amplest meaning History includes every trace and vestige of everything that man has done or thought since first he appeared on earth" (*apud* Fritz Stern, *The Varieties of History* [New York: Meridian, 1956], p. 258).

R. G. Collingwood adopted a parallel position, defining that which serves as the object of history as "*res gestae*: actions of human beings that have been done in the past" (*The Idea of History* [Oxford: Clarendon Press, 1948], p. 9). So long as any action, no matter how trivial, can be the object of the kind of inquiry carried on by a historian, Collingwood held that it is not be excluded from the domain of history. This is clear in his *Philosophy of History* (Historical Association Leaflet no. 79, 1930), where he said that the question of who played center forward on a village soccer team is as much a historical question as who won the battle of Cannae.

5. *The Problem of Historical Knowledge* (New York: Liveright, 1938), p. 9.

6. "The History of Ideas, Intellectual History, and the History of Philosophy," *History and Theory*, Beiheft 5 (1965): 42–47. In a subsequent study, I have discussed some of the problems concerning one type of special history, the history of philosophy, in greater detail ("On the Historiography of Philosophy," *Philosophy Research Archives* [Philosophy Documentation Center, Bowling Green State University, Bowling Green, Ohio], July 1976).

Croce also uses the terms "special histories" and "general history" (*History, Its Theory and Practice* [New York: Harcourt, Brace, 1923], pt. 1, chap. 8, and app. 2). While there are points of contact between his usage and mine, his conclusions are entirely different from those I draw.

7. For example, Herskovits says, "A culture is the way of life of a people; while a society is the organized aggregate of individuals who follow a given way of life. In still simpler terms, a society is composed of people; the way they behave is their culture" (*Man and His Works* [New York: Knopf, 1948], p. 29). Cf. Kluckhohn, "The Concept of Culture" (1945), reprinted in his essays *Culture and Behavior* [New York: Free Press of Glencoe, 1964], in which note especially p. 21.

8. For example, Clifford Geertz distinguishes culture as a system of ideas from the economic, political, and social relations in a society, all of which are to

some degree informed by that system of ideas (*The Interpretation of Cultures* [New York: Basic Books, 1973], p. 362.) Such a system of ideas is characterized by him as "an historically transmitted pattern of meanings embodied in symbols, a system of inherited conceptions expressed in symbolic forms by means of which men communicate, perpetuate, and develop their knowledge about and attitudes toward life" (ibid., p. 89). I find this type of definition too restrictive, since I find it essential, as do many anthropologists, to view language, tools, and crafts as aspects of culture, no less than are, say, religious beliefs.

Kroeber and Parsons, in an attempt to clarify the relationship between the terms "culture" and "society" (or "social system"), also tended to identify culture with values and ideas, though they added to their definition a reference to artifacts ("The Concepts of Culture and of Social System," *American Sociological Review* 28 (1958): 582-83). It is to be noted, however, that this represents a major departure from Kroeber's earlier view as stated in sections 6 and 117 of his *Anthropology*, new ed., rev. (New York: Harcourt, Brace, 1948).

9. In the opening paragraph of his *Primitive Culture* (London: J. Murray, 1871), Tylor used the term "culture" to refer to "all capabilities and habits acquired by man as a member of society" and he included in his discussion all artifacts resulting from those capabilities and habits. (Cf. chap. 7, "Growth and Decline of Culture" in his *Researches into the Early History of Mankind* [London: J. Murray, 1865].) Partly as a result of his evolutionary views regarding societies, he spoke of "culture" and not of diverse, particular "cultures." While not sharing his views on social evolution, I too shall use the term in a generic sense and shall define it as including artifacts as well as ideas and values. In each of these respects, my view is similar to that to be found in Kroeber's *Anthropology*.

10. I quote the relevent passages from "Das Fach 'Geschichte' und die historischen Wissenschaften," Hamburger Universitätsreden no. 25 (1959):

Geschichte im engeren Sinn, allgemeine Geschichte hat es weder mit der Politik, den politischen Abläufen um ihrer selbst willen, noch mit der Kultur *a se* zu tun, sondern mit deren Träger, dem Menschen, sowohl mit dem einzelnen Menschen, der uns stets in gesellschaftlicher Verbundenheit entgegentritt, wie mit menschlichen Gruppen. Eine Geschichte im engeren Sinn haben daher nur Menschen und menschliche Verbände, Familien, Dorfer, Städte, Stände, Klassen, Staaten, Völker, Stämme usw. Menschen und menschliche Verbände ringen um ihre Existenz, behaupten sich selbst; sie handeln in diesem Sinne "politisch." Es sind Sozialgebilde, in denen Herrschaftsverhältnisse bestehen, rechtlich geordnete Machtverhältnisse. [p. 23]

In contrast, Brunner characterized the special forms of historical study in the following way:

Das primäre, zentrale Objekt der historischen Fachwissenschaften ist eben nicht der Mensch und die menschlichen Gruppen, sondern dessen Werke. Hier werden Institutionen, Rechts- und Wirtschaftsordnungen, religiöse und philosophische Lehrmeinungen, Werke der Kunst und der Literaturen, die Sprachen und vieles andere, zuerst einmal abgehoben von ihren Trägern, als Sinngebilde untersucht, interpretiert und dargestellt. [pp. 25-26]

11. In H. P. Finberg, ed. *Approaches to History* (London: Routledge & Kegan Paul, 1962), pp. 41-46.

12. Biographies constitute a special form of historical account, in which the interest is focused on the person who is the subject of the biography. Bio-

graphical studies do not, in most instances, provide an exception to what I have emphasized, since the persons chosen for biographical study are, in general, persons in whom there is interest because of their roles in a particular society or because of their relation to some aspect of its culture. In some cases, however, a person may be the subject of a biographical study simply because of his character, rather than because of his relation to his society or to the culture of his time. Such studies can contribute indirectly to an understanding of the past, but their primary function is likely to be either psychological or (taking the term in its literal and noninvidious sense) hagiographic.

A point of view diametrically opposed to that adopted here is to be found in Frederick A. Olafson's article "Human Action and Historical Explanation," in *New Essays in Phenomenology* (ed. James Edie [Chicago: Quadrangle Books, 1969]). Olafson regards the subject matter of all historical accounts as being human actions, and finds the structure of these accounts to be dictated by the manner in which we analyze such actions.

A similar position is implicit in G. H. von Wright's *Explanation and Understanding* (Ithaca: Cornell University Press, 1971), chap. 1 and 4 (especially pp. 137–39). In assessing von Wright's position, it is to be noted that he confines causal explanation to discovering connections between *generic* characteristics of events or states of affairs, rather than in an analysis of the sufficient conditions of individual occurrences (cf. pp. 38, 43, and 74).

13. *The Problem of Historical Knowledge*, pp. 255–57 and 266–69. As I there pointed out, I had borrowed this concept from a Berlin doctoral dissertation written by K. Milanov. I have recently found a discussion of the same concept in Siegfried Kracauer, *History: The Last Things before the Last* (New York: Oxford University Press, 1969), chap. 5.

14. In "Central Subjects and Historical Narratives," *History and Theory* 14 (1975): 253–74, David L. Hull holds that one should not regard historical narratives as being concerned with a series of connected events but with historical *entities* which have unity and continuity over time. Insofar as general history is concerned, I find myself in agreement with much that he says. However, I do not find him convincing when he holds that this is also true of all histories. In fact, his basic contention that biological species are to be considered as unitary continuing entities seems to me open to doubt.

15. For a stimulating discussion of periodization in relation to chronological time, see Kracauer, *History* chap. 6.

CHAPTER TWO

1. "A Note on History of Narrative," *History and Theory* 6 (1967): 413–19. That article was critically commented upon by Richard G. Ely, by Rolf Gruner, and by W. H. Dray in *History and Theory* 8 (1969): 275–94. Perhaps the most sympathetic assessment of the narrativist view is Dray's "On the Nature and Role of Narrative in Historiography," in *History and Theory* 10 (1971): 153–71.

Neither these articles nor other formulations of a narrativist position by A. R. Louch in *History and Theory* 8 (1969): 54–70, and by Haskell Fain in *Between Philosophy and History* (Princeton: Princeton University Press, 1970), have led me to alter the arguments I used. I find support for some of my arguments in an article by C. B. McCullagh in *Mind* 78 (1969): 256–61. In the balance of this discussion, my criticisms of the narrativist position are retained, but the wider framework within which they are placed may perhaps make them somewhat more acceptable to my critics.

2. To be sure, if an author writes a historical novel, or seeks historical

material as background for his fiction, he will have to engage in preliminary research, and what he writes will have to be compatible with what he has learned. However, his research will not dictate the structure of the story he has chosen to tell; therein lies an essential difference between history and historical fiction.

3. This point is also made by Gordon Leff in *History and Social Theory* (University: University of Alabama Press, 1969), when he says: "The historian methodologically works back from the problem which he has already identified to the circumstances which led up to it" (p. 96) and, again, "Historical explanations begin from what is to how it became such" (p. 100).

The point is also made by Paul K. Conkin in "Causation Revisited," *History and Theory* 13 (1974): 4. He says of the strength of the implicative relationship in causal attributions: "All the strength is retrospective, but so is the vision of the historian. In his causal analysis, if not in his narration, he usually moves back from a significant but somehow puzzling event (the effect) to search out some of its causes, often guided by a detailed description of the event."

4. That Young's aim was to interpret, and not to recount or explain, can be clearly seen in a remark he makes in the introduction to the 1953 edition of *Victorian England: Portrait of an Age* (London: Oxford University Press, 1953): "the real, central theme of History is not what happened, but what people felt about it when it was happening."

Burckhardt's interest in treating the Renaissance in Italy as a single "geistiges Kontinuum," which it was his purpose to reveal through treating its various facets, is clear in the very first paragraph of his book.

5. *King George III and the Politicians* (Oxford: Clarendon Press, 1954), p. 182.

6. *The Foundation of Historical Knowledge* (New York: Harper & Row, 1966), pp. 221–25.

7. See *Explanation by Description: An Essay on Historical Methodology* (The Hague: Mouton, 1968). Newman says: "The thesis of [this] essay will be that historians frequently explain an action by offering a description of that action" (p. 12).

In "The Autonomy of Historical Understanding," in *History and Theory* 5 (1965): 24–47, Louis O. Mink espoused a somewhat similar position. His essay has been reprinted in W. H. Dray, ed., *Philosophical Analysis and History* (New York: Harper & Row, 1966); pp. 178–79 and 180–81 of that edition are especially relevant.

It is also to be noted that in the concluding section of a paper entitled "On the Nature and Role of Narrative in History," Dray discusses the fact that such a view is implicit in the claims of Gallie and Danto, and is explicit in Oakeshott; he expresses his own strong sympathy with it (*History and Theory* 10 (1971): 169 ff.).

8. I first argued this point in "Historical Explanation: The Problem of Covering Laws," in *History and Theory* 1 (1961): 229–42, and then in my book *History, Man, and Reason* (Johns Hopkins Press, 1971), pp. 114–20.

9. For some examples of how economic theory may be important in explaining particular historical changes, see A. G. L. Shaw, "Economics and History," *Historical Studies. Australia and New Zealand* 3 (1949): 277–86. For a more radical approach to the problem, the example of Robert W. Fogel and his fellow "cliometricians" is to be noted.

10. A suggestive example of how one's definition of literature influences the organization of a literary history is to be found in chapter 1, "Prospective," of Oliver Elton's *Survey of English Literature, 1730–1780* (New York: Macmillan, 1928). Particularly relevant is the role that actual speech plays in his definition of literature (pp. 2–3).

A brief and very general discussion of the point is to be found in René Wellek and Austin Warren, *Theory of Literature* (New York: Harcourt, Brace, 1949), pp. 30–31.

11. In what follows, I am confining my attention to the problem of selection insofar as it concerns forms of special history; I shall not consider the question of importance as it arises in other contexts. For example, the term is sometimes connected with the problem of weighing causal factors; sometimes it is identified with whatever criteria a historian may use in selecting a subject matter, and whatever principles of inclusion or exclusion he applies in dealing with that subject. For a discussion of the former problem, see the concluding section of Ernest Nagel, "Some Issues in the Logic of Historical Analysis," which appeared in *Scientific Monthly* in 1952, and is reprinted in Patrick Gardiner, ed., *Theories of History* (Glencoe, Ill.: Free Press, 1959); for a suggestive treatment of the second issue, see W. H. Dray; "On Importance in History," in *Mind, Science, and History*, which is volume 2 of *Contemporary Philosophic Thought: The International Philosophy Year Conferences at Brockport* (Albany: State University of New York Press, 1970).

12. In chapter 1, I called attention to the parallel between the task of a historian in tracing influences and that of the anthropologist in assessing the diffusion of cultural elements, and I shall not labor the point. The anthropologist, of course, suffers under the disadvantage of not having written history on which to rely, and it is therefore especially difficult for him to determine what may have been the point of origin of a particular cultural element and in what direction it spread. Goldenweiser's discussion of the problem, which I cited, affords a useful contrast to the manner in which a literary historian is generally able to proceed.

13. The same situation obtains with respect to the works of any individual author: They are not to be viewed as forming a single linear series in which each work grew only out of the work that preceded it. From work to work an author's experience will have changed, his interest may have been caught by what others were doing, or he may have felt that he had exhausted the vein in which he had been working. These and many other factors may have to be taken into account in order to interpret the relationship between any individual work and the author's life or his work as a whole.

14. What obtains generally with respect to interpretive disagreements applies equally to debates concerning such issues as "the causes of the Civil War," which are not in fact conflicts between differing *explanatory* historical accounts, but between rival interpretive accounts (see Appendix B).

CHAPTER THREE

1. While Bertrand Russell was among the most influential figures in standardizing the prevailing view, it was also a view shared by all positivists. In addition, it was accepted by a number of antipositivist American philosophers, such as J. B. Pratt and Morris R. Cohen.

Among those who rejected this view, Emile Meyerson was for a time the most influential. The view was also repeatedly challenged by idealists, some of whom (e.g., A. C. Ewing and Brand Blanshard) claimed that logical necessity is involved in the causal relationship. Among other forms of challenge, mention should be made of Whitehead's attack on the Humean analysis and C. J. Ducasse's systematic attempt to defend an alternative position in *Causation and Other Types of Necessity*, University of Washington Publications in the Social Sciences, vol. 1, no. 2 (Seattle, 1924). However, none of these succeeded in leading to any basic revision of the dominant view, though Ducasse's position has recently become better known and more widely discussed since its reformulation in his *Nature, Mind, and Death* (LaSalle, Ill.: Open Court, 1951) and in his *Truth, Knowledge, and Causation* (London: Routledge & Kegan Paul, 1968).

2. *Causation in the Law* (Oxford: Clarendon Press, 1959).

3. *The Cement of the Universe: A Study of Causation* (Oxford: Clarendon Press, 1974).

4. It is to be noted that both J. L. Mackie and K. Marc-Wogau also insist that one should distinguish between the causal explanation of a particular case and generalizations concerning cases of a particular type, but do not find that the differences between explanations in the sciences and elsewhere involve different conceptions of the causal relation. See Mackie, *Cement of the Universe*, pp. 121 and 270–71 for summary statements, and Marc-Wogau, "Historical Explanation," *Theoria* 28 (1962): 214 and 215–16.

It is also to be noted that attempts to draw a sharp contrast between history and the sciences is mistaken in still another respect: In some natural sciences, such as geology, inquiries into temporal sequences in the past are of great theoretical importance, providing an indispensable complement to those nontemporal, functional generalizations with which scientists are primarily concerned. T. A. Goudge has made this point clear in an article that has important consequences for understanding historical explanation: "Causal Explanations in Natural History," *British Journal for the Philosophy of Science* 9 (1958): 194–402.

5. In the recent literature of our subject, one of the first to point this out was Michael Scriven. He makes the point especially clearly in "Causes, Connections and Conditions in History," first presented at a conference at the University of Cincinnati, and later published in W. H. Dray, ed., *Philosophical Analysis and History* (New York: Harper & Row, 1966). See especially pp. 242–43.

6. To avoid misunderstanding, I wish at the very outset to say that when I speak of someone's "perceiving" a causal connection it is possible that the person is mistaken, and that such a connection does not exist. To find examples of this one need merely recall one's experience in watching a skillful magician.

7. For example, I assume that even an uninstructed spectator, who did not know the rules of football, would see a difference between the behavior of the players between downs and their behavior during a play, recognizing the latter as a single and unified event in a way in which the intervals between downs, or in a time-out period, are not.

One aspect of an experiment performed by Heider and Simmel may be relevant here. They designed a movie that has as its "characters" two triangles, differing in size, and a circle. These three figures moved in and around a rectangle through an aperture that opened and shut. In general, all subjects interpreted the figures in human terms, and interpreted the rectangle as a house. In the present context, what is relevant about this experiment is that, within the temporally continuous film, particular sets of motions of the figures became segregated as belonging together, with the total flow of motions being seen neither as a disconnected sequence nor as a single event; rather, it was seen as a series of episodes punctuating a flow of action. This is not a point brought out by Heider and Simmel, but as an observer of the film I was particularly struck by it, and my present description of the phenomenon conforms to their account of what their first (uninstructed) group of subjects reported (Fritz Heider and Marianne Simmel, "An Experimental Study of Apparent Behavior," *American Journal of Psychology* 57 [1944]: 243–59).

In this particular paper Heider and Simmel discuss the perception of causation in the film, giving an account very similar to that which has been more fully developed through the Michotte experiments to which I shall later call attention.

8. In this case I must remind the reader that we are here concerned with causal beliefs in everyday life; we are not dealing with the explanations of the motions of the billiard balls that a physicist might give. We shall come to such explanations later. I am here confining myself to what is seen when we say that we saw that a billiard ball moved because it was hit by another.

9. I must repeat that I am not claiming that all cases in which the cause-effect relationship is applied to events in everyday life are of this kind. As we shall see, many conform to the regularity model. I am now concerned only with those in which we believe that we do actually *see the connection* between cause and effect. Furthermore, I must once again say that I am not now discussing how, if at all, *necessity* may be involved in causal connections.

10. In each of the preceding illustrations I have been concerned with cases in which the effect is taken as the end point in a process, but we can ask causal questions concerning continuing processes: Why does the top continue to spin, or the engine continue to run? In these cases, too, our causal attributions refer to what is occurring within the process designated as the top's spinning or the engine's running; it is not some prior event.

11. The following general statement made by A. Michotte, the Belgian psychologist, concerning his experiments on the perception of causation, is relevant here: "It is true that by an analytical and abstract approach such as I have adopted above, it is possible, theoretically, to distinguish two successive events, the movement and the contact. But actually there are not *two events*; there is only one event which develops progressively. As we shall see later, the impact is not really limited to the coming into contact of the two objects; it constitutes a whole *process*, of which the movement and the contact are both constitutive parts. . . . The whole is *one* gradual development" (*The Perception of Causality* [London: Methuen, 1963], pp. 24–25).

Given this statement and the foregoing analysis of cases in which we may be said to perceive causal connections, it should be clear that these cases bear a greater resemblance to the ways in which historians are apt to use the concept of causation than a Humean analysis provides. Thus, the present discussion prepares the way for what is to be said in chapter 5.

12. See Karl F. Duncker, "On Problem-Solving," *Psychological Monographs* 58, no. 270 (1945): 67–68, or Solomon E. Asch, *Social Psychology* (New York: Prentice-Hall, 1952), pp. 101–2.

13. It is to be noted that Hume himself used the resemblance of successive impressions to explain our belief in the continuing identity of objects. I am here using a similar factor to explain continuity in events.

14. In a quite different connection, Bertrand Russell speaks of *similarity of structure* as giving us warrant to infer causal relations. Although his defense of this inductive postulate depended upon considerations of probability and not upon perceptual belief, in both cases the influence of our recognition of similarity in structure is a factor that leads us to regard different events as belonging together in a connected series. (See Russell, *Human Knowledge, Its Scope and Limits* (New York: Simon and Schuster, 1948), pt. 6, chap. 6; pp. 460–64 are particularly relevant.)

15. "On Problem-Solving," p. 67.

16. Analogues to these "explanations" are to be found in many historical works. I find them unsatisfactory, both in history and in everyday life, since the explanation is not couched in terms of actual events, but in terms of what is only a pattern running through them. When such a pattern is particularly striking it is apt to be reified. Instead of being viewed as what results from these events in their interrelationships, it is taken as if it explained them. See chapter 5 for a further discussion of this.

17. If there is no rhythmic pattern, and they bear a fixed spatial relationship to

each other, they will be seen moving as a pair, as if they were rigidly connected. (For example, see Michotte's discussion of the difference between *displacement* and what we experience as movement, in *Perception of Causality*, pp. 315–16.)

18. This question is, of course, a psychological question. In attempting to suggest a psychological explanation of the origins of our causal beliefs, I am merely following the practice of Hume.

19. In his experiments on "qualitative causation" (as distinct from "mechanical causation") Michotte reached an essentially negative conclusion: There was no perception of causation unless a connection was seen between the movement of one object and the movement (or change of shape) of another. I am not denying this negative conclusion. When we switch on a light we cannot claim to *see* the linkage between what occurs at the switch and the fact that the light comes on; it is only past experience that binds these two events directly together. Thus, this is not the sort of example with which Michotte's experiments were concerned: He attempted to find cases in which, independent of past experience, there was a direct perception of some factor linking cause to effect.

20. Even from a phenomenological point of view, the two events do not appear as instantaneous. The motion involved when we switch on a light does not appear to us as instantaneous. Even the light's coming on does not, under scrutiny, always appear instantaneous, as those familiar with "gamma movement" will recognize.

21. Another condition that leads us from one specific case to cases of a particular type is when someone asks us to *validate* our belief that a causal connection did in fact obtain in some particular instance. I am not here dealing with the problem of validation, but only with what is initially involved in our ascriptions of causal relationships. In this connection I might point out that in two passages in which C. G. Hempel criticized my views regarding causation, holding that the causal relation refers to types of cases and *not* individual instances, his argument hinged on the issue of validating our original causal ascriptions. (See "The Function of General Laws in History," as reprinted in Hempel, *Aspects of Scientific Explanation* [New York: Free Press, 1965], pp. 233 n. and 241 n.)

22. This is not to say that lawyers and historians ordinarily use this form of explanation in dealing with the instances of causation with which they are concerned. As I shall note in Appendix B, Hart and Honoré may have too readily assimilated common-sense views with the manner in which causation is used among lawyers. I shall also argue that they have erred in assuming that the procedures of historians are similar to both.

23. Conversely, of course, the onset of a storm can serve as an indicator that changes in barometric recordings have occurred, but for pragmatic reasons we are rarely interested in tracing this particular relationship. Barometers are generally of interest only because they forewarn us of changes in the weather that we do not yet directly detect, or because they help us evaluate other signs that the weather may change.

24. Such cases bear a close resemblance to the cases in which, as I pointed out in the preceding section, what is given in direct experience appears as having a definite rhythmic pattern, and we feel the presence of some underlying but not directly experienced cause.

25. On the other hand, as I have pointed out, there are also many instances in which a Humean model of explanation seems to serve our purposes adequately in ordinary life.

26. The term "mana" entered anthropological literature through R. H. Codrington's *The Melanesians* (Oxford: Clarendon Press, 1891), and became extended in its application by R. R. Marrett's article on "*Mana*" in Hastings'

Encyclopedia of Religion and Ethics (Edinburgh: T. & T. Clark, 1908–26), and by the writings of Durkheim, Lowie, and others. Alternative interpretations of the concept and of the phenomena to which it was used to refer were closely tied to alternative theories of magic and religion in primitive societies. At present a somewhat restricted interpretation appears dominant (see E. E. Evans-Pritchard, *Theories of Primitive Religion* [Oxford: Clarendon Press, 1965], p. 110). For my purposes, however, where the issue is one of causal efficacy and not a theory of religion, and where theoretical issues concerning the role of magic in primitive communities do not arise, it is presumably legitimate to use the term in its more extended sense. For one standard work on mana, see F. R. Lehmann, *Mana: Der Begriff des "ausserordentlich Wirkungsvollen" bei Sudseevolkern* (Leipzig: O. Spamer, 1922).

My use of the mana illustration in the present connection derives from an interesting article by Wolfgang Köhler, "Psychological Remarks on Some Questions of Anthropology," *American Journal of Psychology* 50 (1937): 271–88. A similar point concerning superstition has been made by William Ruddick in "Causal Connections," *Synthèse* 18 (1968): 49.

27. For example, Hume says in *An Inquiry Concerning Human Understanding*, sec. 7, pt. 2: "One event follows another, but we never can observe any tie between them. They seem *conjoined*, but never *connected*" (Selby-Bigge edition [Oxford: Clarendon Press, 1966], p. 74).

28. It is in such cases that Hume speaks of "secret powers." See *Inquiry Concerning Human Understanding*, sec. 4, pt. 2, pp. 32–34.

CHAPTER FOUR

1. *English Works of Thomas Hobbes*, ed. W. Molesworth (London: Bohn, 1839–45), vol. 1, chap. 9, pp. 121–22.

2. In his well-known article "Causal Relations" (*Journal of Philosophy* 64 [1967]: 691–703), Donald Davidson was also concerned with causal explanations of particular events, and in this connection he cited a similar example. He was, however, critical of Mill's inclusion of all relevant conditions as elements in the true cause of a particular event. However, that point was not essential to the main thrust of his argument (see p. 692).

3. In this connection it is apposite to cite J. L. Mackie's defense of Mill against the criticisms made by Hart and Honoré. Speaking of what Mill termed "the philosophical view" of causation, in which any distinction between "cause" and "mere conditions" disappears, Mackie says: "Since what we recognize as a cause, rather than a mere condition, commonly depends on what we know—or what we knew first—or what is closely related to our interests, there is much to be said for Mill's refusal to distinguish 'philosophically speaking' between causes and conditions. As an analysis of ordinary language, this would be wrong; but from a theoretical point of view, as an account of causal processes themselves, it would be right" (*The Cement of the Universe: A Study of Causation* [Oxford: Clarendon Press, 1974], p. 120).

4. Mill offers an account of why we single out some *event* as the cause of an effect, and why, in contrast, we designate *continuing states* as being merely attendant conditions. He says of the latter that they "might therefore have preceded the effect by an indefinite length of duration, for want of the event which was requisite to complete the required concurrence of conditions: while as soon as that event . . . occurs, no other cause is waited for, but the effect begins immediately to take place: and hence the appearance is presented of a more immediate and close connection between the effect and that one antece-

dent, than between the effect and the remaining conditions. But though we may think proper to give the name of cause to that one condition, the fulfillment of which completes the tale, and brings about the effect without further delay; this condition has really no closer relation to the effect than any of the other conditions has. The production of the consequent required that they should all exist immediately previous, though not that they should all *begin* to exist immediately previous" (J. S. Mill, *A System of Logic*, bk. 3, chap. 5, sec. 3). (For this variant of the passage, see *Collected Works of J. S. Mill* [Toronto: University Press, 1973], 7: 328.)

5. C. J. Ducasse, *Nature, Mind, and Death* (LaSalle, Ill.: Open Court, 1951), p. 108. This volume contains Ducasse's fullest explanation of his theory of causation, but (as I have pointed out) it can be supplemented by an earlier monograph, *Causation and Other Types of Necessity*, University of Washington Publications in the Social Sciences, vol. 1, no. 2 (Seattle, 1924), and by his later collection of studies, *Truth, Knowledge, and Causation* (London: Routledge & Kegan Paul, 1968).

6. This passage comes from the 14th edition, s.v. "tuberculosis." The account of the pathology of tuberculosis given in the 15th edition is more detailed, but is entirely compatible with the point here being made. Equally clear is the account in the *American Encyclopedia*, where the etiology is discussed in terms of the host-parasite relationship.

7. In a different context (namely, in attacking the notion of the "accidental" in history), Michael Oakeshott makes a similar point (cf. *Experience and Its Modes* [Cambridge: At the University Press, 1933], p. 140; also, pp. 129 and 142).

Alexander Gerschenkron, the economic historian, distinguishes between what he terms "nonfacts" and "counterfacts" (*Continuity in History and Other Essays* [Cambridge, Mass.: Harvard University Press, Belknap Press, 1968], pp. 53–54). If I understand him correctly, this parallels the distinction I here wish to draw.

8. Cf. H. L. A. Hart and A. M. Honoré, *Causation in the Law* (Oxford: Clarendon Press, 1959), pp. 35–36 and 37 for their use of this example.

9. The most influential statement of the supposed difficulty has probably been that of Bertrand Russell in his essay "On the Notion of Cause," in *Mysticism and Logic* (New York: W. W. Norton, 1929), pp. 184–85.

10. It is obvious that in this discussion, and elsewhere, I have been assuming that the notion of what constitutes "a process" is not hopelessly obscure. I do not believe that it is, and I see no reason to think that it raises special metaphysical difficulties that are not paralleled in those cases in which we claim to know what we mean by "an object," "an event," "a state of affairs," etc.

At this point I should also indicate that my present account of the cause-effect relation differs from the manner in which I stated my position in *The Problem of Historical Knowledge* (New York: Liveright, 1938). There I spoke of "events" and "sub-events" rather than speaking of the end point in a process and what led up to it. In correspondence and conversations (long ago), Hugh Miller, formerly of the University of California at Los Angeles, pointed out to me some difficulties inherent in my earlier formulation. I should like to think that my present way of formulating my views of the relation between cause and effect has overcome those difficulties without giving up what was basic in my earlier position, and without having engendered serious new difficulties.

11. For example, see Michael Dummett, "Can an Effect Precede Its Cause?" in *Proceedings of the Aristotelian Society* suppl. vol. 28 (1954): 27–44, and "Bringing About the Past," *Philosophical Review* 73 (1964): 338–59. Also, see Richard Taylor's discussion of the issue in his two articles entitled "Causation,"

one of which appeared in *The Monist* 47 (1963): 287–313, and the other in the *Encyclopedia of Philosophy*, s.v. "causation." For further references, see G. H. von Wright, *Explanation and Understanding* (Ithaca: Cornell University Press, 1971), p. 185, n. 18.

12. If I understand him correctly, this point would be endorsed by Wesley Salmon, who, in discussing his own and Reichenbach's view of causal relevance, says: "One very basic and important principle concerning causal relevance . . . [is] that it seems to be embedded in continuous processes" ("Theoretica Explanation," in Stephan Körner, ed., *Explanation* [Oxford: Blackwell, 1975], p. 132).

13. For an attempt to draw a distinction between casual laws and laws that connect properties, see Ducasse, *Nature, Mind, and Death*, pp. 127–28.

14. "Making Something Happen," in Sidney Hook, ed., *Determinism and Freedom in the Age of Modern Science* (New York: New York University Press, 1958), pp. 23–24.

15. On this point, see Hart and Honoré, *Causation in the Law*, pp. 36–37.

16. In "The Function of General Laws in History," as reprinted in *Aspects of Scientific Explanation* (New York: Free Press, 1965), p. 232.

17. For example, in Hempel's illustration we must exclude the possibility that the owner will start his car in order to warm its engine, or that he will add an antifreeze solution as the temperature drops to the freezing point. The sequential aspect of the series of occurrences would surely not be denied by Hempel, even though this aspect does not become apparent in his schematic account of how initial conditions and laws are used in explaining a given effect.

18. Cf. Ernest Nagel, "Determinism in History," *Philosophy and Phenomenological Research* 20 (1960): 293–94; also, his *Structure of Science* (New York: Harcourt, Brace, 1961), pp. 594–95. In both places he uses an example of determinism that was formulated by L. J. Henderson in *Pareto's General Sociology* (Cambridge, Mass.: Harvard University Press, 1937), chap. 3.

19. To relate this and what follows to more technical discussions of the issue involved, I find myself in agreement with J. L. Mackie when he characterizes the various factors entering into the cause of an effect as being what he terms "*inus* conditions," and also with what I take to be Michael Scriven's meaning when, in reviewing Ernest Nagel's *Structure of Science*, he says that causes are "contingently sufficient." I shall quote the summary statements given by each.

Mackie says: "In the case described above the complex formula '(*ABC* or *DGH* or *JKL*)' represents a condition which is both necessary and sufficient for *P*: each conjunction, such as '*ABC*,' represents a condition which is sufficient but not necessary for *P*. Besides, *ABC* is a *minimal* sufficient condition: none of its conjuncts is redundant; no part of it, such as *AB*, is itself sufficient for *P*. But each single factor, such as *A*, is neither a necessary nor a sufficient condition for *P*. Yet it is clearly related to *P* in an important way: it is an *insufficient* but *nonredundant* part of an *unnecessary* but *sufficient* condition: it will be convenient to call this (using the first letters of the italicized words) an *inus* condition" (*Cement of the Universe*, p. 62).

In holding that causes (by which he means specific conditions) are "contingently sufficient," Scriven says: "They are part of *a* set of conditions that does not guarantee the outcome, and they are non-redundant in that the rest of *this* set (which does not include all other conditions present) is not alone sufficient for the outcome" (*Review of Metaphysics* 17 [1964]: 408).

Scriven then introduces five refinements of this account (pp. 408–12).

20. In "Causation" (*Monist* 47 [1963]: 287–313), Richard Taylor takes a different position. He argues that each of the conditions that, together, are necessary for the production of a given effect must also, when taken individually, be regarded as necessary.

CHAPTER FIVE

1. *Experience and Its Modes* (Cambridge: At the University Press, 1933), p. 141.

2. Both W. H. Walsh and W. H. Dray contributed discussions of Oakeshott's views regarding history in a volume of essays entitled *Politics and Experience* (London: Cambridge University Press, 1968), edited by Preston King and B. C. Parekh, and presented to him on his retirement.

3. *Experience and Its Modes*, p. 127.

4. From "The Autonomy of Historical Understanding," originally published in *History and Theory* 5 (1965): 24–47; reprinted with minor revisions in W. H. Dray, ed., *Philosophical Analysis and History* (New York: Harper & Row, 1966), where this passage appears on p. 178.

5. Dray concludes an article entitled "On the Nature and Role of Narrative in Historiography," in *History and Theory* 10 (1971): 153–71, with a section contrasting Mink with Oakeshott, and with other narrativists; he, too, finds Mink's position on this point especially congenial.

In the *Review of Metaphysics* 21 (1967–68): 667–98, Mink reviewed the books of Gallie, White, and Danto, but in that essay he did not develop his own views beyond what was contained in his earlier article.

6. Cf. Patrick Gardiner, *The Nature of Historical Explanation*, (London: Oxford University Press, 1952), pp. 89–90 and 96–97; W. H. Dray, *Laws and Explanation in History* (London: Oxford University Press, 1957), pp. 32–37; Arthur Danto, *Analytical Philosophy of History* (Cambridge: At the University Press, 1965), p. 234 and, for a parallel example, pp. 234–35.

7. See "Causes, Connections and Conditions in History," in Dray, *Philosophical Analysis and History*, pp. 242–43. Scriven, however, does not speak of the part-whole relationship between any one element in the causal conditions and the total effect; rather, he speaks of the cause as "physically identical and only conceptually distinct" from the effect.

8. There are, of course, other biographical studies, such as literary or scientific biographies, in which some facet of culture, rather than the institutional aspects of a particular society, provide the primary context in terms of which the life and work of an individual are viewed. Some biographies, depending upon the career of their subject, may fuse these interests; others may focus on the subject in relation to an interpretive thesis regarding the characteristics of the period in which he lived.

9. In contrast to this, as I pointed out in chapter 2, a special history involves a historical study of some type of cultural product, tracing the connections and the changes in examples of it; it is not the primary task of special histories to deal with the nature and changes of the society or societies that either produced or have preserved these products.

10. C. V. Langlois and C. Seignobos, *Introduction to the Study of History* (London: Duckworth, 1925), p. 214.

11. I might here point out that any events prior to the particular series of events under investigation are *not* to be viewed as determining its characteristics, except indirectly. Thus, while they may be part of the cause of its cause, they are not to be included among the causal features responsible for *it*.

12. This was a relatively common point of view among social psychologists, of whom William McDougall was one. Among social anthropologists one finds it represented in B. Malinowski, *A Scientific Theory of Culture* (Chapel Hill: University of North Carolina Press, 1944), though not in his earlier works.

In three articles to be cited in n. 30, below, I have argued against a related view, "methodological individualism," which holds that societal facts are to be understood and are to be explained in terms of the behavior of individuals.

13. This remark also applies to most attempts to use psychoanalytic theories in historical explanations. While some historians hold that such theories may be fruitfully applied both in biographical studies and in explaining the persistent patterns of action of various political figures, many of the actions with which historians are concerned involve the decisions of individuals concerning whom there is insufficient knowledge to warrant a concrete application of psychoanalytic theory.

14. Alan Donagan, in "Historical Explanation," *Mind* 66 (1957): 163, uses a similar argument as that given above to explain the heuristic value of generalizations.

What has been said may also remind the reader of Michael Scriven's thesis that the generalizations historians use are "truisms." (Cf. "Truisms as the Grounds for Historical Generalizations" in Patrick Gardiner, ed., *Theories of History* [Glencoe, Ill.: Free Press, 1959], pp. 443–75.) However, Scriven interprets these truisms as relating to what individuals *normally* do, and he therefore calls them "normic generalizations." I do not believe that, as a rule, the generalizations historians use are meant to refer to what is normal behavior, or to what normally happens, in either the statistical or the quasi-normative sense of the term "normal." Therefore, in spite of a superficial resemblance between what I here say concerning the looseness of the generalizations used by historians and the views brought forward by Scriven, I wish to separate my position from his.

15. In part, its importance for discussions of historical methodology lies in its ability to provide an alternative to Carl Hempel's view that because of the looseness of their generalizations historians offer only "explanation sketches," not explanations. (Cf. "The Function of General Laws in History," sec. 5.4, reprinted in *Aspects of Scientific Explanation* [New York: Free Press, 1965], p. 238.)

16. The only work I know that makes a serious attempt to define the parameters of this type of problem and to elicit conclusions is *Size and Democracy* by Robert A. Dahl and Edward R. Tufte (Stanford: Stanford University Press, 1973).

17. E. B. Tylor, "On a Method of Investigating the Development of Institutions," *Journal of the Royal Anthropological Institute* 18 (1889): 245–69.

18. George C. Homans and David M. Schneider, *Marriage, Authority, and Final Causes* (Glencoe, Ill.: Free Press, 1955). For the summary statement of their hypothesis, see p. 28.

19. One of the most stimulating attempts to provide such a law seems to me to have been Robert Michels' development of Mosca's theories. According to Michels, there is a basic principle of political organization that—in a manner reminiscent of Marx—he called "the iron law of oligarchy" (*Political Parties* [New York: Free Press, 1966], pt. 6, chap. 2; cf. *First Lectures on Political Sociology* [Minneapolis: University of Minnesota Press, 1949], pp. 141–42). It was his contention that there was inherent in the necessity for political organization in society an inescapable tendency for control to be exercised by a minority group. He phrased this most concisely as follows: "Organization implies the tendency to oligarchy. In every organization, whether it be a political party, a professional union, or any other association of the kind, the aristocratic tendency manifests itself very clearly. The mechanism of the organization, while conferring a solidity of structure, induces serious changes in the organized mass, completely inverting the respective position of the leaders and the led. As a result of organization, every party or professional union becomes divided into a minority of directors and a majority of directed" (*Political Parties*, p. 32). In *Union Democracy* (Glencoe, Ill.: Free Press, 1956), S. M. Lipset, M. A. Trow,

and J. S. Coleman examined the International Typographical Union in an effort to explain why it, alone among labor unions, provided a conspicuous exception to Michels' iron law of oligarchy. (See their first chapter, "Democracy and Oligarchy in Trade Unions.") Their answer involved certain of the structural features of this union, but their explanation of the development and persistence of these features demanded an appeal to various historical occurrences: The cumulative effects of these occurrences changed the initial conditions present for each subsequent stage in the development of the union, thus negating the applicability of Michels' law. For their brief discussion of this basic theoretical point, see pp. 393–94 and 402–3.

While Michels' formulation and defense of his position was overburdened by a concern with problems of socialism and democracy in modern political life, and was therefore not formulated in terms that make it readily applicable to all forms of society, one can conceive of a more generalized statement of it which could be applied to all forms of organization and not to modern forms of political life alone.

I might add that one conventional generalization I have cited, concerning size of population and direct democracy, can itself be considered only a special case of Michels' "law," as he himself attempted to show in the chapter of *Political Parties* entitled "The Mechanical and Technical Impossibility of Direct Government by the Masses," from which the above quotation was taken. (See also pt. 5, chap. 1 of that work, on "The Referendum.") However, in his explanation of why the iron law of oligarchy holds, Michels offered two basic principles, only one of which depends upon "tactical and technical necessities"; the other rests on assumptions as to psychological changes that individuals undergo when they assume roles of leadership (*Political Parties*, pp. 400–401). Only the first of these, and not the psychological assumption, seems to me likely to have universal applicability.

20. Cf. W. B. Gallie, *Philosophy and the Historical Understanding* (New York: Schocken Books, 1964), pp. 107–8.

21. Once this distinction is drawn, so that not all occurrences that may affect various aspects of life in a particular society are regarded as belonging within its own history, the temptation to view the whole human past as constituting a single history should disappear. However, idealists such as Oakeshott will, on metaphysical grounds, of course reject any such distinction between external and internal relations.

22. As we shall see, general histories that are primarily interpretive in structure fall between special histories and other forms of general history in this respect.

23. While the term "genre" is usually used only in referring to stylistic types in the arts, I believe that its use can be extended to other fields. One can, for example, say that different types of philosophic problems and different methods of approaching these problems resemble the diversity to be found in different literary genres or in different genres in the plastic arts. So, too, in the sciences there are many sorts of problems to be investigated, and there is also variety in the styles of investigation that different scientists follow. In different periods some types of problems and some styles of investigation may be more dominant than others, just as is true in the arts.

24. It is said—and probably correctly said—that in a primitive society (that is, in a nonliterate society) tradition is more rigorously followed and innovation is more restrained than in other societies; as a consequence, a greater degree of continuity in the culture of that society is to be expected than would otherwise be the case.

In addition, the greater the contact of a society with other societies, the more opportunity there is for cultural interchange and, therefore, the more are innovations and discontinuities likely to occur.

25. *English Literature in the Sixteenth Century Excluding Drama* (Oxford: Clarendon Press, 1954), p. 56.

26. In this connection one may note that there is some evidence that economic factors, rather than the exploitation of new scientific discoveries, play a dominant role in developing major technological innovations. For a defense of this thesis, see Jacob Schmookler, *Invention and Economic Growth* (Cambridge, Mass.: Harvard University Press, 1966), especially chap. 3. In any such study there is, of course, the problem of defining "major technological innovations" in a way that does not prejudge the issue, and Schmookler's case studies might be challenged on this ground. Nevertheless, his study calls attention to the role played by economic factors—as distinct from scientific advances—in fostering technological change.

27. I say "concrete explanations" since I think it entirely possible that one might be able to set up general principles relating to stylistic change in the arts, and perhaps in other fields of cultural history as well. Such principles might refer to changes in fashion due to factors such as the satiation of taste for a style when that style has been dominant for a time, or because of factors such as a tendency for styles to be vulgarized as their influence spreads. However, such general principles—if any are to be found—would only explain why there is change and would not concretely explain the direction in which the change took place.

28. In *English Literature in the Sixteenth Century*, C. S. Lewis made some very apposite remarks on how the word "Renaissance"—which was originally used by humanists conscious of living in a *renascentia* in which Greek was recovered and there was a revival of classical Latin—became debased by the inclusion of other elements which were quite independent of the new classical learning. As he said, "Where we have a noun we tend to imagine a thing. The word *Renaissance* helps to impose a factitious unity on all the untidy and heterogeneous events which were going on in those centuries as in any others. Thus the 'imaginary entity' creeps in. *Renaissance* becomes the name for some character or quality supposed to be immanent in all the events, and collects very serious emotional overtones in the process. . . . No one can now use the word *Renaissance* to mean the recovery of Greek and the classizing of Latin with any assurance that his hearers will understand him. Bad money drives out good" (pp. 55–56).

29. For example, this is the view of Melville Herskovits in his well-known text in social anthropology *Man and His Works* (New York: Knopf, 1948), pp. 21–28. For a philosophic discussion of "methodological individualism" and some of its alternatives, see "Holism and Individualism in History and Social Science," by W. H. Dray, in the *Encyclopedia of Philosophy*.

30. I argued against methodological individualism in "Societal Facts," *British Journal of Sociology* 6 (1955): 305–17, and in "Psychology and Societal Facts," in *Logic, Laws, and Life*, ed. Robert G. Colodny (Pittsburgh: University of Pittsburgh Press, 1977). In "Societal Laws," *British Journal for the Philosophy of Science* 8 (1957): 211–24, I attempted to show that a rejection of methodological individualism does not entail an acceptance of the type of societal law that Popper, Isaiah Berlin, and other methodological individualists have assumed that it does.

31. Frederick A. Olafson, "Human Action and Historical Explanation," in *New Essays in Phenomenology*, ed. James Edie (Chicago: Quadrangle Books, 1969), see especially pp. 366–67.

32. It is instructive to note a discussion of the element of novelty in early English drama in F. P. Wilson's *The English Drama 1485–1585* (Oxford: Clarendon Press, 1969). In speaking of Henry Medwall's works he says: "As the author of *Nature* Medwall would barely merit a mention in the history of

our drama, but as the author of *Fulgens and Lucrece,* the first purely secular English play that has survived, he is a significant figure. . . . The discovery of this play in 1919 caused almost as much surprise as the recent discovery of an historical play dating from the great period of Greek drama" (p. 7). But Wilson immediately adds: "No doubt Medwall's play seems to us more original than in fact it was," and he traces a whole series of works of different types that also were popular in character and were both secular and quasi-dramatic. To this he adds the concluding comment, drawn from a remark of Sir Edmund Chambers: "So we build up the past." It is this that an experienced cultural historian is in a position to do, but the novice is not.

CHAPTER SIX

1. For both cognitivists and noncognitivists moral judgments are valid only if they are objective. For the distinction between the validity and the truth of moral judgments, see chapter 6 of my book *The Phenomenology of Moral Experience* (Glencoe, Ill.: Free Press, 1955).

2. In the concluding section of "Some Issues in the Logic of Historical Analysis," Ernest Nagel suggested various ways in which historians attempt to estimate the relative importance of two causal factors in a situation. I would be willing to accept each of the five ways Nagel differentiated, but I wish to call attention to the fact that he failed to include the type of assessment I have indicated. Were he to have included this type—but his general conception of causal explanation perhaps made it impossible for him to do so—his final position might have been less discouraging than it was. (His article was originally published in *Scientific American* in 1952; it is reprinted in Patrick Gardiner, ed., *Theories of History* [Glencoe, Ill.: Free Press, 1959], pp. 373–85.)

3. In the first three sections of chapter 25 of *The Open Society and Its Enemies* (Princeton: Princeton University Press, 1963), Karl Popper argues that *theories* have no place in history: There are at best *general interpretations,* which he also calls quasi-theories. This contention is based on two premises, each of which I take to be false. First, Popper assumes that a genuine theory can be formulated only if one has already established empirical laws, but, as I have indicated, this was not the case with Darwin's evolutionary theory. Second, Popper assumes that the laws upon which theories regarding history would necessarily depend will take the form of saying that, given an occurrence of type *a,* an occurrence of type *b* will always follow. However, as I have elsewhere tried to show, sequential laws of this type constitute only one of the kinds of laws that might be used in understanding societal change; yet it is the only type that Popper considers when he rejects the possibility of establishing laws concerning history. (See my article "Societal Laws," *British Journal for the Philosophy of Science* 8 (1957): 211–24; reprinted in W. H. Dray, *Philosophical Analysis and History* [New York: Harper & Row, 1966].)

4. Cited by Eileen Power, "On Mediaeval History as a Social Study," in *The Study of Economic History,* ed. N. B. Harte (London: Cass, 1971), p. 115.

5. The passage reads as follows:

It is always difficult, and frequently impossible, to bring to the point of inductive testing a *system* of explanation of a *system* of interrelated facts. "If Keynes was really to be successful" (remarks Sir Roy Harrod in his *Life of Keynes*) "he should have been able, it is argued, to refute, say, Mr. D. H. Robertson by showing a set of facts which the Keynesian doctrine would fit, while the other would not. Unhappily, the state of economics is not so advanced." Both of two alternative systems of explanation may fit most of the facts (and those it did not

—an adherent might hope—could be explained away with further research or reflection). In complicated disputes, it is not detailed theories, but rival attitudes to the world that are in collision. [*Times Literary Supplement* (London), 2 May 1975, p. 471]

6. To be sure, if one were to interpret Hegel's philosophy of history as being concerned only with the development of the notion of political freedom, and not with the growth and decline of those great societies whose destinies he traced, this stricture would not hold; however, such an interpretation of what his philosophy of history was about would seem to me untenable.

As to the views of Comte and Spencer regarding historical methodology, see my book *History, Man, and Reason* (Baltimore: Johns Hopkins Press, 1971), particularly pp. 88–89.

7. In my opinion, there can be relevant "outside" evidence for or against any form of general aesthetic theory: Appeal can be made to historical and psychological facts, as well as to phenomenological investigations, all of which can go far toward resolving such disputes. However, I shall not press the point here.

8. First in "The Intelligibility of History," *Philosophy* 17 (1942): 128–43; then in *Introduction to the Philosophy of History* (London: Hutchinson, 1951), pp. 23–24 and 59–64.

9. *Philosophy of the Inductive Sciences* (London: J. W. Parker, 1847), 2: 36. This part of that work was republished as *Novum Organum Renovatum*, and the passage occurs on p. 60 of the edition published by J. W. Parker in London in 1858.

10. *Introduction to the Philosophy of History*, p. 23.

11. Ibid., pp. 31–33. Cf. "The Intelligibility of History," p. 130.

12. *Introduction to the Philosophy of History*, p. 62, and "The Intelligibility of History," p. 133.

13. Morton White's treatment of colligation in *The Foundation of Historical Knowledge* (New York: Harper & Row 1965), pp. 252–54 and 257–64, is even more explicitly opposed to the possibility of objective historical knowledge, as I have defined that term.

14. See *Introduction to the Philosophy of History*, pp. 59–64.

15. Although Erwin Panofsky was by no means skeptical of the validity of most art-historical periodizations, one of his essays, "The First Page of Giorgio Vasari's 'Libro': A Study on the Gothic Style in the Judgment of the Italian Renaissance," admirably illustrates the point I am making. See his *Meaning in the Visual Arts* (Garden City, N.Y.: Doubleday Anchor, 1955), pp. 169–225, and especially section 5 of that essay.

CHAPTER SEVEN

1. Cf. chap. 2, sec. 3. What was said there holds not only of interpretive accounts of particular periods, my primary concern in that discussion, but holds also of interpretive biographies and interpretive studies of, for example, the works of an individual author. In this connection I might cite a passage from J. A. Passmore, "The Objectivity of History":

Some little time ago, I wrote a book which purported to be an interpretation of Hume's philosophy. One reviewer addressed me somewhat as follows: "a possible interpretation, but other interpretations are equally possible." How is one to reply? . . . What happens is something like this: an interpretation is suggested by certain passages in Hume; that interpretation is then confirmed by passages I had not previously so much as noticed, which the proposed interpretation serves to illuminate. Or I discover that passages I previously could not understand now make good sense. . . . If a reader is convinced of my interpretation, this will be because he has himself been puzzled by passages in Hume, and my interpretation solves his puzzle for him. [*Philosophy* 33 (1958): 106–7]

E. D. Hirsh's bold yet careful study *Validity in Interpretation* (New Haven: Yale University Press, 1967) should be consulted by anyone concerned with problems in the authentication of interpretations.

2. To reply in advance to an apparent exception that might spring to mind, I remind the reader of what I said in Appendix B concerning the problem of "the cause of the American Civil War": Affixing of praise or blame presupposes detailed, structured historical knowledge and is not itself an investigation of causes, as I use that term.

3. I have dealt with this at greater length in an article appearing in a Spanish symposium on the philosophy of history. In translation it was entitled "Historia y Universalidad" and it appeared in *Revista de la Universidad de Madrid* 12 (1963), no. 45.

4. See chapter 1, section 1. Hempel's paper, originally published in the *Journal of Philosophy* in 1942, is reprinted in *Aspects of Scientific Explanation* (New York: Free Press, 1965).

5. In *Laws and Explanation in History* (London: Oxford University Press, 1957), pp. 67–68.
For my own criticism of Hempel concerning the same point, see "Historical Explanation: The Problem of 'Covering Laws,' " *History and Theory* 1 (1961): 233–38.

6. In "Historical Explanation," pp. 239–41, I criticized Dray in the same way, and developed the point at somewhat greater length. At that time, however, I failed to see—as I now see—that there are cases in which tracing a series of events, such as those constituting a campaign, may provide an adequate explanation of a particular state of affairs. However, I wish to emphasize that in such cases one must not assume (as Dray tends to do) that the relevant events form a single linear series. On this point, see chapter 2, section 1, and also an article, "A Note on History as Narrative" (*History and Theory* 6 [1967]: 413–19), in which I developed the point in a more precise way. Dray responded to the latter article in *History and Theory* 8 (1969): 287–94.

7. This is admittedly a crude statement of the factors that might be involved. For example, in speaking of "economic factors" I might be referring to the conditions obtaining either at the source of emigration or at its goal. For a careful study of one case of immigration, see Simon Kuznets, *Immigration of Russian Jews to the United States: Background and Structure*, Perspectives in American History, vol. 9, 1975 (Cambridge, Mass.: Harvard University, Charles Warren Center for Studies in American History, 1976). In that study (pp. 86–89), Kuznets cites comparable cases that suggest that his findings are generally applicable and are not confined to the case at hand.

8. When laws are mistakenly assumed to state an invariant connection between specific types of occurrences, it is plausible to hold not only that historians do not use laws to explain events, but that no one can cite any example of a well-formulated law that a historian could possibly use. When, however, it is understood that in the natural sciences, too, events are not explained by deducing them directly from a law—that an analysis of the initial conditions is essential before a law can be successfully applied—it will become apparent that there may be a great many generalizations upon which historians can and do rely in explaining events.

9. See Appendix B for my argument that the lawlike connections with which Hart and Honoré, and also Hume, were concerned are fundamentally different from any basic laws characteristic of an advanced science.

10. On phases and component parts as two different but compatible ways of looking at the structure of continuing events, see chapter 5, section 1.

11. A somewhat analogous situation is to be found in the development of the much younger discipline of cultural anthropology, though its theories have tended to shift more rapidly than have those in history, where evidence concerning particular societies has always been more readily available.

When this difference is taken into account, what Clifford Geertz has said concerning his discipline can be used in substantiation of my claim regarding history. He said: "Rather than following a rising curve of cumulative findings, cultural analysis breaks up into a disconnected yet coherent sequence of bolder and bolder sorties. Studies do build on other studies, not in the sense that they take up where the others leave off, but in the sense that, better informed and better conceptualized, they plunge more deeply into the same things. . . . Previously discovered facts are mobilized, previously developed concepts used, previously formulated hypotheses tried out; but the movement is not from already proven theorems to newly proved ones, it is from an awkward fumbling for the most elementary understanding to a supported claim that one has achieved that and surpassed it" (*The Interpretation of Culture* [New York: Basic Books, 1973], p. 25).

In histories, the new sorties that are most apt to change previous interpretations involve examining the same events on a different scale, or examining other facets of the same events. When this is so, shifts in interpretation do not warrant a denial of objectivity.

APPENDIX A

1. I have developed this argument at greater length, and with more attention to detail, in "The Distinguishable and the Separable: A Note on Hume and Causation," *Journal of the History of Philosophy* 12 (1974): 242–47.

2. I have examined at least some of them in the third chapter of *Philosophy, Science, and Sense-Perception* (Baltimore: Johns Hopkins Press, 1964).

3. See the opening paragraph of bk. 1, pt. 3, sec. 4 of the *Treatise of Human Nature*.

4. A. Michotte, *The Perception of Causality* (London: Methuen, 1963). In this connection. I have particularly in mind his "entraining" experiments—for example, p. 21, experiment 2.

APPENDIX B

1. H. L. A. Hart and A. M. Honoré, *Causation in the Law* (Oxford: Clarendon Press, 1959).

2. *Causation in the Law*, pp. 8–9.

3. *Causation in the Law*, p. 9.

4. *Americans Interpret Their Civil War* (Princeton: Princeton University Press, 1954).

5. In my opinion, what follows casts serious doubt on the thesis supported by W. H. Dray in an article entitled "Some Causal Accounts of the American Civil War," *Daedalus* 91 (1962): 578–98. The thesis of that article, and much of the article itself, are also to be found in chapter 4 of Dray's *Philosophy of History* (Englewood Cliffs, N.J.: Prentice-Hall, 1964).

6. To be fair, I must point out that in distinguishing between the explanatory and the attributive contexts in which causal judgments are made, Hart and Honoré acknowledge that it is sometimes necessary in the law to offer explanatory accounts before attributive judgments can be made (*Causation in the Law*, pp. 22–23). Further, in the same passage they admit that such preliminary inquiries may sometimes be difficult, but they add that "such searches for explanation are not the source of the lawyer's main perplexities." This suggests that when they speak of "the lawyer" they have in mind primarily the judge, and not the investigative officers of the court. This should suggest how misleading it may be to view historians as if their interests were essentially like those that Hart and Honoré find to be characteristic of "the lawyer."

INDEX

About the Author

Maurice Mandelbaum is Andrew W. Mellon Professor of Philosophy at the Johns Hopkins University. He is the author of THE PROBLEM OF HISTORICAL KNOWLEDGE: AN ANSWER TO RELATIVISM; PHILOSOPHY, SCIENCE, AND SENSE PERCEPTION: HISTORICAL AND CRITICAL STUDIES; THE PHENOMENOLOGY OF MORAL EXPERIENCE; and HISTORY, MAN, AND REASON: A STUDY IN NINETEENTH-CENTURY THOUGHT.

Library of Congress Cataloging in Publication Data

Mandelbaum, Maurice H   1908–
   The anatomy of historical knowledge.

     1.   History—Philosophy.   2.   Causation.   I.   Title.
D16.9.M26   901   76–46945
ISBN 0–8018–1929–6

DATE DUE

GAYLORD   PRINTED IN U.S.A.